Teaching, Learning, Assessing

A Guide for Effective Teaching at College and University

Teaching, Learning, Assessing

A Guide for Effective Teaching at College and University

edited by Kara Smith, Ph.D.

mosaic press

Library and Archives Canada Cataloguing in Publication

Teaching, learning, assessing : a guide for effective teaching at college and university / edited by Kara Smith.

Includes bibliographical references.

ISBN 0-88962-866-1

1. College teaching. 2. Effective teaching. I. Smith, Kara, 1967-

LB2331.B69 2006   378.1'25   C2006-905298-0

Publishing by Mosaic Press, offices and warehouse at 1252 Speers Rd., units 1 & 2, Oakville, On L6L 5N9, Canada and Mosaic Press, PMB 145, 4500 Witmer Industrial Estates, Niagara Falls, NY, 14305-1386, U.S.A.

info@mosaic-press.com

Mosaic Press in Canada:
1252 Speers Road, Units 1 & 2,
Oakville, Ontario
L6L 5N9
Phone/Fax: 905-825-2130
info@mosaic-press.com

Mosaic Press in U.S.A.:
4500 Witmer Industrial Estates
PMB 145, Niagara Falls, NY
14305-1386
Phone/Fax: 1-800-387-8992
info@mosaic-press.com

www.mosaic-press.com

Many thanks to
Dr. Glen Rideout, King's College University, Canada, and
Dr. Scott Kissau, North Carolina University, U.S.A.

Table of Contents

Teaching, Learning, Assessing

<u>Theory</u>

2. HOW WE TEACH

<u>Starting</u>

Table of Contents

Wayne Tousignant
Larry Morton

3. HOW WE ASSESS

FOREWORD

I was excited to have been asked to write a foreword for *Teaching, Learning, Assessing,* not only because it is a book prepared for teachers by teachers in higher education, but because of its applicability and usefulness to both the college and university professor. For the many teachers of higher education who hold teaching at the heart of their profession, thinking about teaching and learning and continuously exploring methods that contribute to students' success is a common process – it is what good teachers do.

There are undoubtedly many faculty members, even the most seasoned professionals, who have at times needed support and encouragement in developing strategies that promote student learning. Creating educational environments that focus on student learning is not as easy as preparing great course outlines or entertaining students for hours on end. Quality education starts by focusing on learning activities and requires faculty to recognize that learning is the first priority in every educational exchange. Continuously reflecting on strategies and engaging in process that lead to improved instructional performance contributes to expanded student learning and ultimately greater student success and retention.

Not only are the thoughts, ideas and suggestions presented in this manual applicable to most of today's large, diverse higher education classrooms, but they are also a compilation of best practices in teaching and learning and provide a foundation for continuous improvement. As important as it is for teachers to engage in activities that encourage the examination of their own teaching practices, so it is for teachers to engage in opportunities to work closely with peers to improve one another's teaching. A book for teachers by teachers provides this peer-to-peer opportunity and further promotes the establishment of positive learning environments in our college and university classrooms.
Teachers will be engaged and challenged by actively reflecting on the processes and practices presented herein.

Tina Di Simone, Vice President Academic
St. Clair College of Applied Arts and Technology

Introduction

Every faculty or department has a unique set of members. There are members who love to teach, those who prefer to research, some who serve on every committee, some who write, those who are business minded; there are administrators, those that are new and green, those who are about to retire; there are union people, activists, some famous and newsworthy, ones that are favoured by students, award winners, family members, friends and foes alike. As diverse as the characters in a faculty, so are teaching personalities within a school. Our faculty is no different. The experience of teaching varies with each new class and each new semester. There is not one syllabus that stays the same, nor one delivery that remains constant. *Voices* (Newton et al, 2001) illustrates this varied experience beautifully. What is it like to be one voice amongst a multitude of distinct voices? It can be isolating, but in most supportive environments it is a rich, stimulating relationship.

The faculty members who have written this manual are distinct in their own right. Each has a personal approach to teaching which has grown and emerged through years of teaching and active reflection. The group consists of seasoned teachers of teachers. They train teachers. Many have taught at every level of the educational system - public schools, colleges, universities, graduate schools, and research institutes. Between them, they possess 461 years of teaching and teacher training experience. Their liaison, and research, with secondary schools, colleges, and universities, puts them in a unique position. They can, at once, provide informed advice for new faculty about 'where first year students have been', 'where they are now', and 'where they want to go'. Their teaching suggestions are informed by educational research in both secondary and higher institutes in the Sciences, Social Sciences, and Humanities. As a result, the writing within reflects the diversity of teaching methods available to new faculty. It is a snapshot of the kaleidoscope of teaching in higher education.

Many of the authors within struggle to find alternatives to the traditional lecture format. Although there are many undergraduates who do prefer the lecture to seminar, lab, or discussion (Brinkley et al, 1999; McKeachie, 2002), much learning is acquired in more student centred classes (Bligh, 2000) as the chapters by Laing, Glassford, and Crawford argue. This 'student-centred' approach to college teaching is often referred to as constructivism. A constructivist approach to teaching is common and current. It involves listening to the *voices* of the students (Cranton, 1998; Newton et al, 2001) and engaging students through connections, actively acknowledging their societies and worlds. As defined by both Crawford's and Morton's chapters, a constructivist approach to teaching is as collegial as a good faculty. The instructor, as Egbo suggests, surveys the class: **Who** is there? What is their prior learning? As a teacher, you may ask, "What would you like to learn from this course?" Course outlines are constructed to include the requests and needs of the learners (see Tobin's chapter). Evaluations and assessments are constructed to link negotiated content with negotiated outcomes. Thus, the focus is on the learner. Learning, for the student, and teaching, for the faculty member, is created, or constructed, based upon the members of the class community (see Shantz's chapter). The focus of teaching is on the promotion of inquiry, interpersonal skills with members of the class, knowledge of the class, and reflective practice.

For a teacher, reflective practice is invaluable. What was good about this class, lesson, or course? What kinds of things could have been done differently, better? How would I restructure the course next time to accomplish more of the class's (both teacher's and students') goals? What skills do I want students to have learned from this course? How can course content be linked to perceived professions? These are not easy questions. Many authors have grappled with them. If the experience of teaching and learning can be thought of as an ecosystem, then one might recognize the ever-changing environment of the 'course'. Subject matter changes, views alter, new research is disseminated, and society shifts. Louis Schmier's "Random Thoughts", a weekly narrative on the changing mindset of one teacher at North Dakota University, embodies this change. Recognizing that the ground is not permanent is an important acknowledgment in the journey of teaching.

This short manual provides an overview of a group's teaching approaches within a faculty. Chapters are organized in a step-by-step manner according to what we do as instructors "before we teach", "how we teach", and "how we assess". The kinds of issues an instructor needs to consider before and while planning a course (Tobin) includes what prior knowledge the students possess (Smith, Oakley), and which groups, interests, and needs are present in the class (Egbo, Shantz). Once the course outline is complete, delivering the material is challenging and takes lots of practice. Starr, Laing, and Glassford provide ways of beginning classes, and suggest methods for encouraging community building, discussion and inquiry. Crawford illustrates step-by-step ways, and examples of, student-centred teaching practices and ways to encourage active, hands-on learning. These chapters are a survey of ideas. They are personal, educational frameworks of faculty, developed through practice. Much is provided for new faculty as a set of instructions on "how to teach"; however, these are really only generative heuristics. New faculty are encouraged to taste the sampling of teaching within, begin to create their own personal teaching style, and read further into those teaching areas which are of most interest. There is much literature on teaching and learning, and many cross-references to this canon within the chapters of this manual. An extensive teaching bibliography has been provided at the back of this monograph for those faculty requiring deeper knowledge.

When a teaching idea has been created, or something has been done particularly well, it is called "best practice". Some of the best practices for Biology, Mentoring, On-line Courses, and Teaching Large Classes have been outlined in the latter part of section 2. Lee's chapter, for example, illustrates how one instructor uses common, everyday experiences to make basic Biochemistry processes immediately relevant to her undergraduates. Salinitri's

Mentoring program is unique to North America. Tousignant, who has been organizing on-line courses for faculty for years, provides new instructors with excellent advice on how to easily integrate this into a course. And Morton, who also has a keen interest in technology and learning, as a psychologist, describes ways for faculty to make large lectures feel more intimate.

The final two sections of this manual deal with topics that are ever-present on our minds. How do we mark our students? And when will we find time to research and publish? Marking, evaluating, assessing students is an ongoing, and sometimes, frustrating issue. How can we measure performance accurately? How do you measure a skill, or level of inquiry, rather than straight, factual knowledge? Clovis introduces some answers to these controversial questions, and invites readers into the theoretical debate. Ableser, who is actually an advocate of "Portfolio Assessment", lists the multitude of assessment options available to faculty. This list is a wonderful resource for those who are looking for a new, or alternative, way of marking.

The effort new faculty put into teaching is not wasted. Good teaching is at a premium in today's academy. Teaching is the foundation of public support for Colleges and Universities (Pocklington & Tupper, 2002). Intrinsic rewards from students in years to come, and publishing opportunities in this venue are frequent. A good teacher is always recognized, and the work and time spent creating a meaningful course is not only a distinguished job, but a thoroughly enjoyable one as well.

Use the chapters and content within this book to whet your appetite for the field of Teaching and Learning. It is a varied collection of people, writing, teaching, and learning. Welcome.

BEFORE WE TEACH

The majority of teaching work happens before students even step into the classroom. Ask experienced teachers why they are successful, and they will say, "organization". This section of *Teaching, Learning, Assessing* describes how teachers and schools can help students transition from secondary learning to higher inquiry. It provides valuable insights into how to make a classroom warm and inviting; on how to motivate learning; and on how to make students love coming to class by fostering a relationship of mutual respect. Creating the optimal environment happens by organizing one's thoughts regarding the audiences we have. For e.g., are students there because the course is mandatory or because they chose it as an option? Who are they? From where do they come? This is illustrated in everything we do as instructors - from the course outline, to our daily agenda, to how we speak and conduct ourselves. These are things we consider before we teach.

What Did They Learn in High School?
by Kara Smith

Last year's entrance numbers from Statistics Canada indicated that just over 85% of students entering a college or university did so directly from high school. The remaining 15% were composed of working students, part-time students, foreign graduates, and mature students. The following chapter offers the beginning instructor a brief overview of the type of learning and content which students acquired in their secondary school experiences. Each province and state in North America has separate subject requirements for secondary school diplomas, so this chapter will not provide depth in any one of these areas. The requirements specific to the institution or the area in which new faculty teach may be found on government web sites. For example, in Ontario, curriculum covered is published on the site: www.edu.gov.on.ca . Foundational courses in high school, such as English (où Français), Math, and Science equip students with a basic level of knowledge in each of these areas. Professors refine this knowledge and develop a discipline-focused rigour much greater than the broad, secondary school education.

As instructors, we often forget how "young" first year students really are. They are not the mature, deep thinkers we ideally imagine them to be. Mentally, they are not even adults yet. For most, this is their first time away from home, their first time away from their parents. This is their first time managing money, making meals, finding shelter, juggling a job, and trying to fit in with new friends without a pre-established network of support. Many, many basic physiological needs take priority over their classes.

If one considers Maslow's Hierarchy of Needs as an, albeit antiquated, indication of learning priorities at university and college, then three levels of needs stand before the student's ability to concentrate in class. Simply being able to eat, find a place to live for daily shelter, and being able to feel as if s/he belongs, all take precedence over lectures. As Oakley attests in the next chapter, it takes the average student six months to adjust to new living conditions, and longer to adjust to the changes in the way they must learn at college and university. This being the case, most students (unless they are living at home) do not perform at optimum academic levels during their first year of college or university.

In high school, the day to day "management of learning", and administration of assigned work, is completed for the student by someone else - the teacher. Most colleges and universities require that students learn on their own. Most first year students indicate that this, coupled with new domestic responsibilities, is one of the most daunting tasks they have ever faced. High school teachers organize daily learning for students. Simple concepts are broken

1

down into micro lessons and spaced over the period of one week. In secondary school, students are frequently reminded of tests and assignments; daily practice for tests and feedback for assignments often occur the week or month prior to any evaluation or assessment. Learning, in general, is handled in smaller doses in high school, and most students depend upon their teachers to remind them of their duties. This is not often the case in higher education. Here are some of the differences between learning in high school and learning in college/university for those students who enter higher education directly from secondary school:

High School	College / University
Parents care for Physiological/Safety needs	Students responsible for any/all needs
Average class time - 1 hour	Average class time - 3 hours
Average teaching style - discussion/group work	Average teaching style - lecture
Learning style utilized - kinesthetic	Learning style utilized – aural
Average evaluation worth - 3% of final	Average evaluation worth - 35% of final
Test Practice/Reminders - 5 per test	Test Practice/Reminders- 0 per test

In all, students must adapt to a distinct style of learning in university or college. In high school, in general, classes are shorter- concepts are broken down into micro sections which are each delivered in the form of a hands-on lesson involving several learning styles - visual, oral/aural, and kinesthetic. Evaluations and performance feedback are provided frequently and students are reminded of their tests, as well as receiving practice evaluations, or the opportunity for individual feedback on rough work, prior to any actual graded assignment. These features of high school learning are rare in college and university learning. In higher education, students must learn to manage their own 'micro lessons' and self-evaluation. They must assign themselves daily questions for practice; they must conduct practice tests themselves; they must force themselves to write rough drafts and receive feedback on the quality prior to a due date *without* being asked. They must remember when a midterm is, and prior to such a large test, be prepared to organize a study and reading schedule for themselves without having the benefit of a teacher doing it for them in class daily. They must, in essence, switch from kinesthetic, participatory learning in small doses to aural, theory learning in large doses. In college and university, students must re-learn how to learn.

Most college instructors ask, "What did my students learn in high school? What do my students already know?" Having this information allows the instructor to use prior knowledge as a basis for new learning (as Ian Crawford describes in his chapter on "improving learning"). Not all subjects are compulsory in secondary school, but three main subject areas receive more attention than others. They are: English, Mathematics, and Science. Following a secondary school diploma, most students have acquired the following concepts in three basic areas:

ENGLISH	MATH	SCIENCE
How to write a 5-paragraph essay How to write a short story Appreciation of 3-5 types of poetry forms. How to present to a class. The plot lines and themes of 5 Shakespeare plays. Appreciation of, at least, 2 Canadian novelists.	Reasonable computational ability for +, -, x, / without a calculator. Estimation skills based on mathematical models. Use calculators appropriately. Apply strategies for problem solving. Appreciate the need for mathematics in a variety of settings. Communicate (orally and in writing), mathematical solutions to problems in a clear and accurate way.	Force Mechanics Planets 20 Elements Chemical Reactions Cells The Body Living versus Non Living Ecology

As a prerequisite for a high school diploma, Canadian History and Geography is studied until Grade 10. This covers the formation of the country. Physical Education is studied until the end of Grade 11, at which point, students have a broad foundation in health issues, and two common sports, basketball and volleyball. French is required until the end of Grade 9, and most students fossilize their language learning long before this, and do not retain much beyond the verb "avoir". Music and the Arts are optional courses. Students who have a desire to continue in a particular area of study will likely complete their courses for secondary school in that subject area. Chemistry, for example, may be studied until Grade 12; and Visual Arts may be studied in various forms until the end of high school, if it is so opted. Subject foundations of English, Math, and Science are in place when students arrive at college, however, much will need refining as they acquire new knowledge and methods for applying this knowledge in a specific area of study. A more complete outline of "what students learned in high school" is available on government web sites {www.edu.gov.on.ca} and through the students themselves. As Crawford outlines in this book, one of the simplest ways of finding out what your students know and what they need to know, "the one minute paper", is by asking them. Survey them to derive this information, then begin to refine your course to include it. Instructors teaching introductory level courses provide a transition between former knowledge and new knowledge; former learning styles and new learning styles.

Instructors in college and university have significant influence on the direction of a student's enthusiasm, drive, and direction. As an instructor, you can stimulate students' interests. You can motivate them to want to manage what they are learning and to monitor the quality of what they are producing.

Salinitri's chapter indicates how vital mentoring can be for first year students. A new instructor can coach and guide young students to discover the intrigues of the discipline. This is the transition they need to make. The classroom you construct will make this academic nirvana possible.

Remember that most of your students are still someone's child. Remember that the method by which they were required to learn, and by which they were evaluated in high school is distinctly separate from that of most first year university or college classrooms. Keep an open mind towards new styles of teaching and methods of learning, and do not be afraid of experimenting in the classroom to bring the discipline to life. At the higher level, subjects hold a great deal of excitement - pass this passion on.

To further teaching:

Sacks, P. (1996). Generation X goes to college: An eye-opening account of teaching in postmodern America. Chicago: Open Court Publishing.

Schmier, Louis. (2002). Random Thoughts. (A weekly listserv newsletter on teaching.) North Dakota University. acadv@listserv.nodak.edu

Schönwetter, D.J. (2002). Becoming a successful student. Communique, 2(2), 23-25.

Schönwetter, D.J. (2002). Equipping teachers with strategies to engage inquiry in first year students. Unpublished paper delivered at 2002 Society for Teaching and Learning in Higher Education (STLHE) Conference, McMaster University, Hamilton, Ontario.

First Year Students in Transition: What Institutions Do to Help
by Beth Oakley

Oakley provides a profile of the first year student, a clear outline of orientation support programs and highlights the needs of first year students. This transition from secondary school to post secondary institution is difficult for students, both academically and socially. Before a new instructor sees the students, they have already been exposed to a number of services on campus – libraries, writing centres, student centres, finance offices, job centres, and transition programs. Transition and orientation programs provide first year students with the skills necessary to be successful in their new environment. Students are exposed to resources that assist them with completing research, studying effectively, managing their time, and navigating the post-secondary environment. Knowledge about the available services on campuses is invaluable to instructors who can save time by referring students to available resources when they are most needed. If students have access to a writing centre for help with completing research reports, for example, there is no need for the instructor to cover this in class. Instructors who act as mentors may also refer students to appropriate campus services for follow-up and additional, in-depth help. Being a good teacher means knowing where to find help when you need it.

First year students today arrive at university and college with varying degrees of life experience and academic preparedness. They also bring with them certain expectations developed through family interactions, the influence of high school teachers and guidance counsellors. At university, they are quickly thrust into a world that demands that they exhibit responsibility. This new learning environment imposes on students a new set of life and learning skills, and a level of independence far greater than what was previously expected of them. Increased academic expectations, financial burden, competitiveness, and fear, make it difficult for first year students to cope with these complex changes.

How can faculty, staff and administration work together to create an environment that supports and assists first year students to enhance their chance for success? Universities have to begin by understanding the identity of first year students before they can consider the best way to assist them with setting a course for success in post secondary education and beyond. This chapter will outline some practices that instructors might implement in order to assist students with the transition to post-secondary education.

Why Transition Support?
Developmental psychologists have long understood the important role that personal development plays in young people's lives. Gaining an awareness and understanding of student development theory might help instructors to anticipate the challenges facing first year students (Chickering, 1990). Traditional

post secondary educators may presume that secondary school graduates ought to arrive at university with the knowledge and skills required to be successful in their post-secondary education and that providing transitional programs only serve to 'spoon feed' students. The reality is that very few first year students are ever fully prepared for the multitude of transitional issues that they will encounter. Their best chance for success occurs when they are made aware of services and support programs and are shown how to utilize them.

Just as successful job applicants might reasonably expect to be provided with a framework of responsibilities and some type of employee orientation, likewise new students require a basic foundation that outlines the skills and strategies to help them to become successful in this new learning environment. For most students, university or college is their first encounter with having to be responsible for their own learning.

In the last one to two decades, an increasing number of universities and colleges have recognized the need for a variety of orientation programs for first year students. Universities no longer assume that students are naturally prepared to handle the rigours of this new environment. First year students are particularly vulnerable to failure or to experiencing difficulties and especially during the first few weeks (Astin, 1993; Levitz & Noel, 1989; Tinto, 1987). Retaining students is beneficial to institutions as well as to students. Therefore, it stands to reason that if universities and colleges hope to improve the rate of retention, they must take action to improve first year student performance.

Types of Transition Support

The success of the first year student is largely dependent upon the efforts of all departments and individuals working in concert. Faculty, staff, administration, student affairs officers, academic advisors and student government must all work to achieve this common goal of focussing on improving the quality of services to students in order to move towards a more student oriented culture. This chapter will outline some of the more common services on university and college campuses and suggest ways that instructors might utilize them and make effective recommendations to students.

Prior to attending classes for the first time at university, students will communicate with a number of departments including liaison and recruitment, the office of the registrar and departments responsible for orientation programming. These initial encounters may set the tone for the students' overall impression of the university, but this is only the beginning. New students may or may not be aware that support services include; academic advising, transition support courses, learning skills workshop, information centres, writing centres, library and technology services. Although students are initially exposed to these services during orientation, they may need to be reminded of them when it is more relevant to them throughout the course of their first year of study.

Liaison and Recruitment Services

Frequently the first contact between the post secondary institution and the potential student occurs by way of a liaison and recruitment event. Liaison staff is knowledgeable about the campus and provide extensive information about various programs and services. What can faculty do to help with this initiative? Faculty have a critical role in the recruitment and retention efforts of the institution. The liaison office relies upon dedicated and enthusiastic faculty who are eager to discuss their field of expertise with prospective students, related university programs and career opportunities at open houses and show case days. Those who exhibit a genuine interest in their field and are willing to share their enthusiasm with prospective students at various events both on and off campus are always an asset to university recruitment efforts.

Summer Orientation

This is typically the first way that all campus services and staff come together in one location to welcome future students and their parents. Orientation allows new students to meet faculty, staff and fellow students. It allows them to gather the final bits of information before committing to the institution. It sets the tone of the campus, enables students to tour the facilities, to get answers about academic programs, administrative procedures and more. It is often the day that students register for courses and finalize plans for residence accommodations and food services. Orientation allows new students to meet senior students who can answer questions and ease their anxieties. It lessens the shock of arriving on campus in the fall to an unfamiliar and often intimidating environment. In addition, most orientation programs today include a component for parents and family members that allow the families to understand their role as emotional supporters of their sons and daughters and most importantly, assist them with the process of letting go.

Faculty support during orientation is critical in that it allows students to communicate about course selection and career options with those who know the programs first hand. It also serves as the first contact for students and their instructors and allows them to see that faculty are genuinely interested and approachable.

Fall Orientation

More and more universities and colleges are adopting a week long orientation program to compliment their summer orientation. Fall orientation is meant to be an extension of the orientation that began in the summer to welcome students to their new environment and enable them to acquire a sense of connection from the beginning, thereby increasing the likelihood for their success. Fall orientations incorporate both social and academic activities and usually involve several days of varied activities. Events may include team building exercises, games, competitions, transition presentations, community events, and information sessions. Other activities might include student success workshops, faculty meetings, welcoming convocation, sponsored meals and mentor opportunities. The emphasis of these events is usually based on educating and informing, but more importantly aims to provide students with a sense of connection to their new environment. Until students feel socially connected, they will not be ready to prepare themselves academically.

Many universities and colleges are increasingly committed to ensuring that the majority of these welcoming events are alcohol free due to the fact that more and more first year students are under the legal drinking age. The goal of fall orientation week is to ensure that first year students will feel more at ease and connected to their colleagues, have gotten to know some of the faculty and have become more familiar with campus services and support areas. This outcome is essential for student retention.

Faculty assume an essential role during fall orientation by collectively planning and implementing program specific information sessions for their student body. The aim of these sessions should be to welcome their cohort to campus, initiate discussion about course requirements, program expectations and possible career goals, and to encourage students to seek assistance before they encounter serious academic distress. An additional benefit is that many students acquire a sense of belonging to a supportive faculty. As a follow up to this initial contact, faculty and departments should work towards developing other strategies to support their students throughout their academic careers.

First Year Transition Courses

More and more universities are offering student transition courses. Some institutions require all first year students to enrol. Whether mandatory or optional, the large majority of campuses offer it as a credit course, which is the key to students valuing the course. Most student success courses include a learning skills component covering topics such as time management, exam strategies, note taking and text reading. There is the opportunity for self-reflection through assessing ones learning style, examining values and goals and journal writing. Students learn how to apply practical topics such as stress management, responsible drinking, health issues, career, personal and finance planning and general university processes and procedures. There is ample opportunity for student to student and student to faculty interaction through web discussions and face to face meetings. Ideally, this type of course should provide the student with the opportunity for close student/faculty interaction, so a small class size (25 students) is essential to the success of the course.

Faculty who teach this type of course need to be at ease with establishing an exceptional rapport with first year students and should be well versed about first year student issues. First year students generally exhibit varying degrees of maturity and academic readiness and faculty must be prepared to respond to the different ranges by developing engaging teaching strategies. Obviously this can present a challenge for faculty but also many rewards.

Learning Skills Workshops

Through weekly classroom interactions and assignment and test reviews, an instructor may recognize when a particular student is struggling with academic skills. Most post-secondary institutions offer some form of workshop series or individual support service designed to help students to improve skills in specific areas such as text reading, note taking, time management, presentation skills, exam preparation, studying and memory and other strategies. These workshops are available to students to provide ongoing support throughout their academic careers. Online study skills modules are increasing in popularity and they allow students to learn these skills at their own pace and on their own time. Instructors who refer students to these services may be helping students to develop new skills that will continue to be beneficial throughout their entire academic experience.

Tutoring Services

Many campuses offer some form of tutoring assistance program that matches tutors with students who may require additional academic support in a particular area of study. This is a valuable service for students because it allows for peer interaction and one-to-one support that may not be available in the traditional classroom setting. Faculty that encounter exemplary students and refer them to the tutoring office, provide a beneficial service for students who may need extra assistance. Tutoring services hold faculty recommendations in high regard and most require potential tutors to provide a faculty endorsement. Not only does the knowledgeable student gain experience and income, but the struggling student gains valuable peer support in the process. The instructor also benefits from this program because the tutor frees up time that the instructor might normally have had to devote to helping students during office hours.

Student Information Centres

In this era of computers and automated telephone systems, students still appreciate having a place where they can get face to face information or directions about campus services. These services allow students to ask questions, get directions, have contacts made with other departments on their behalf. Its other function is to diminish the potential for "run around" which may accompany the process of trying to find answers to questions in the typical university bureaucracy. Student information centres provide students with one stop shopping and take pressure off faculty who are called upon by the student to give answers to general university questions. The faculty save time because they don't need to stop and figure out what the student needs and where the student should go for help. Information centres also become a valuable resource for faculty who may be unfamiliar with many of the campus services and university policies.

Library Orientation

Over the past several years, libraries have become increasingly user friendly places. Workshops, reference help centres, inter library loan services and online journals enable students to navigate through the mountains of resources and build confidence in their ability to conduct valuable research. Instructors can help their students to fully utilize the library by placing course materials on reserve or on their websites. In classes where research assignments have been assigned, instructors might consider inviting the library experts to the classroom to present on-line demonstrations to make the students' first experience with research less intimidating.

Technology Services

Technology is and will continue to be an essential component to every university and college. Students successfully use it to research, participate in on-line courses, access course information, correspond with faculty and peers and complete the majority of assignments. Ideally, instructors can use it to add variety and quality to the traditional lecture style class. Although making classes more innovative and interactive may initially take extra time and effort, those who are dedicated to meeting this end will probably make both the learning and teaching experience more satisfying. Campuses today provide technological support, and tutorials that enable even the most technologically timid instructor to feel comfortable and confident with introducing students to new ways of learning.

Other Essential Services

Writing centres provide important services for students at all stages of their academic careers. Most offer information and workshops on essay writing, research strategies and thesis techniques. Instructors have an obligation to be alert for students with writing difficulties and encourage them to seek the assistance of this centre. International students may also benefit from English as a Second Language (ESL) classes usually administered through the campus writing office.

The instance of psychological difficulties among our first year student population continues to increase. Student counselling centres are staffed by qualified professionals who assist students with coping with the stressors of academics and everyday life. In addition to professional staff, peer mentors can also act as a valuable resource. Instructors should maintain a keen eye for students who display troubling behaviours or cues either verbally, in written assignments or email communications. Student counselling staff is always available to consult to ensure prompt referrals.

The number of students with documented disabilities requiring academic accommodations at universities and colleges is also on the increase. Ministry guidelines (Ontario Disability Act and the Ontario Human Rights Code) provide direction to universities and colleges with regard to the processes associated with accommodating students. Faculty are instrumental in the process of providing appropriate accommodations and partnering with disability service areas to ensure equal access to education for this population of students.

Academic integrity offices are increasing at university campuses to address the need to combat plagiarism and other forms of academic dishonesty. This office provides faculty and students with resources related to maintaining academic integrity and minimizing cheating. Students suspected of compromising academic integrity are referred to this area for discipline. Since the issues associated with academic integrity may be unclear to first year students, faculty are encouraged to discuss with their students what constitutes cheating.

Profile of the First Year Student

This new generation of students learns differently than students did twenty years ago. Today's first year students have grown up in a technological age which has brought them sophisticated video games, MTV, remote controls, the internet, chat rooms and online social networks. They are accustomed to having their needs met instantly with a simple push of a button or a click of a mouse. They are master multi-taskers and are quite proficient at it. This has a direct impact on their expectations for higher education and their learning styles.

Today's students may have less tolerance for situations requiring longer periods of attention and concentration and are sometimes more difficult to engage. First year students in particular may struggle with the ambiguous nature of some course content at the post-secondary level. Hours of text reading and lectures present serious deterrents for many of them. The traditional university lecture is no longer an effective teaching method for many. Although traditional instructors may believe that students need to be more accountable and responsible, the fact is that they are products of their fast paced, multi-tasking environment. Instructors of post-secondary students may need to consider these factors in their teaching approach. Establishing a more active and learning centred environment which recognizes individual learning styles may enable students to be more academically successful.

The ultimate challenge for the college and university instructor today is to find ways to get students more involved in their learning. Students appear to be more stimulated and receptive to learning with technological presentations, hands on opportunities and small group interaction. This can be achieved using technology such as clickers, power point presentations, or providing web resources. Developing new teaching strategies is only limited by the instructor's imagination.

There is no doubt that first year students may still be developing critical thinking skills, but effective instructors will consider ways to assist them rather than express displeasure at this new generation of learners. Most universities and colleges provide opportunities for instructors to participate in forums to address the challenges of student apathy toward learning and develop solutions to overcome this trend.

Mature and Part Time Students

Mature and part time student enrolment is on the rise at most post-secondary institutions. Mature students often arrive at university with more clearly defined goals and a more ambitious attitude toward learning. The reasons for their return to school are varied. Some are pursuing a degree to obtain an improved quality of life, and others are seeking promotion within their companies and others merely want to learn for the sake of learning. Mature students can be a welcome addition to the classroom and instructors can benefit from their presence by encouraging them to be active contributors to the course.

More students are attending school part time not by choice, but rather due to increased financial restraints. With increased tuition costs, students must work more hours to finance their education. Some attend part time because they have family or other obligations. Still others simply find it more manageable to succeed academically.

In addition to traditional lecture style classes, an increasing number of campuses are offering distance and on-line courses. This allows for more flexibility in terms of how students choose to learn and allows individuals to pursue their degree more independently from the traditional method of being on campus to learn. Deadline dates for submission of assignments is often more flexible allowing the students to complete course work up until the end of the term. This new learning environment creates more flexible opportunities for part time and mature students.

International Students

As the world becomes a smaller place and technology increases, more and more students from abroad are choosing to come to North America to pursue their degrees. This population of students has unique needs and challenges and may find it difficult to adjust to the differences in culture, climate, language barriers and academic expectations. These students take an increased risk by leaving their families, culture and home and they may require additional campus support. Most universities and colleges have an international student centre helping students to assimilate, meet other international students and obtain assistance with writing and language skills, or second language (ESL) courses. Writing centres on campus often offer ESL courses as well.

It is likely that the international student population will continue to increase on many campuses in the years to come. Faculty must be cognisant of the differences among all students and be ready to provide clarification or additional support and guidance where appropriate. The campus as a whole should recognize that international students provide the community with the ability to learn and interact with individuals who are different from themselves and help students, staff and faculty to appreciate the diversity of different lifestyles and points of view.

Residence Students

For students who choose to live in residence, most encounter their first experience with personal independence. Some will adjust well to this new lifestyle but inevitably, most will struggle with some part of the process. The initial feelings of excitement and independence can quickly be replaced by feelings of loneliness and homesickness. Students learn that living with a room mate creates new stressors and often necessitates compromise and maturity. First year residence students often report having difficulty studying in this environment. If they are not disciplined with their time, they can get trapped into the temptations of dorm life at the expense of good grades. They may find it difficult to strike a balance between social and academic discipline. Instructors who take the time to meet with their students throughout the semester just may have a slightly positive influence on a student's academic conscience or at least become aware of warning signs.

Commuter Students

Students who continue to live at home and commute to school experience a different set of challenges. Sometimes they struggle more with developing a sense of independence because there are certain family dynamics for which they are still responsible. Commuters may feel less in touch with the university campus because there is a lack of camaraderie compared to that which is found in residence. This group is more likely to attend class and then immediately leave the campus. Despite their best efforts, universities often struggle to find ways to get commuter students involved. Commuting to and from campus can in itself be a time consuming activity as can the challenge of parking. Instructors who create opportunities for their students to meet outside of the classroom may be creating an opportunity for commuters to get more involved in campus life.

Why Do They Come to University?

There are numerous reasons that students choose to pursue a post-secondary education. Among the most notable is their desire to gain valuable skills and a degree that will enable them to be more marketable. For some the choice is not their own, but one instilled in them by their parents. Still others decide based on the fact that their friends are attending and so they too feel pressured to get a degree. Some simply choose to exercise this right of passage which allows them the opportunity to move away from home to enjoy the freedom from parental constraints. Society dictates that attending university or college is the next logical step after high school for those who have aspirations for success.

Many students leaving secondary school are not fully aware of the exact direction of their goals. They may be quite certain about the decision to attend university or college but are still uncertain about their final academic or career aspirations. Most universities offer programs and services that help students to work towards defining their future goals.

Parents

With the arrival of the millennial students come the boomer parents who are highly involved in the lives of their students (Howe & Strauss, 2000). With the increased costs of post-secondary education and students arriving at university younger than ever, comes the sense of being entitled to be truly invested in their children's education. Students beginning university generally do not view their parents as meddlers but rather as an essential support. From the initial application procedure, to orientation and sometimes well beyond first year, many students continue to rely upon their parents to give advice, ask questions of university personnel, and problem solve for them. A very large number of students are in daily contact with their parents by way of instant messaging, cell phones and the internet. As a result, this can greatly stifle students' ability to become independent problem solvers. Their parents are often their first choice for advice and direction whether or not they reside in the same city.

Post-secondary educational institutions recognize parental investment and have responded accordingly. Many institutions now provide parents and family members with a special orientation program, website, monthly e-newsletter and contacts for answering questions and lending support throughout their students' first year. Universities should recognize that parents are best served as partners in the transition process, and offer advice about how to guide their children to independence to ensure their success into adulthood and their future career goals.

Why Are Some Students More Successful Than Others?

There are numerous factors that determine a student's success at university and college. For many students the biggest barrier to pursing an education is financial. The need for students to work an increased number of hours to fund their education may result in compromised academic performance levels; especially if they lack good time management skills to balance their many obligations.

Students with ambition, well defined goals and a strong work ethic will have an easier time adjusting to university. Developing and following an effective time management plan is probably a student's best chance for meeting with success. Secondary to this, but equally important is the students' sense of family support. Parents and family members play an essential role in a student's ability to succeed and effective supporters understand that there is a balance between being supportive and allowing the student to achieve a measure of independence and personal responsibility.

Students who take an active role in campus life tend to be more successful than those whose only goal is to obtain a degree. Campus involvement has also been shown to increase student retention (Astin, 1977, 1985). Universities and colleges have a responsibility to provide out of class opportunities for students to ensure that they receive the most value from their education. Students who are involved are not only more positive about their educational experiences, they are also more able to enhance their leadership skills, their ability to work as a team and to establish more personally meaningful relationships (Kuh, 1991).

Volunteering, community involvement, internships, and athletics are just some of the valuable ways that students can enrich their post secondary experience and enhance their resumes. Faculty can encourage students by keeping them informed about possible opportunities for research, part time employment, work study or volunteer opportunities within their areas.

Changes in the Learning Environment

It is important that we examine the learning environment from which they came so that we can begin to understand how their post-secondary experience will impact them. Most students have recently come from a high school environment where the average class size was less than 40. Upon arriving at university, they are thrust into a classroom which in some cases has greater than 200 students. In secondary school, they knew all of their teachers by name and

14

the teachers knew them. The reality of the first year classroom rarely allows for much personalized student to instructor interaction.

The high school environment is largely student centred. The learning process is directive in its approach. At university and college, students must exhibit almost complete independence for their learning. At university and college, the focus is not on memorizing facts, but more about how to reflect, criticize and analyse. The student is expected to be a leader in the learning process. First year students may have the most difficulty with developing writing and critical thinking skills because up until this point, they were told *how* to write and *how* to think. They may have difficulty when they realize that frequently in university instructions for assignments are less detailed and directive and require more reflective and subjective responses than they did in high school.

The culture of the university classroom is undergoing an unsettling change. Frequently students arrive late to class, leave early, engage in side conversations, allow their cell phones and pagers to ring, surf the internet and may be less than diligent in attending class on a regular basis. Students may misinterpret their new sense of freedom. In high school, students were held accountable for their attendance and submission of assignments. Once at university, students are accountable for their own choices.

What can instructors do to alleviate this disruptive classroom conduct? Faculty have a right, and in fact, an obligation to provide students with guidelines outlining acceptable classroom etiquette, so that all students are able to exercise their right to learn without disruption. Students may perceive that it is their right to come and go as they please because they are paying for their education and they may weigh the benefits of attending class against other obligations in their lives. They may also choose not to attend class if they feel that it is not worth their time. Outlining instructor expectations and deadlines clearly in the syllabus is one way to achieve this. By the same token, faculty have an obligation to their students to be punctual for class, hand back assignments and provide feedback in a reasonable amount of time, and communicate clearly and effectively to their students.

How Can Faculty Assist First Year Students With Success?

Universities and colleges must work harder to find ways to involve students in campus life. Instructors need to take more responsibility for getting to know the students whom they teach. This can be an enormous challenge considering the size of many first year classes, but it is not completely impossible. Perhaps a more realistic goal is for each instructor to commit to getting to know a handful of students at a time.

Aside from teaching, most instructors have an obligation to undertake research. Instructors might begin by conducting informal, non-academic research about the university campus itself. The best opportunity to reach out to students is by being informed and aware about current student issues and services on campus that can provide support to students in distress. No one would reasonably expect instructors to have all of the answers, but by being informed about the campus, they can become an essential part of the process and an excellent reference point for the student in need. This initiative can have long lasting effects on the future of individual students who otherwise might go unnoticed and uninformed.

Many campus programs would welcome faculty involvement, some requiring only a minimal amount of time but having maximum effect. Summer orientation greeters, academic advisors, convocation platform participants or special guests at social and academic events are all ways that faculty can show their support to students in small but significant ways. Most universities offer new faculty orientation programs which can provide invaluable information to the new instructor, or act as a refresher for someone who has been on campus for a number of years but may be unfamiliar with recent changes.

The face of the college campus is changing and will continue to change dramatically over the next decade. Increased competition among universities and colleges will require that we all work together to support students at every stage of their academic careers. As educators of young adults, we should not only feel a sense of obligation to undertake this worthwhile commitment, but we should also share in sense of satisfaction when we witness the transition of the awkward, inexperienced first year student to the confident, mature and knowledgeable graduate and contributing member of society.

To Further Teaching:

Astin, A. W. (1993). What matters in college? Four critical years revisited. San Francisco: Jossey-Bass.

Astin, A. W. (1985). Achieving educational excellence. San Francisco: Jossey-Bass.

Astin, A. W. (1977). Four critical Years. San Francisco: Jossey-Bass.

Chickering, A. W. (1990). Education and identity. San Francisco: Jossey-Bass.

Chickering, A. W. (1974). Commuting versus resident students: overcoming the educational inequities of living off campus. In L. Upcroft, J. Gardner, and Associates. (eds). The freshman year experience. San Francisco: Jossey-Bass.

Howe, N., & Strauss, W. (2000). Millennials rising, the next generation. Vintage Books (New York).

Kuh, G., (1995) The other curriculum: Out of class experiences associated with student learning and personal development. The Journal of Higher Education, 66 (2) 123-155.

Levitz, R., & Noel. L. (1989). Connecting students to institutions: Keys to retention and success. In M. L. Upcraft & J. N. Gardner (Eds.), The freshman year experience (pp. 65-81). San Francisco: Jossey-Bass.

Noel, L., Levitz, R., Saluri, D., & Associates. (1986). Increasing student retention. San Francisco: Jossey-Bass.

Tinto, V. (1987). Leaving college: Rethinking the causes and cures of student attrition. The University of Chicago Press: Chicago.

Upcroft, L., Gardner, J., and Associates. (1989). The freshman year experience. San Francisco: Jossey-Bass.

How to Plan and Organize a Course for the First Time
by Ruthanne Tobin

When Tobin wrote this chapter, she was a new faculty member herself. In a step-by-step guide, she takes the reader through the process of preparing a course outline. Two of Tobin's wonderful pieces of advice in this section are "consulting with other faculty members for examples of old course outlines" and with publishers regarding "exam copies" of textbooks and Access Copyright laws. New faculty often feel isolated in this time consuming process, but just as research is built upon an existing body of knowledge, so is teaching (Prégent, 1994). Someone has taught the course before. Old course outlines and methods exist. Seeking such collegial support builds networks.

For new professors, few tasks are as daunting as the planning and organizing of a course which they are about to teach. Much of the trepidation and challenge of designing a course, and then writing an outline for it, stem from a desire to make the course coherent, cohesive and comprehensive the first time that it is presented. Many experienced professors will tell you that it frequently takes two or three times through a course before they are comfortable with its shape and substance. Organization of the course, and the subsequent revision of the course outline or syllabus each time we teach it, is a process of continuous improvement for most of us. Our own experiences with the course, the feedback from our students, and our students' achievement in the course, all contribute to the necessary refinements.

While nothing can take the place of this experience, the initial organizing and planning can be much more successful, efficient and rewarding if you follow a few basic guidelines. In this chapter, you will find an outline of some essential guidelines for organizing a course for the first time and a description of some of the key decisions to be made and essential elements to be included in a course outline or syllabus. Whether you are teaching your first course ever, or a first course at a new university, some of these suggestions will help you get off to a smoother start.

Don't Go It Alone: Gathering Resources and Knowing the History of the Course

As with any other task, we need to gather the tools and resources before we begin. Foremost at this stage is that you should not attempt to go it alone. This is the best time to elicit support and advice — most of your colleagues will recall only too well their first forays into college or university teaching.

Don't skip the obvious first step of carefully reading the course description in your university calendar. Remember, the information in the course calendar is all that your students have available to them at course selection time. Also, scan the descriptions of other related courses in your discipline in order to extract the key differences between the courses and to help you place your course in a larger context of a student's program.

Become familiar with the key dates from both your university calendar and your faculty's internal calendar, which may have an impact on your course outline. This is particularly important if your faculty is involved in co-op programs, practica or internships which will create natural parameters around assignments and may influence the time of core concepts required in students' applied work, and due dates.

The next step is to contact the chair of your department for copies of course outlines constructed by other professors so that you can see the parameters that others in your field have set in order to cover, or uncover, the content of a particular subject area. The administrative assistant to your faculty's chair generally keeps course outlines dating back several years. Ensure that you get two course outlines written by two different professors from recent years so that you get a broader view of how this course was handled before you arrived. Also ask for a copy of the evaluation sheet that students will be using to assess your course. Items that are included on the student evaluation will give you some indication of what your university and your faculty consider to be sufficiently important about teaching and learning.

One effective way of getting organized is to use a one- or two-inch binder for each course that you teach. Entitle the binder: "Administration of Course 260" and insert the sample syllabi, a photocopy of the calendar description, important faculty dates, information you have gleaned about popular textbooks and your notes from talking to other faculty members about the course.

Making the Most of Sample Course Outlines

The main purposes of perusing sample course outlines are to give you some starting points for shaping your own course, and to consider some sensible framing parameters. The most useful information you could glean includes suggestions for student textbooks, assessment and evaluation ideas, clarity in the wording of course objectives, and exposure to what others in your field thought were important topics or concepts. If your samples of syllabi have been written by colleagues who are still within your department or faculty, ask if they would meet briefly with you to discuss things they may have changed or refined since their last official revisions of their course outlines.

If you come across a course outline that articulates the course objectives particularly well, or has a clever way of handling assignments, consider contacting the professor and asking if you may adopt this section. Some professors add a note at the end of their course outlines such as: "I would like to acknowledge the contributions of Dr. Elizabeth Smith in preparing this course outline." This not only appropriately acknowledges the contribution of others, but also sets a collaborative tone which is highly desirable in college and university teaching.

Three Initial Decisions about Your Course

There are at least three initial decisions which you must make about your course. Firstly, what do you want students to know or understand at the end of your course that they didn't know or understand at the beginning? In other words, what are the big ideas/ concepts/ core course objectives or essential understandings of your course?

Secondly, what resources should students purchase, or be able to access, in order to prepare for your classes, assignments or exams and to achieve the core objectives. Thirdly, how will you assess or evaluate your students' knowledge and understanding of the core concepts?

Often, novice professors choose a popular textbook based on recommendations within their faculty or from sample course outlines. So-called *desk copies* of textbooks can be obtained free of charge from the publisher if you intend to use that text for your students. Some publishers may require that the order for your students' texts be placed at the same time. The administrative assistant to the Chair of your department often will handle such textbook orders for you. You may also contact publishers of textbooks in your discipline directly, and then explain that you are new to teaching in the field and would like to peruse some of their textbooks. Describe to them the types and levels of courses that you are teaching, or are likely to be teaching.

The pre-existing organization of a text book is a major advantage when compared to using a compilation of readings. A book's structure may aid in shaping your course or making the subject matter more easily understood. Some textbooks also come with an instructor's manual, which may include some blackline masters and chapter tests, and may even offer some suggestions on how to present the material. A note of warning though — the quality of such manuals varies considerably, so make sure you evaluate it first hand and, if possible, ask the opinion of other professors.

The disadvantage of textbooks is that they are rarely a perfect fit with your course objectives. Professors new to teaching a particular course often trade off the lack of ideal fit for the organizational framework that a textbook provides for their students and the time difference that compiling a series of readings would entail at this particular stage of their career. At later stages, as professors become discontent with the unavailability of what they consider to be comprehensive, user-friendly texts, they sometimes compile their own readings and may publish their own textbooks to meet this need.

At the very beginning of our careers, most of us are grateful for a well-organized text that is a reasonable fit with our course objectives, and we accept the need to supplement the text with other readings. The term texts or readings is used in the broadest sense; in addition to books and articles you may also wish to use music, film, painting, architecture, primary documents, virtual course kits etc.

A couple of perennial pet peeves of students concerning required textbooks are the price (over which you have no control once you have made your selection), and professors who rarely refer to the text and/or whose in-class lectures, discussions and collaborative groups do not relate to the information in the text. Both of these concerns can be avoided by careful consideration of how the textbook fits with your course content, and by stating clearly to students that part of class time will be devoted to elaborating or discussing the readings, and part will be focused on other aspects of the course, not all of which are mentioned in the textbook. Consider asking students their opinions at the end of the course about the textbook and take this information into consideration in making your decision the next time you teach the same course.

Ensure that you determine the budget your faculty or department permits for photocopying of student handouts. It is not uncommon for universities to require professors to collect a small photocopy fee at the beginning of the course to defray costs. It is critical that you state in the course outline the amount that will be charged to students for photocopying. Of course, no discussion of photocopying would be adequate without mention of the Access$^{©TM}$ laws (formerly CANCOPY). Short versions of the Access Copyright laws can be obtained from your chair, or from their website {http://www.accesscopyright.ca}. Most government institutions such as colleges and universities purchase collective licensing for copyright materials. For one annual fee, they are entitled to photocopy sections of print material for educational purposes. The percentage of a book, journal, or reference material institutions are allowed to photocopy under this agreement varies; as a result, you must disclose the number of pages from a particular text which you intend to photocopy so that the institution can verify whether they have paid for the right to do so or not. If you are an author, collective licensing benefits you annually. By registering with Access$^{©TM}$ access spot checks the number of times an article or book of yours has been either checked out of a library or photocopied, and as a result, you receive a small amount of remuneration for that public use of your work. Thus, becoming familiar and abiding by Access$^{©TM}$ may avoid embarrassment or legal repercussions and will also influence your textbook and materials selection decisions.

Universities generally have well honed procedures for student access to articles, books, journals, and other materials, through the reserve readings section of the library. With some notice, library staff will locate books and articles that you want to place on reserve reading so as to avoid subjecting your personal copies to the wear and tear of student use. In the case of an obscure article, or to accelerate the process, you may choose to provide the library staff with best quality copy you have available. Library staff usually requires a few days processing time to put materials on reserve for your students and often ask you to indicate the maximum length of time any student may sign out the materials. Usual options are a two-hour loan or overnight sign-out.

If possible, in consideration of students' financial needs, you may also consider placing a copy of the textbook (other than your own desk copy) on reserve for your students.

One other option at some universities is a *course pack* of course reading materials. This is a selected group of readings chosen by you that is copied, compiled and bound for your students and sold at the bookstore. This option is not recommended for most novices since it requires a fair amount of time to make the selections and to verify copy laws, as well as proper acknowledgement and permissions before sending it to the university printer. It also requires quite a broad understanding of the best and most comprehensive research relevant to your course. Few novice professors possess either the required breadth or time to construct a course pack. It is included as an option here because occasionally someone on your faculty may have already assembled a course pack which you may wish to consider using.

The method you plan to use to evaluate your students is another decision that you need to make prior to putting together your course outline. You can be sure that this will be the first section of your course outline to which most students will refer, so they can discover what they need to do to be successful in the course. The evaluation method you decide to use must be one that can equitably assess the extent of each student's knowledge or understanding of particular concepts that have been stated in your course objectives. You must determine the evidence that you need to collect that will prove to you what they know. Assessment (gathering data) and evaluation (making judgments about the gathered data) are always concerned with "the two P's" - purpose and possibility. The purpose of any assignment is to lead students to a greater understanding of the course objectives. It must also be possible for you to be able to mark each assignment fairly. An assignment may have a clear purpose, but it may not be possible for you to give a proper evaluation to every student simply because of the number of students that you teach or supervise. In other cases, it may require too much time for you to be able to give adequate feedback on an assignment in order to provide every student with the information they need to improve their work and clarify their understandings.

Here too, it is important to draw on your resources. Ask your colleagues how many and what types of assignments are typical in your faculty. For example, Chris Clovis and Judy Ableser do a fine job of discussing this in Section 3. of this manual. If the rationale for the number and type of assignments is not clear to you, make sure you ask why the current practice is what it is. Some practices arise from years of experience and refinement, while others are the result of "We've always done it that way" mentality. Sometimes faculties will have decided on informal policies of a particular number of assignments based on the credit value of the course. When meeting with a colleague to discuss your course, it is always a good idea, after you have asked your specific questions, to add one more: "What else may be helpful for me to know about how courses are taught, evaluated or organized in this faculty?" Give your colleague sufficient time to reflect so as to allow a thoughtful answer.

So far, you have discovered the history and parameters of your designated course in your department/faculty by analyzing sample course outlines and talking to colleagues and your Chair. You have made three critical decisions regarding your core objectives for the course (i.e. what students are expected to know or understand by the end of this course); you have selected both the required and the recommended textbooks or materials that your students will use; and finally, you have determined the number and type of assignments that your students will be required to complete in order to show their understanding of the course objectives. You have selected assignments that have a clear purpose in helping students understand the course content and which you believe can be evaluated adequately. With this groundwork completed, you are now ready to write the course outline.

Writing the Course Outline

A course outline is a contract between a professor and students which states what the professor will do and what the students are expected to do. At the end of this chapter, you will find samples of course outlines which are less useful than the ones you have gathered explicitly for your course but which may give you some formatting ideas, typical assignment descriptions and a sense of how courses are framed.

A course outline is intended to describe your framework for delineating how you have organized a particular body of information or knowledge and the workings of the class, or how each class is structured to facilitate an understanding of this knowledge. If you have not clearly delineated in the course outline both what you will do and what students are expected to do, communication difficulties may arise. Ideally, no changes should be made to the course outline after it is distributed to students without discussion and class consensus.

The essential components of a course outline can be summarized as: where and when to find you (General Information); when and what you will cover in this course (Topics, Core Concepts and Objectives); when and how you will evaluate student understanding of the core concepts of this course (Assignments & Evaluation); and what will happen in the event that students do not meet the delineated expectations of the course (Notes). An example of a typical course outline is given below.

Example of a Course Outline

Education Department St. Francis Xavier University P.O. Box 5000 Antigonish, Nova Scotia B2G 2W5	Dr. Ruthanne Tobin Office # 204 Phone: 867-5406 <rtobin@stfx.ca> Office Hours: Tuesday 10:30- noon Thursday 10:30 –noon Before and after classes and by appointment.

Education 414 Curriculum & Instruction in Language Arts 11 (three credits)
Winter, 2001   Tuesday and Thursday

Course Description (Academic Calendar, p.62)

"This course is designed to prepare prospective elementary teachers to teach the language arts: reading, writing, speaking, listening, and viewing. Also included is whole language programming, children's literature, authentic assessment, and organizing the classroom for language instruction across the curriculum. Throughout this course, the practical influence of various language arts theories is emphasized."

Required Text

Tompkins, Gail. Teaching Writing: Balancing Process and Product 3rd ed. Prentice-Hall, 2000. (We will be covering specific chapters only

General Information

Course outlines begin with the name of your university, the faculty, your name, email, your office location and phone number and your office hours. Most universities have minimum guidelines on how many hours faculty members must allocate for meeting with students. Some suggest that faculty keep scheduled office hours equivalent to the number of teaching hours. Preferably, these hours should be posted near your door and printed on your course outline. In other universities, because of idiosyncrasies of student schedules, the policy is to have students book an appointment with professors at times that are mutually convenient, by contacting you by email or telephone. Be sure to check your faculty contract and ask about the standard procedures within your department. If these practices vary considerably within your faculty, ask your Chair what the expectations are in this regard.

Clearly, what is most important is that when students do come to find you at your appointed office hours that you are there. Also be reminded that no matter what questions or concerns students bring to you, they have also come for some reassurance of their performance or potential performance in your class. Show by your demeanor that you are glad they stopped by, and if appropriate, validate their willingness to seek clarification or help. Consider phrases such as: *"I'm glad you came by"*; *"You seem to be making sense of this"*; or *"You're on the right track"*. Of course, if this is not the case try: *"It's good to get clarification on this"* or *"As you study/practice/read more I'm sure it will make more sense to you"*. This is still important even if their question was answered twice already in class and written in your outline or other handout. Learners are often dealing with competing stimuli in class and they don't always make sense of content until they have an immediate need to know, such as during completion of an assignment or when they can talk it through with someone.

To make the best use of office hours, it is wise to encourage students in class to read their course outlines attentively and, if possible, write down their queries before they come to see you. This helps them clarify where they need help. Frequently, it may lead them to discover the answer to their inquiry in information that you have already provided. Keeping a copy of your course outline and any recent handouts on your bulletin board or other handy spot for easy reference also helps in meetings with students who know they need help but are less prepared or focused.

Students sometimes have difficulty ending a conversation with their professors. Whenever you see this happening with your students, and you feel that their questions or concerns have been answered or at least addressed, or their comments have become circular, help them close off the conversation by repeating that you are glad they came by, or by inviting them to return when they have considered what you have discussed or have done further reading. With a student who is particularly unskilled at ending conversations, consider standing as you make these comments.

If you have been pre-empted in getting to do the course outline due to the lateness of your appointment to the university or to some other challenge that accompanies relocation, the critical thing is to get some information down in each of the categories we have discussed. For example, include two or three of your course objectives, a couple of sample topics and a very brief description or naming of the assignment with a note that says: "Students will receive a more detailed description of this assignment in one of the early classes". This gives you time to gather your resources and to elaborate more clearly on what you expect students to do.

Topics, Core Concepts and Objectives

This next section of the course outline is intended to show some sequence or structure to how the course will unfold. A list of topics to be covered, perhaps with dates and readings, is very helpful in allowing students to plan their study and reading times. On the other hand, if you are teaching a course for the first time, you may find this too confining until you know how long a topic will likely sustain the interest of the students and/or how long it will take to reach your objective. If you want this flexibility, consider listing the topics with tentative dates and a note indicating that you will be making some adjustments according to student needs.

A second paragraph needs to address what formats or strategies you will be using during the class. Some examples may include small interactive talking groups, lectures, labs, tutorials, field experiences, large group discussion and debates.

Assignments and Evaluation

Elsewhere in this book is a discussion of evaluation, which will address many of your questions. It is worth noting here the possibility of giving a brief description of each of the assignments or tests with a sentence or two indicating that a more detailed description of the assignment and/or criteria for marking will be discussed well in advance of the due date. If all the information about assignments is given in the syllabi, students sometimes become overwhelmed by the volume of information and pay less attention to areas more critical to course success.

Notes

This section is intended to tell students what will happen if they do not meet the expectations you have outlined above. It gives them specific information about your policies, guidelines or conditions regarding attendance in classes or labs, make-up exams, options (if any) on missed or failed tests, penalties for late assignments, etc. The dilemma in writing this section is to give enough specific information that students know what to expect, but allows enough room for you to exercise discretion in your dealings with them. This is never easy. There is always a trade-off between setting policies in writing and dealing with individual circumstances as they arise. Professors address this by encouraging students to communicate with them if there are extenuating circumstances that hinder their performance. Any professor who has worked with undergraduates has heard a fair share of woeful, albeit sometimes doubtful tales, yet it is also true that grandparents do die (and in the current face of blended families, the credence of this reason/excuse has grown significantly); serious illnesses do occur; relationships end painfully; and yes, occasionally technology fails when we need it most. While many of our students are young adults with school and perhaps part-time work as their main time absorbers, increasingly we are also enrolling students in our classes who are parents; more than casual part-time workers; caregivers for their aging parents; and many who serve in multiple other roles. Will these competing demands factor into your thinking around how to respond when students do not meet the expectations outlined in your course outline? How will you show your understanding of fairness and equity? Thinking through your own balance between accountability and flexibility is very important. Discussing this balance with a colleague can give you invaluable insights into the challenges of working with learners in successful ways.

Introducing the Course Outline/Anticipating Questions

Although counter-intuitive, the best time to present the course outline is often not at the beginning of the first class, but toward the middle of that class. The reason many professors find this more effective is the realization that discussion of the course outline generally initiates the topic of evaluation and assignments which may not help in establishing the relaxed tone you desire at the beginning of the first class. Many professors start with some general information about why the course is interesting, relevant, worthwhile or important, in order to generate some enthusiasm about the content. A joke or personal anecdote can also set a relaxed tone prior to introducing the details of the course outline. Others in smaller classes (30-40) use an ice-breaker, whereby students have the opportunity to meet a few other students by participating in an activity such as "Find someone who recently visited a different province this summer; someone who speaks three languages; someone who...". Experienced professors acknowledge this as a valuable part of establishing a tone conducive to learning. In larger classes (60-100 students), professors have students turn to the person on either side of them and tell them one piece of information about themselves pertaining to this course. For example, you might have students ask one another why they enrolled in your course.

Once you distribute the course outline, accept the reality that many students will invariably switch to the page that answers that pressing question *"What do I need to do?"*. You will likely need to draw their attention to the course description, the objectives and the topics list in order to proceed with the debriefing of the course outline. Your efforts in organizing the course outline will be much more effective if you walk the students through each section. Walking them through does not mean reading every word aloud, but engaging them in some of the key ideas. Profs successfully do this by asking students to read the course objectives and identify the one that they already know something about. If your course is a true introductory course, try asking them which objective/concept/topic most interests/intrigues them or which makes the most sense. As soon as we ask learners to make some decisions, to compare or contrast or to offer an opinion, they are much more likely to be engaged. Placing them in a passive role of having them track along and "listen" while you read the course outline will not likely accomplish this.

Anticipating Questions and Uncertainties

In the section on required texts and readings, make sure you have found out from the bookstore the cost of the book and whether there are used copies available or not. There will be questions that arise on the first day that it will not be possible to address until the students get some teaching and understanding of the course. Alleviate some uncertainty by telling them that there are parts of the course outline which will make much more sense as they get initiated into the content. Some students "jump the gun" and try to settle their uncertainties before it's possible or desirable to do so. It also helps to lightly remind students or indicate to them that some confusion and uncertainty is part of the learning process and that developing a tolerance for a certain amount of ambiguity is a sign of intellectual growth. This by no means suggests that as instructors we do not strive to be clear in our teaching and direction, but as we well know, not all learning occurs in a sequential or linear fashion, but rather occurs in highly contextual and recursive ways.

At the end of the first class, assign the course outline as part of the required reading for the next class, indicating to students how much better equipped they will be to do well in this course if they know the overall framework.

Student Evaluation of Your Course

Avoid the common error of waiting until the very end of the semester to find out what students are thinking about your course. About a third of the way through the course, it is a good idea to get a broad indication of misunderstandings, concerns or validations about your course. This need not be time consuming. Consider asking students to anonymously list two things that they have enjoyed or found interesting about the course to date and one suggestion on how you might improve it for the course duration. Or ask students to tell you the two main points that you made in today's class. Encourage them to be as specific as possible, providing them with a few examples, such as: "I'm finding the textbook user-friendly"; "I wish the readings went on reserve earlier"; "I can't quite read your handwriting on the overhead"; or "The PowerPoint presentations go by a little fast".

Some things you will not want or be able to address, while others are easily improved if you have the information. Students appreciate that you take their opinions into account at a time when they can still benefit from any improvements. If you teach several sections of a course, or a large number of students in one course, consider taking only a sample feedback from a couple of sections or select student numbers at random to give you an indication. Remember, even if you decide to give an opportunity for every student to provide early feedback, you don't need to read more than a sample to get an indication of how your students are experiencing the course.

As with all new endeavors it is important to ask for help when you can most use it and view course syllabi as living documents that change over time as you respond to the needs of your students and your own experiences of what is effective in your discipline.

To Further Teaching:

Jerowski, S. (1994, July). Assessment and evaluation. Paper presented at the University of Victoria, Victoria, British Columbia.

Wiggins, G. & McTighe, J. (1998). Understanding by design. Alexandria, Association for Supervision and Curriculum Development, The Canadian Copyright Licensing Agency. Retrieved November 3, 2002), from http://www.accesscopyright.ca

Teaching for Inclusion in University Classrooms
by Benedicta Egbo

When course planning, one must consider the deeper seeds of learning rooted in equity. If you are an instructor at an institution with a diverse student population, then you must also begin to consider ways of making your subject relevant to everyone. Since we, as instructors, tend to approach our subject areas on the basis of our lived experiences, it is often possible to exclude groups with whom we have [seemingly] nothing in common. Students learn best when the material has some relevance to their own experiences and backgrounds. Finding these links with students is critical and best done prior to teaching. Through an overview of the theory involved, Egbo succinctly outlines some practical methods for creating inclusive classrooms. "Who is in my class?" she asks. The answers to this simple but far-reaching question will help instructors make the preparations and connections that allow for inclusive teaching and learning in university classrooms.

Introduction

Like other institutions of learning, universities are increasingly becoming diversified learning environments. Demographic trends and predictions suggest that university classrooms in Canada will become even more diversified in the near future as a reflection of cultural and linguistic diversity among students in the first two tiers of our educational systems. Juxtaposed with other socio-demographic variables such as gender, class, differential learning styles etc., university teachers must now find ways of meeting the challenge of teaching to include everyone in such an amalgam of student population. Paying particular attention to three related aspects- gender, minority empowerment and critical classroom language, this chapter explores how instructors can make their classrooms more inclusive learning environments. The key stance adopted in the chapter is that professors need to create alternative visions of their classrooms beyond orthodox practices and pedagogies that quite often, do not reflect the socio-demographic realities of contemporary university classrooms. The fundamental goal of inclusive teaching in university classrooms is to value, nurture, and draw on the diverse experiences and perspectives of all students for the purposes of critically engaging them in the teaching and learning process.

In discussing the strategies, I adopt a contingency approach- that is, the specific strategies adopted by individual professors will vary according to teaching contexts and other variables such as class size, academic discipline and the degree of diversity among the student population. It should however be emphasized that while subject differences may result in variations in strategies, every discipline lends itself to critical and just classroom practices whether the discipline is education, engineering, history, mathematics, psychology or sociology. As a consequence, the discussion here transcends disciplinary boundaries and each suggested strategy is potentially adaptable to every subject area. For practical convenience, I discuss the strategies from a temporal framework– pre-instructional activities, instructional activities and post-instructional analysis.

Pre-instructional Activities

The pre-instruction phase includes all preparatory planning and activities that precede the actual lecture or seminar. In addition to routine content-related preparations, this stage is particularly crucial for instructors who wish to teach for inclusion and empowerment because the extent to which they succeed depends on what they do at this stage of the process beginning with critical self-analysis. There is a growing body of literature on faculty professional development that cites critical self-analysis as a method for improving practice (Biggs, 2003; Kreber and Cranton, 2000; Gibson, 1998). The argument by experts in favour of self-examination (which in turn, leads to reflective teaching) is based on the belief that teachers who engage regularly in self-reflection as well as closely monitor their classroom activities can easily diagnose and subsequently modify undesirable practices particularly those that may contribute to the alienation of subordinated groups such as women and minorities whose world views are not represented in mainstream knowledge. Critical reflection also provides professors with opportunities to interrogate the moral and philosophical assumptions that inform their teaching practices including the way they use language in class. Knowing ourselves is an integral aspect of inclusive practice because not all are our practices are as "neutral" or "value-free" as we would like to think.

An important starting point for critically analyzing ourselves and our teaching is the construction of practical questions that will facilitate the development of inclusive and empowering classroom strategies. The following are examples of some pertinent questions that professors can ask themselves early in the process:

- what are my preconceptions of other groups in society particularly those that are different from mine?
- in what ways do my personal history and world views affect my teaching practices?
- how do I relate to people that are different from me especially among my students? E.g. male, female, racial and linguistic minorities?
- in what ways am I contributing to the silencing of the voices of some groups in society especially those that are represented by my students?
- in what ways do I reinforce stereotypes through my teaching practices?
- what kinds of resources do I use in my teaching? How relevant are they to the lived experiences of *all* my students especially those from traditionally marginalized groups?
- what are my expectations for my students and how committed am I to the success of *all*?
- how current am I with research in the area of inclusion, equity and power relations in society in general and university classrooms in particular?
- what does the research say?

- how often do I reflect on my teaching?
- how can I improve my teaching?

It is conceivable that professors who engage regularly in this kind of self-reflection are likely to become critical teachers who work towards inclusion in their teaching environments. However, to be exceptionally successful, self-reflection should be considered as an integral part of the preparatory activities for every class rather than as additional work in an already tight schedule.

Instructional Activities
This is the phase in which the instructor delivers the actual lecture or seminar beginning with an important activity I refer to as *"environmental scanning"*.

Environmental Scanning
I use this term to describe the process of appraising the student composition of a class beginning with a simple question but often ignored question "who is in my class?" While at first glance, such an activity may appear only remotely connected to the crucial task of completing an often ambitious syllabus within a matter of weeks, personal experience has shown that without initial assessment and understanding of who we are teaching, preparations for instruction cannot be adequately made since such scanning provides instructors with valuable information that is necessary for the effective planning of subsequent lectures. In other words, the "findings" of such scanning should help professors make informed decisions or revisions (as the case may be) with regards to appropriate pedagogical strategies, materials, language, assessment formats etc. to be used during lectures over the course of a semester or year. Although it sounds rather cumbersome, in practice, systematic classroom scanning need not continue after the first few classes in a new semester since it is essentially diagnostic and therefore no longer necessary once the instructor becomes reasonably familiar with the students in his or her class.

I have found through personal practice that opening and closing activities are also critical to the success of any lecture particularly one that aims to include, empower and critically engage all students. In their discussion of strategies for empowering female students, Litner, Rossiter and Taylor (1992) recommend beginning a class with apparently trivial and inconsequential conversations that are in reality, important acknowledgement that the professor and the students share similar human experiences. Such exchanges, designed to put students at ease, may be nonverbal such as a smile or a nod. They may also be brief but pleasant conversations about such mundane issues as campus parking and the weather (a common ice breaker). According to Litner et al., professors' acknowledgement and affirmation of student presence are critical because many walk into the classroom feeling apprehensive and alienated especially minority groups who already feel excluded from mainstream society. As Kreizinger (2006) points out, the key to empowering students is making critical connections even on the first day of class. Besides letting students know that they are valued members of the class, professors can also empower their students by using inclusive language.

Pedagogy and language of inclusion

The adoption of strategies that are cognisant of the interplay between power and knowledge construction in the classroom, as well as the fact that students learn differently, is crucial in any program that aims to be inclusive. Unfortunately, some professors, especially those at the early stages of their career and those who have not had any formal training in the methodology of teaching, enter the classroom without a basic knowledge of what constitutes inclusive or critical pedagogy, i.e., teaching that acknowledges other people's ways of knowing while simultaneously critiquing the predominantly mainstream ideologies that are routinely transmitted to students. Of course, it is not realistic to expect professors to integrate every student's learning style into their teaching practices especially given the time and resource constrained environments that university classrooms have become. It is however important for instructors to bear in mind that real differences exist in how students learn and to strive towards respecting these differences regardless of the discipline or subject area.

An equally important inclusive strategy is the use of participatory language in the classroom. Researchers have gathered overwhelming evidence that shows that collaborative dialogue in the classroom contributes significantly to students' learning. Unfortunately research also shows that discursive practices tend to be exclusionary at all levels of education thus limiting the participation of some groups of students such as women and minorities in classroom discussions. Although significant strides have been taken towards challenging and changing the status quo, many researchers agree that the language of the classroom does not often reflect women's ways of knowing since female discursive practices are different from the dominant male norms. Unfortunately, language plays a key role in the maintenance of uneven power relations in society (Corson, 1993).

With regards to university classrooms, Shor (1992) distinguishes between dialogical or participatory communication as opposed to teacher talk in which teachers dominate classroom discussions. Participatory classroom discourse is important because it is student-centred and aims to facilitate the development of critical thought and inclusive communication which engage rather than disengage students. By contrast, teacher talk is "the one-way discourse of traditional classrooms that...alienates students, depresses their achievement and supports inequality in school and society" (p. 85). Because teacher-talk tends to suppress critical thought, students become disinterested and put up resistance that sabotages their desire to learn. The following comments from a female participant in a study that examined power relationships in university classrooms (Kramarae and Treichler, 1990) illustrate the point:

> The professors dominate the scene, sort of not making students want to speak and interact unless the students feel very secure; and there are some students ... who do feel very cer-

tain of themselves and want to make a show of themselves (p. 44).

Commenting on teacher behaviour during a particular lecture as part of the same study, another female participant offered the following view "[I felt] the professors [were] just judging your viewpoint, you know, standing there like the tribunal, making you feel like a moron" (p. 44).

My general point here is that professors who truly want to make their classrooms inclusive learning environments, must create opportunities to dialogue with all students regardless of class size although arguably, the number of students in the class will determine the amount of time allotted to such discussions. Instead of teacher talk, professors should strive towards making the classroom a community of learners where knowledge is created collaboratively with their students. In brief, professors who plan to infuse empowering pedagogy and inclusive language into their classrooms practices should do the following:

- create a learning environment that provides all students with ample opportunities to express themselves and share their views, i.e., allow the "voices" of all students to be heard
- use language sensitively i.e., use non-racist, non-sexist language and anti-bias language
- adopt participatory and democratic discursive practices.
- strive towards integrating various teaching techniques into their lectures
- show empathy and sensitivity when presenting materials that reinforce stereotypes, e.g., prevailing stereotypes of women, minorities and other marginalized groups (if possible, avoid using such material)
- encourage positive teacher-student and student-peer interactions

Group work
A time-tested strategy that fosters participation and inclusion in classrooms is group work. There is general consensus among educators that small group discussions for instance encourage cooperative and collaborative behaviour among students. Group work also promotes the involvement of students such as self-conscious language minorities, who would otherwise not speak in the larger group. My own experience shows that group work and discussions do indeed provide valuable opportunities for students to interact among themselves thus creating a climate that enhances the quality of classroom experience for all. One strategy for facilitating group work especially in large classes, is to randomly group students (using the class list) even before the first class. The list should then be posted strategically around the classroom or lecture hall. By the end of the second lecture, students should be familiar with members of their groups thus making it easy for them to organize for in- or out-of-class group activities. Although class size is often considered a determinant factor in decid-

ing whether or not to include group work in the classroom activities in universities, class size does not impede grouping students for assignments, in-class discussions etc. On the contrary, experts believe that group work and discussions enhance the quality of teaching and learning even in large classes.

Post-instructional Analysis

Like the first stage, this stage is reflective but, the focus here is on determining how successful the instruction was including the strategies that were used. It is in effect, the stage during which an instructor decides on which strategies to reinforce, refine, modify or eliminate either because they worked very well or failed to contribute to inclusion in any meaningful way. Because it provides opportunities for self-critique, post-instructional analysis can also reveal valuable information about ourselves and our teaching that can only become evident after the fact. Gibson (1998) for instance, provides a compelling narrative of the unravelling of the intersections of her own personal beliefs and ideologies on the one hand, and her teaching practices on the other, through a reflective analysis of a class she had taught to a group of graduate students. The class discussion had focussed on the learning pace and social separation of ethnoculturally different students. Through post-instructional analysis, Gibson realizes how she had "retreated" from discussing with her students, the political implications of some taken-for -granted school practices such as tracking. She contends that her confrontation with "self" and the interrogation of her own practices, exposed prejudices which had been submerged, leading her to conclude that "encounters with self as a cultural entity, as a teacher, and as a learner are critical components in the construction of culturally relevant pedagogy" (p.361) Some guiding questions for post-instructional analysis include, but are not limited to the following:

- did I achieve the goals of inclusion that I had planned to accomplish?
- why was I successful or why was I unsuccessful?
- to what extent did I succeed in involving *all* my students?
- did I provide the students equal opportunity to express themselves?
- who did I call on to respond to questions and why?
- which teaching strategies should be reinforced in subsequent lectures?
- which strategies require modification?
- did I dominate class discussions?
- did I use language appropriately?
- was knowledge jointly created with my students?

To be very effective, post-instructional analysis should be conducted immediately after each class when the proceedings are still fresh in the professor's mind. Post-instructional analysis is by no means a time-consuming activity especially once the process becomes an integral part of a professor's teaching practices. Furthermore, if the analysis is properly done, the answers to the questions listed above should provide useful insights that will facilitate the planning of subsequent lectures. It should be emphasized that although conceptually separate, the three phases discussed here are interconnected since the process is rather cyclical. For example, while pre-instructional activities set the stage and inform professors' activities during lectures, insights gained from post-instructional analysis will in turn, guide preparations for subsequent lectures or seminars thus beginning the cycle again as figure 1 illustrates.

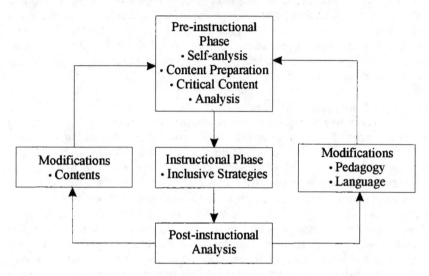

Figure 1: A Practical Model of Inclusive Teaching

Other Practical Inclusive Strategies
Out-of-class consultations

Quite often, students thrive in less threatening environments than the classroom. Arranging mandatory one-on-one or group (for large classes) consultations (besides tutorials) within the first few weeks of class is an effective way of engaging and dialoguing with students especially those that are reluctant to participate in class. I have found this strategy to be very effective in "loosening up" quiet students. Time and time again, students have told me during one-on-one discussions that they are often intimidated to speak in class. This strategy is particularly useful for engaging language minority students who sometimes feel self-conscious and therefore find it difficult to speak freely in class. In my experience, participation in class discussions among some of my students tends to increase after such consultations. But, besides increases in participation, out-of-class contacts have the potential of improving educational achievement among some groups of students especially minority students (Hurtado et. al., 1999). In sum, if we expect our students to engage our course content, we must first engage them in critical dialogue both in and outside the lecture hall.

Related to, although less effective than one-on-one contact, is e-mail correspondence which offers faculty another medium for maintaining ongoing dialogue and consultations with students. I use this strategy to encourage my students to ask questions or to seek additional help. Like direct consultations, e-mail exchanges can be extremely time consuming particularly in large classes. But, faculty that is committed to making a difference can find creative ways of minimizing the volume of work. For example, rather than responding individually to all questions particularly those that are of a general nature, instructors can identify commonalities in students' e-mail queries and then use them as the basis for in-class discussions with the entire group. As in direct faculty/student consultations, the value of e-mail communication lies in the fact that it provides students who would not normally speak in class, an alternative forum for sharing their thoughts on a regular basis.

Learning Students' Names

A corollary to one-on-one consultations is learning and remembering students' names. This strategy lets students know that they belong, that the class is their turf as well the instructor's (Litner et. al., 1992). Thinking back to our own university experiences, we can all remember the classes that were particularly inviting as well as those that were less welcoming. One distinguishing factor would be, I suspect, the extent to which professors referred to students by their names especially those from non-mainstream backgrounds. But, the value of learning students' names as an inclusive strategy is supported by more than anecdotal evidence. A study by Denzine and Pulos (2000) found that knowing students names is an important determinant of students' perceptions of instructors' approachability, so much so that the researchers recommend that faculty should let students know when they forget their names. They also suggest that instructors use name plates and other memory aids to help them remember the names of their students.

Organizing Seating Arrangements

While this would be quite challenging in large lecture halls and amphitheatres, arranging students' seating in such way as to create comfortable and informal learning environment has been known to increase students' interest and participation in class. I have found in my own practice that informal seating arrangements tend to give students a sense of inclusion which in turn, encourages increased interaction with each other. The end result is that students become much more relaxed and willing to participate in class discussions, group projects and other activities.

Different Assessment/Evaluation Options

Constructivists have long acknowledged that students learn and construct meaning differently. It seems logical to assume that differential learning styles should also be reflected in the types of assessment strategies that professors and indeed, all teachers adopt. More importantly, assessment format matters since different formats will produce different results (Biggs, 2003). Providing assessment options is vital in contexts of student diversity since that increases the chances of every student finding at least one approach that is congruent with his or her learning style, cultural background or ways of knowing. But, a word of caution; in providing students with choices in assessment methods, professors must be careful not to replace cognitively challenging assignments with watered-down options. The trick is to provide students with equally challenging choices.

Conclusion

While this chapter has presented some practical guidelines to help instructors make their classrooms more inclusive learning environments, the point should be made that teaching for inclusion is by no means an easy task. First, it is time consuming and requires sustained effort. Second, the huge pressures that university professors face (particularly those that are new to the field) may understandably, act as impediments to adopting progressive practices that aim to empower all students. But, professors who are committed to integrating the voices of, and lived experiences of their students into their classroom practices, can change the status quo. Simply put, the prospect and promise of inclusive teaching in university classrooms depend on the commitment of faculty. It is however worth pointing out that nothing substitutes for expert and in-depth knowledge of the subject matter nor indeed, good teaching in any academic discipline. I would in fact argue that inclusive practice is an integral part of effective teaching especially in contexts of student diversity.

Finally, the overall goal of instructors who aim to teach for inclusion should be to provide a sense of ownership or belonging to students in the classroom. This is even more critical for women, racial and language minority students who come to school already disadvantaged. As I pointed out at the beginning of the chapter, strategies will vary according to contexts and disciplines but, taken together, the strategies discussed here will provide a critical starting point for professors who wish to infuse inclusive strategies into their classroom practices as part of a dynamic instructional program.

To Further Teaching:

Adams, M. (1997)Pedagogical frameworks for social justice education. In M. Adams, L. Bell and P. Griffin (eds). Teaching for Diversity and Social Justice (New York: Routledge).

Bellamy, L & Guppy, N. (1991). Opportunities and obstacles for women in Canadian higher education. In J. Gaskell and A. McLaren (eds). Women and Education. (2nd edition). Calgary: Detselig Enterprises.

Biggs, J. (2003) Teaching for Quality Learning at University. Berkshire (UK): The Society for Research into Higher Education & Open University Press

Corson, D. 1993. Language, Minority Education and Gender: Linking Social Justice and Power. Clevedon: Multilingual Matters/Toronto: OISE Press.

Denzine, G. & Pulos, S. (2000). College students' perceptions of faculty approachability. Educational Research Quarterly 24 (1): 56- 66.

Egbo, B. (1999) Options, Relevance and Voice: Transforming Minority Students' Educational Disempowerment through Critical Teaching. Paper presented at the annual conference of the Canadian Society for the Study of Education at the Université de Sherbrooke, Quebec, June 7-9, 1999.

Hurtado, S. Milem, J. Clayton-Pedersen, A, and Allen, W. (1999), Enacting Diverse Learning Environments: Improving the Climate for Racial/Ethnic Diversity in Higher Education. ASHE-ERIC Higher Education Reports 26 no 8 1-116.

Gibson, L. (1998) Teaching as an encounter with self: Unravelling the mix of personal beliefs, education Ideologies and pedagogical practices. Anthropology and Education Quarterly 29, (3), 360-371.

Kramarae, C. & Treichler, P. (1990) Power relationships in the classroom. In S. Gabriel and I. Smithson. Gender in the Classroom: Power and Pedagogy. Urbana: University of Illinois Press.

Kreber, C. & Cranton, P. (2000). Exploring the scholarships of teaching. The Journal of Higher Education, 71 (4) 477-495.

Kreizinger, J. (2006) Critical Connections for the First Day of Class. The Teaching Professor 20, (5), 1.

Litner, B., Rossiter, A. & Taylor, M (1992). The equitable inclusion of women in higher education: some consequences for teaching. Canadian Journal of Education 17 (3) 302.

Sadker, M. & Sadker, D. (1990). Confronting sexism in the college classroom. In S. Gabriel and I. Smithson. Gender in the Classroom: Power and Pedagogy. Urbana: University of Illinois Press.

Shor, I. (1992). Empowering Education: Critical Teaching for Social Change Chicago: University of Chicago Press.

Williams, (1990). Is the post-secondary classroom a chilly one for women?: A review of the literature. Canadian Journal of Higher Education 20 (3): 30-42.

Creating a Positive Culture and Climate in the University Classroom
by Doreen Shantz

Grounded in the social sciences, Shantz provides one instructor's method of creating an inclusive, positive climate, or atmosphere, within a classroom. College instructors who create lessons, or lectures, for their students try to ensure that the students' experiences are meaningful ones. Competent learning arises out of clear, successful experiences with the subject matter. A highly successful teacher herself, who actively engages her students, Shantz bases her techniques on the similar theories of McGlynn (2002) and Timpson & Burgoyne (2002).

Introduction

Creating a positive culture and climate in the classroom is a basic task that is required in order to be an effective university / college teacher. The concept of culture when applied to the classroom helps to examine the classroom as a human community and explore the various components that already exist (Glickman, Gordon & Ross-Gordon, 2001). Culture refers to the underlying values, beliefs, and traditions that are then translated into behaviour (Daresh & Playko, 1995). It involves many assumptions and shared norms. Climate then is the feel of a group or place. It can be defined as the personality of the group and is based on the culture (values, assumptions, beliefs). The climate in the classroom will be dependent to a great extent upon the teaching and learning philosophy of the teacher. Therefore it is important to sit down and draft your philosophy of teaching and learning. What do you believe is the role of the learner? of the teacher? What interaction should take place between teacher and learner? learner and learner? The answer to these questions will start to shape your philosophy and provide insights into what kind of culture and thus climate you want to establish in your classroom.

Teachers play many roles and your philosophy will determine to what extent you play the various roles of a teacher. They can be divided into three broad categories. The teacher as the: instructional expert, manager, and counsellor (Moore, 1995). In the role of the instructional expert you will plan, guide, and evaluate learning. The instructional expert needs to make decisions about instructional strategies, determining what topics can best be presented by what strategies. (The need for variety in lesson planning will be addressed in a later section of this chapter.) As the manager, you will make decisions and carry out actions required to maintain an effective learning environment. The manager needs to be organized and well prepared so that class time is used efficiently and not wasted. As the counsellor you need to be a sensitive observer of human behaviour. The counsellor needs to be aware of motivation theories and realize that students will learn what they want to learn and will have great difficulty learning material that does not interest them (McKeachie, 1994). The motivation of students is closely linked to the principles of adult learning.

Principles of Adult Learning

University / College students are usually young adults and they are beginning a phase of independence. Stephen Brookfield (1986) has suggested six principles of effective practice in facilitating adult learning:

1. Participation in learning is voluntary; intimidation or coercion have no place in motivating adult participation;
2. Effective practice is characterized by respect among participants for each other's self-worth - including teacher and learners;
3. Facilitation is collaborative, with learner and facilitators sharing responsibility for setting objectives and evaluating learning;
4. Praxis is at the heart of effective facilitation, with learners and facilitators involved in a continual cycle of collaborative activity and reflection on activity;
5. Facilitation aims to foster in adults a spirit of critical reflection. Educational encounters should assist adults to question many aspects of their lives; and
6. The aim of facilitation is the nurturing of self-directed, empowered adults who will function as proactive individuals.

The above characteristics of adult learning need to be addressed as much as possible by university or college teachers when planning lessons. Specifically it could mean the following:

1. Giving students some choice in assignments - topic, format, scope;
2. Making journals a mandatory part of the course and giving credit for journal writing;
3. Providing opportunities for students to collaborate with one another (see following section on Variety);
4. Treating students with respect at all times and not patronizing them in class as a group, or in individual interactions.

University / college teachers also need to be aware that students learn in different ways and at different speeds. Therefore lessons must be delivered in many ways.

Lesson Variety

Several kinds of learning are going on in the classroom. The first and most often stressed is figural - subject matter content; however there are others. Some examples are: cognitive or conceptual structures (the development of organized conceptual relationships); skills and strategies for learning and thinking; motives for learning (interest, curiosity, a sense of progress); self-efficacy (feeling competent to use current learning and to learn more); interpersonal or group skills (leadership, cooperation, giving and receiving help) (McKeachie, 1994). Varying your teaching can be effective in helping students understand their own learning processes. Many students find a two hour class an eternity (along with some professors). To make this time productive it is necessary to vary your presentation style as much as possible. Divide your class into two - one hour segments. The first can be utilized for information giving (lecture), assisting students to learn and remember specific facts, and organize the facts in such a way as to make sense of them. The second hour can be utilized for participation (group work), assisting students in applying the concepts to situations, analyzing the information, synthesizing or putting it together in a meaningful way, and evaluating it and making critical judgments (Gibbs, 1992). The combination provides an opportunity to share vital information, as well as encouraging students to collaborate and discuss issues, This technique can work with a class of any size; however, the larger the class the more prepared and organized you must be. In the lecture portion of the class allow for audio and visual presentation strategies. The ideal lecture will present information for auditory learners - e.g. lecture, and for visual learners - e.g. power point, overheads. The group assignments and discussions will appeal to the manipulative learners. As mentioned earlier, preparation and organization will be very important, particularly if you have a large class.

The following two sections discuss in detail the lecture portion and the group discussion / assignment time.

Lecture
The lecture portion of your class must be very organized. Two key features of good lectures are clarity and enthusiasm (Good & Brophy, 1997). Clarity is essential if students are to understand concepts. Enthusiastic teachers assist students in developing enthusiasm of their own and enable students to ultimately achieve at higher levels. "Personal strategies to enhance motivation included being sincere, positive, enthusiastic, and supportive" (Jacobsen, Eggen & Kauchak, 1999, p.7).

Another thing to carefully examine when preparing lectures is the amount of material covered. Professors who are experts in their field often overestimate the amount of material that students can reasonably absorb. Overloading students makes it more difficult for students to comprehend, and retain information. The overhead or powerpoint can be used effectively to help students concentrate and stay focused. Prepare lectures so that points are presented succinctly and logically. Request that students do the assigned readings prior to class so that lecture material can be better absorbed.

The organization of lectures can be made easier by starting with the concepts you plan to teach and then deciding which strategy will be most effective. Some common principles for organizing, used by lecturers are: cause and effect; time sequence; parallel organization such as phenomenon to theory to evidence; problem to solution; pro versus con to resolution; familiar to unfamiliar; and concept to application (McKeachie, 1994). Choosing one of these principles based on the content and goal will be helpful.

The use of personal experiences is very beneficial in maintaining students' interest. Personal anecdotes can be utilized to emphasize concepts and assist students in retaining information. It is also a good way of creating a more personal connection with students, which is very difficult in a large class. Personal anecdotes when related to the lecture material and appropriately inserted can be very effective.

Humour can be an indispensable tool in promoting a positive relationship with students. It reduces negative feelings and improves student perceptions of the teacher, contributing to improved attention, retention, and learning (Jacobsen, Eggen & Kauchak, 1999). Humour can create renewed interest in the lecture. Humour can also be utilized to diffuse tension when presenting sensitive topics or concepts.

Group Assignments

Learning can be categorized into three broad hierarchical categories: category one represents facts; categories two represents concepts and principles; and category three represents thinking skills (Moore, 1995). The lecture portion can assist students with categories one and two, and group assignments can be extremely helpful with category three. Group work can: stimulate higher thinking; teach problem solving; integrate various types of information; and increase positive interaction amongst class members (Good & Brophy, 1997). The following suggestions are provided to assist in planning and organizing group assignments for large classes.

1. Prepare all group assignments before the first class. At the first class distribute a copy of all assignments to all students so they have their own personal copy and can prepare accordingly.
2. Provide each group with a duotang fore recording group assignment responses. Provide only the amount of space that you think is needed for a complete response.
3. To ensure that students work as a group, and to discourage the submission of irrelevant material, insist that the assignment be done in class. Encourage students to prepare for their group assignment, and bring the necessary materials to class.
4. Insist that all assignments be completed in the one hour time slot and handed in at the end of class.
5. Prepare a general rubric or marking scheme that can be utilized for making the assignments. Mark each assignment out of three or four rather than out of 100.
6. Vary the assignments to include case studies, and the relevant application of concepts that are discussed in the lecture.
7. Assign ten percent of the grade for self and group evaluation. Ask group members to evaluate themselves and other group members out of ten (done confidentially) based on a number of criteria. Some of these criteria could be: leadership, cooperation, attendance, preparedness, verbal participation, assuming responsibility for completing assignments, and resolving conflicts appropriately. This will encourage

students to attend thus eliminating the need to take attendance, and also clearly outlines students how they can be a productive group member.

Students can choose their own groups or groups can be assigned. There appear to be an equal number of pros and cons to each method. One reason for assigning groups is to control the number of students per group. Ideally student groups of four work very well. If your class is too large to work with groups of four use six. Any more than six members becomes rather unproductive foe effective group work. Before the first class, assign each student on your class list to a group. Post these lists around the classroom prior to class (e.g. Group 1, Group 2) so that students can meet with their group very briefly during the first class. Plan an introductory assignment to enable group members to begin to get to know each other. This may include things like sharing email addresses, telephone numbers and outlining three words that describe you. This kind of activity begins to facilitate group interaction. If you have a large class, book other classrooms that can be utilized for the group portion of the lesson. Devise some method for collecting the assignments at the end of class. Also, a graduate assistant is very useful in helping to mark weekly group assignments.

Respect for Students
Another very significant way to create a positive culture in your classroom is to respect the students. Respect develops when we believe that others are capable of solving their own situations and problems (Gazda, Asbury, Balzer, Childres, Walters, 1991). It is characterized by supporting others in their efforts rather than patronizing them by doing things for them. In most cases students will have less information about the subject area and probably fewer experiences than you; however, their thoughts, comments and questions must be respected. It is somewhat difficult in a large class to deal with student questions; however, the benefits of answering communicate respect, and outweigh refusing to do so. The following suggestions are offered for dealing with questions in a large class (McKeachie, 1994):

1. Inform students that questions are permitted and welcomed;
2. Repeat any questions before answering them to ensure that everyone has heard the question;
3. Complete a section before entertaining questions. Sometimes questions raise points that will be addressed later. If such a question is asked, write it on the board or overhead to ensure that it is not disregarded or forgotten;
4. If a question is asked to which you don't know the answer, record it and prepare a response for next class;
5. Students may sometimes disagree with you and pose a threatening question. Do not become defensive, simply express the fact that there are many opinions and explain the source of your information. In certain circumstances it may be appropriate to declare the student correct, to state that there are many opinions, or to suggest that students

discuss the concept with other academics and peers to get various ideas on the topic.

Things to Avoid
There are a number of things that should be avoided in the classroom.

1. Pontificating - Students are not impressed with professors who act in a pompous manner and pretend to be infallible. Professors who bring this demeanour to the class often turn students off very quickly. This haughty manner creates a negative atmosphere and caused students to attack the professor.
2. Tangents - These can be successfully avoided by planning lectures carefully and thoroughly. Tangents wastes time, confuse students, and interrupt the flow of the class.
3. Pet Topics / Soap Boxes - Most professors have certain topics that are of extreme importance to them. It is not productive to constantly be talking about these "pet" topics. Discuss them when appropriate and when carefully incorporated into you lesson. Avoid them at other times. Also if you have a certain personal bias towards a topic, declare that bias so students can interpret your comments in that light.
4. Sarcasm and Cynicism - Do not let cynicism turn your lectures into negative sessions. The constant use of cynicism communicates a lack of personal sincerity and encourages students to adopt a negative impression of your course content. Sarcastic comments are also negative and communicate disrespect. Sarcasm should be avoided both in class, and in individual student encounters. Positive language is so much more effective.

Conclusion
Creating a positive culture and climate in your classroom is a complicated and important task. Developing a sound educational philosophy, paying attention to the principles of adult learning, developing variety within your lesson, and respecting the students in your class will all assist in mastering this task.

To Further Teaching:
Brookfield, S. (1986). Understanding and Facilitating Adult Learning. San Francisco: Jossey-Bass.

Daresh, J. C., & Playko, M. A. (1995). Supervision As a Proactive Process Concepts and Cases (Second Edition). Prospect Heights: Waveland Press Inc.

Gazda, G. M., Asbury, F. R., Balzer, F. J., Childers, W. C., Walters, R. P. (1991). Human Relations Development A Manual for Educators (Fourth Edition). Boston: Allyn and Bacon.

Glickman, C. D., Gordon, S. P., & Ross-Gordon, J. M. (2001). Supervision and Instructiona; Leadership A Developmental Approach (Fifth Edition). Boston: Allyn & Bacon.

Good, T. L. & Brophy, J. E. (1997). Looking in Classrooms (Seventh Edition). New York: Longman.

Jacobsen, D. A., Eggen, P., & Kauchak, D. (1999). Methods for Teaching Promoting Student Learning (Fifth Edition). New Jersey: Merrill.

McGlynn, A.P. (2002). Successful Beginnings for College Teaching: Engaging your students from the first day. Madison, WI: Atwood Publishing.

McKeachie, W. J. (1994). Teaching Tips (Ninth Edition). Lexington: D. C. Heath & Company.

Moore, K. D. (1995). Classroom Teaching Skills (Third Edition). New York: McGraw-Hill Inc.

Timpson, W. M., Burgoyne, S. (2002). Teaching and Performing: Ideas for energizing your classes. Madison, WI: Atwood Publishing.

HOW WE TEACH

In Western classrooms, regular discussion and debate epitomizes an ideal learning environment. There is a large ongoing research project at the University of Windsor, Canada, in 'informal logic'. Informal Logic, run by Dr. Ralph Johnson, studies how to bring the classical rules for argument into the everyday classroom, and World.

Developing a respectful relationship with students by learning their names, learning how to motivating them to discuss, debate, and answer questions critically, are some of the ways teaching is motivated. It is not easy getting students to talk and engage in the subject area, and yet the authors in this section of *Teaching, Learning, Assessing*, prove that linking subject content to the students' every day lives is a critical aspect of learning to retain information. It awakens their spirits to the discipline. The instructors in this section use prior learning to anchor new information and theories to the students' memories and minds. Crawford's two chapters on learning in this section focus on the importance of this link - active, kinaesthetic learning; that is, using a series of active tasks to aid the learner in grasping and remembering text.

The 'Best Practices' in this section of *Teaching, Learning, Assessing* provide actual classroom examples from Biochemistry, administration, on-line learning, large lecture learning, and graduate classes. The examples in this section describe how professional instructors stimulate discussion, and organize active learning with their own students. It also provides very candid thoughts on these changing styles of learning.

Morton's chapter on large classes, in particular, provides more than 14 examples of how to make a "large class seem smaller", or more intimate, for the students who are often lost in the crowded lecture hall.

For all of us who love the journey of learning, 'how we teach' illustrates how this is done from the other side.

What's in a Name?
by Elizabeth Starr

There is so much power in knowing a name. It allows you to know someone. It allows the student to feel known. It invites participation in the discourse. It is a simple concept, and yet difficult to implement when you teach between 100-500 students a year. "How can I possibly learn all those names?" Starr does it, and provides her own constructivist methods for doing so (some of which are also outlined by McKeachie, 2002 and Brinkley et al, 1999). Many of the authors in this manual, such as Laing and Glassford, state that learning students' names opens gateways to learning. You can call on them in class, or for discussion. They feel included and committed to their own learning.

The first lecture has arrived. You are faced with anywhere from 20 to 200 or more anonymous students, waiting for your words of wisdom–a daunting prospect even for experienced lecturers. At the beginning of every new course there is always at least a touch of anxiety for every professor as each wonders what a new "batch" of students will be like. "Will I be able to interest them in the subject matter? Will they be thoughtful students and come up with interesting questions and insights? Will they like me? Will I be able to "connect" with them?" These concerns can be overwhelming for novice professors, however brilliant they may be in their subject area.

Invariably part of the anxiousness is the fact that you simply know nothing at all about the students, not even their name. The students, on the other hand, very quickly begin to get a feel for you–they learn your name, your particular areas of interest, your teaching style, your expectations. This seems to set up a rather unequal personal knowledge base that I find slightly disconcerting and is one reason why I make an effort to learn students' names immediately.

The effects of anonymity has an empirical base in the social psychology area. Its effects have been studied in connection with crowd behaviour, deindividuation, decision making and social facilitation among other topics (Lea, Spears, & de Groot, 2001). There is much less of a research base dealing with anonymity in a university context: on the relationship between professor and student, student contributions and participation in class, and the nature of learning in classes in which the professor knows students' names (Smith & Malec, 1995). Despite the lack of a research base, most professors feel that it is helpful, if not essential, to learn as many student names as possible, that it *does* make a difference to classroom atmosphere, and make some efforts to accomplish this task. In a study examining the techniques used by sociology professors to learn names, Smith and Malec (1995) found that 83% of those surveyed did make a "special" effort to learn names.

The purpose of this chapter is to examine some of the reasons why learning names is an important task and worth the effort, and secondly, to provide the novice professor with some practical ways to achieve the task with differing class sizes.

The Whys

Why bother making the effort to learn names of potentially hundreds of students who you may only see for one term? Will it really make a difference to your teaching? To your control of the class? To your students' perception of you as a person, or as a professor who cares about his or her students? Will it affect the atmosphere and learning environment of the class? Does anyone really care? I believe the answer is "yes" on all counts.

First of all, although some students may prefer anonymity and seek out large classes with the express intention of remaining anonymous (Erickson & Strommer, 1991), most students prefer to be identified as a person, and are pleased and often impressed if you are successful in learning their names (or at least make an effort to learn them), remember their names, and are even able to use them out of the context of the class (the ultimate test!). Whether you are right all the time is of less importance than the effort put forth. Goldsmid and Wilson (cited in Smith & Malec, 1995) report that one of the five attributes of superior teachers most often mentioned by students is their sincere interest in students as persons. Making an effort to learn student names is the most basic step in demonstrating one's interest in a student as an individual and is really the least that a professor can do. Most students automatically see you in a more favourable light when you regard them as more than an anonymous face in the crowd. This alone makes it worthwhile to expend effort at learning names. However, there are other reasons why learning names is an important task.

The newly graduated high school student.

Students arriving at university straight from high school have many major changes happening in their lives at once–living away from home for the first time perhaps, living with roommates, negotiating a large campus with classes in many different buildings, and being responsible for their own learning without anyone telling them what they should be doing or when they should be doing it. These are just a few of the many adjustments these young students need to make.

Another major adjustment for new students to make is getting used to the anonymity of universities. Whereas most teachers and fellow students at high school knew them by their name, universities seem far more interested in their student number than their name. Unimaginable class sizes only serve to compound their sense of anonymity.

When Ontario eliminated the fifth year of high school in 2003 students entering university became even younger than traditionally was the case. These students may find it even more difficult to adjust to the anonymity of universities than the "older" high school graduate and a professor's effort to learn names may be even more appreciated as they adjust to their new world.

Class management.

School teachers have always known the importance of knowing students' names, and *not* knowing names is one of the most difficult aspects of substitute teaching. Teachers know that knowing students' names makes a difference in classroom management and control and is an aid in leading effective discussions. If students know that the teacher knows their names, most are less likely to exhibit disruptive behaviour and seem to feel more personal responsibility for "behaving" and participating.

Although discipline is presumably less of a problem at the university level, the effect of anonymity is not fundamentally different. Students whose names you know are more likely to contribute to class discussions, answer questions and generally be involved in the class, whereas students whose names you *don't* know are more likely to be passive listeners, whisper in class, fall into a confused slumber, or fail to show up at all (Kolstoe, 1975). Because they are anonymous there isn't any sort of a personal bond to make them feel that part of the success of a given class is their responsibility. The reverse is true for students whose names you do know in my experience.

School teachers have learned that an effective method to regain the wandering attention of a student is to call on them by name for a comment, an answer to a question, or use their name in an example you are providing to the class. Ignoring a persistently whispering or obviously inattentive student is to passively condone the behaviour.

The same technique is also effective at the university level for the same reasons, but knowing a student's name is key. It is much more effective to say, "Now, let's imagine that Madeline here is someone who _____. Madeline, what would *you* do in that situation?" than to say, "You, in the fourth row...no, not you, but you with the blue sweatshirt...no, beside you...yes, you." Somehow the "umph" has gone out of the point you were trying to make in your up-to-now scintillating lecture in the latter example! In both situations of course, drawing attention to a specific student or calling out their name must not be used to embarrass the student.

Lecture facilitation.

Another reason to learn student names can simply be a question of "delivery" and this is particularly important in lectures with 80 or more students. Because it is more difficult to keep the attention of such a large class, the pace and rhythm of the lecture are extremely important. If student attention is lost it is difficult to reclaim it. Being able to call on a student by name (even if it's only because they have a nametag in front of them), rather than by a, perhaps ambiguous, point that may need to be verbally clarified, or a "yes, you over there, with the green shirt," can help you maintain your pace, line of thought, and the students' attention. And even if you *are* reading a nametag, it is still more personal than the "yes, you" method, and of course the more practice you have saying the name, the more likely it is that you will remember that person's name without the tag on a subsequent occasion.

Interestingly, in their study of sociology professors' learning of student names, Smith and Malec (1995) found that female professors were significantly more likely to use name learning tactics than male professors. They interpret this finding in light of research by Gilligan who states that females are more likely than males to be concerned with "...the ongoing process of attachment that creates and sustains the human community" (cited in Smith & Malec, 1995, p. 283). Smith and Malec (1995) propose that the community of the classroom is sustained by the attachment provided by learning student names.

The How

How can this seemingly impossible task of learning so many names be accomplished in a single term, only to have to start all over again with new courses in a new term? This is an almost impossible undertaking unless all your classes are exceedingly small, you have an exceptional memory, or you are able to devote an extensive amount of time to the task. In the real world there is rarely enough time, people tend to have average memories, and undergraduate classes often have between 80 and 400 students. So, no–you are probably not going to learn all the names of all the students in your large classes. It *is* possible, however, to learn the names of all students in classes of 35 to 40 or so, and to learn a good proportion of names in classes up to about 90, and be able to "fake it" for many more by reading nametags. What is more important than succeeding at the task, in my opinion, is that your students see that you are making an effort.

Being able to learn the names in certainly going to be more or less easy depending on the size of class, the size of the institution, and the type of program or course. For example, if the course is part of a "self-contained program" in a self-contained building, you are more likely to see the students in the hallways throughout the day and exchange pleasantries, aiding in the name-learning game. On the other hand, if the course is one that is open to all students at the institution (such as an introductory psychology or English course), you are less likely to ever see the students outside of class time which definitely impedes name learning. However, even in huge classes, it *is* possible to learn a substantial number of names with an acceptable level of effort.

Essentially all name learning techniques, regardless of class size, come down to rehearsal–constant repetition of names whenever the chance arises–every time students put up their hands, every time they come up before or after class to talk with you, every time you converse in the hallway with students, and every time students come to your office. Start the conversation by asking their name and use it in the conversation and at the end of it. If you don't remember their name (or never did know it), ask. I make it a policy to never converse with a face without having a name attached to it. It's just that simple. I have yet to meet a person who remembers the name of every acquaintance, and yet everyone seems to think that only *they* are afflicted with this difficulty. I have come to the irrefutable conclusion that, like everyone else in the world, I am not going to remember everyone's name, so it's okay to just admit it, apologize and ask again. It is far easier to ask students to repeat their names when you are first unsure of them, rather than at the end of the term after 6 office meetings and 4 after-class discussions when you *should* know their name and they think you do. By following this simple rule myself (and one that takes no extra time on my part), I have been able to learn a good proportion of names in my classes of 85 students and all names of students in classes of 35 or less.

There is no question that it is easier to learn the names of students in smaller classes than in huge lectures, and the amount of time needed to accomplish the task is in reasonable bounds. It follows that the greatest number of feasible techniques are most useful for smaller classes. Smith and Malec (1995), not unsurprisingly, found a significant difference in the number of name learning tactics used by instructors of classes up to 75 students and those of classes deemed "very large"–up to 150 students, with instructors of smaller classes using about 6 different strategies and instructors of very large classes using 4.4 strategies. Instructors of "huge" classes (greater than 150) used name learning tactics too rarely to be included in the comparison in this study.

Many of the ideas presented below are ones that either I, or colleagues of mine at the University of Windsor find helpful when trying to learn names. Other ideas come from the Teaching and Learning Center website of the University of Nebraska-Lincoln (n.d.). Needless to say, a combination of name learning tactics will yield the greatest number of names learned.

Techniques for smaller classes (up to 35 students).

1. One technique I use with classes of up to about 35 students, is a name game that is fun and definitely breaks the ice. Everyone stands in a circle and the first person says what their name is and what they like, both beginning with the same letter. For example, Regis may say "My name is Regis, and I like rowing." The next person begins with the first person and what they like and add their name and what they like. This continues around the circle with each subsequent person beginning with Regis and saying everyone's name and what they like before adding their own. Of course I am the last person and have to remember all students and their "likes." I may then say the names out of order to be sure I'm matching a name with a face. I find this a very effective method and not only do I learn the names, the rest of the class does as well. Although I may forget some names because of the sheer number of students in other courses, and I only see them once a week, many names are remembered and when supplemented with name tags, I find it only takes about 3 classes to be sure of the names. In one course, a group of students incorporated the game into a presentation on mnemonics and had remembered what everyone in the class "liked" from the first class 10 weeks earlier! The one danger with this technique is that you may remember what a student "likes" more easily than their name!

2. Another fun "circle" method that helps everyone get to know each other's names is to throw a ball back and forth to people in the circle where the holder of the ball has to say their own name and the name of the person to whom they will throw the ball. A variation on this is after

people have introduced themselves and some aspect of themselves (favourite food, unusual hobby, etc.), they throw a ball of yarn to a person in the circle (maintaining hold on the end of it) stating their name and aspect. That person keeps hold of the yarn but throws the ball to another person and so on. Eventually the whole class is "connected." The process can then be repeated in reverse as the yarn is untangled. By the end everyone should know everyone's name and at least one interesting bit of information about them.

3. Another idea is a sort of scavenger hunt. In this method everyone (including the professor) is given a list of items or aspects of people to find and they have to talk to everyone in the class and write the name of a person who has that item or meets that description (e.g., someone who wears size 10 shoes, someone who has been to Europe, etc). Each name can only be used once.

4. A commonly used, but also effective method of learning names in smaller classes is to have students pair off and interview each other for about 10 minutes and then introduce each other to the rest of the class.

5. Many professors have students fill out information cards and sometimes attach pictures of the student to their card and review the cards frequently.

6. There are many variations on the use of seating plans to learn student names. This is an effective, tried-and-true method that can be enhanced by reviewing the plan immediately after class and trying to visualize each student. In the next class you can then concentrate on those whose names failed to elicit faces. Alternatively, attaching photos of students to a seating plan, or writing in something about the student learned from initial introductions on the seating plan can also speed up name learning.

7. Much work that students do in a Faculty of Education is group work and some professors have found it helpful, once the groups are formed to take pictures of the group with name tags and create a file folder for each group in which notes, etc. are kept. Name tags are also worn for the first few weeks. This technique has allowed professors to learn the names of all 240 students in multiple sections.

8. In smaller classes, passing out handouts and assignments individually each time, rehearsing names as you go is also helpful.

Techniques for larger classes (up to 100).

Some of the ideas presented above may also be possible in larger classes or multiple section classes without using excessive amounts of class time although some adaptations may be necessary. It is still possible to get to know a good proportion of names in larger classes with time and some effort. I find that the being able to personalize larger classes in any way possible is well worth the effort and helps to engage the students.

1. I find the most helpful method in classes of this size is simply to have students make freestanding nametags in the first class using old file folders that have been pre-cut into 3 inch strips and heavy markers that I supply. I ask that they bring these to every class. At the beginning of every class I ask them to use their nametags, or I model by putting up a nametag for myself and draw attention to it. I may use different methods every week to remind students to bring their name tags and for the first month or so I bring markers and extra tags for those who have forgotten. However, by consistently insisting on nametags, it does become a habit. Then I try to make sure that I always use their names when they have a question or comment, and incorporate their names into examples I may be using.

2. Because I begin a multi-section course with a simulation that requires four volunteers, I have the volunteers wear nametags around their necks so that throughout the simulation I can be sure to always call them by name. I rarely forget the names of those students and just build from there. This method also has the advantage of being an integral part of the course rather than a time-consuming extra.

3. If circumstances permit, arrive at class early so you can chat with different groups of early arriving students. Ask their names, rehearse them, and find out something about the students--what program they're in, what other courses they're taking, and so on. Ask about pronunciation of names, comment on spellings, notice that there seem to be a lot of "Edwards" in the class--anything that makes you use the names or notice what name goes with whom, is helpful, and of course the more "person" you can put behind a name, the more likely you are going to remember the name.

4. Another method of getting know students in larger classes is to require office visits for all students, perhaps setting up a schedule where two or three students come at once and just use the time to get to know their names, a bit about them and any course concerns (Smith & Malec, 1995).

Techniques for very large classes (over 200)

Certainly it will be nearly impossible to learn all names in huge classes in the course of a term without exorbitant effort and time. It is in these classes where your effort (if not your success) is particularly appreciated by students. In classes of this size students rarely have real desks so the use of nametags becomes impossible even if you did have the osprey vision required to see them past the fourth or fifth row. It is also in classes of this size that professors are more likely to use Powerpoint presentations necessitating the dimming of lights. Since night vision goggles are rarely part of standard issue to professors, other methods of learning names become necessary. By combining some of the previously mentioned techniques with those that follow, you will certainly learn substantially more names than would otherwise be the case.

1. Assuming the lecture hall has proper tables, it may still be helpful for students to have name tags in front of them, particularly if you lecture from places in the classroom besides the front. Moving around the classroom will allow you to see, use and learn additional names among a host of other advantages.
2. McKeachie (2002) suggests inviting students to coffee after class, or to pass out invitations to a few students every class to join the professor for coffee and to get acquainted.
3. Other professors of large classes have students say their names before they state their question or comment.
4. It may be possible to divide a large class of 250 or so into working groups of 8 or 9 students and have them work on particular questions or projects in different parts of the lecture hall. As you circulate, you can begin to get to know student names group by group, a much easier task than trying to learn names en masse (Teaching and Learning Center, n.d.).

...And The Rewards

Learning student names is certainly worth the effort from both your students' and your own perspective. From the students' perspective, I believe that knowing their names or making a consistent effort to learn as many names as possible makes you more approachable in their eyes and takes away the all too frequent anonymity of university, especially for students fresh from high school. It tells students that you care about them as individuals and that you see them as individuals.

From your perspective, knowing the names of the students you're teaching, whether in small or large classes, helps to makes you feel like you're teaching individual people instead of an anonymous crowd. It helps to make the learning relationship slightly more personalized which both you and your students can appreciate. Students really do appreciate your efforts to learn names and as a result, are more responsive and involved.

To Further Teaching:

Erickson, B. L., & Strommer, D. W. (1991). Teaching college freshmen. San Francisco: Jossey-Bass.

Kolstoe, O. P. (1975). College professoring. Carbondale: Southern Illinois University Press.

Lea, M., Spears, R., & de Groot, D. (2001). Knowing me, knowing you: Anonymity effects on social identity processes within groups. Personality & Social Psychology Bulletin, 27, 526-537.

McKeachie, W. J. (2002). McKeachie's teaching tips (11th ed.). Boston: Houghton Mifflin.

Smith, D. H., & Malec, M. A. (1995). Learning students' names in sociology classes: Interactive tactics, who uses them, and when. Teaching Sociology, 2, 280-286.

Teaching and Learning Center, University of Nebraska-Lincoln (n.d.). Learning students' names. Retrieved June 23, 2006, from http://www.unl.edu/gradstudies/gsapd/instructional/names.shtml

Nurturing Discussion in the Classroom
by Donald Laing

Donald Bligh's book, What's the use of lectures? *(2000), points out that there is empirical evidence that students learn more from participating in discussions than from listening to lectures (see also Brookfield, 1999). Laing supports this claim, and describes his own step-by-step method of creating active, engaging discussions and debates within the college classroom. Just as the writing process requires time for individual thought and group exchanges, so does the discussion process. " Individual to Small Group to Large Group" creates a full, participating class.*

There is widespread consensus among those who think about teaching in universities and colleges that it is valuable for students to have opportunities in the classroom to discuss the content of their courses with their instructors. Informed by constructivist learning theory, which stresses that learners actively build their own knowledge, and supported by considerable research (Gall and Gall, 1990), the consensus holds that discussion in the classroom increases students' interest in learning and helps them to integrate new knowledge more effectively into their minds, to make use of it at higher cognitive levels, to think more actively about course content, and to communicate their thoughts more capably. What is envisioned in this consensus is, of course, genuine discussion in which professors and students take part in purposeful and focussed sequences of oral interactions during which they exchange information, questions, judgments, beliefs and feelings in relation to a relevant topic. It is how to promote this genuine form of discussion that we will consider in this chapter.

Before we do, it is worth noting that discussion in the sense just put forward may not be as common as we would wish in classrooms at any level of education. There is a body of research built up over fifty years that consistently tells us three things: (1) that teachers tend to dominate classroom discourse, typically talking about 80% of the time; (2) that about three-quarters of the students say little or nothing in class; and (3) that teachers predominantly ask questions that call for simple recall of information. Admittedly, most of this research has been done in elementary and secondary schools and the truth is we do not have many studies of actual teaching behaviour in universities and colleges. However, the studies we do have at the tertiary **level** strongly suggest that the same tendencies hold there too (Karp and Yoels, 1976; Barnes, 1983; Fischer and Grant, 1983; Smith 1983). Recently, an observational study of 20 social science and humanities professors teaching classes of third- and fourth-year students (class size $M=28.95$, $SD=6.86$) found that on average only 26.10% of the students talked and that they did so for only 5.86% of class time, a figure elevated considerably by the fact that in two classes they talked for 20% and 23% of the time (Nunn, 1996, p. 250). Thus, for all our talk about the value of discussion, it may be that "discussion" sometimes amounts to little more than professors interrupting their lectures for a few minutes to ask students to recite information that they have picked up from earlier lectures or their assigned reading. As Roby has observed, such discussions are really more accurately thought of as "quasi-discussions," for while they have the virtue of having at least some student participation they lack the "fruitful, reflective interactions" that arise from genuine discussions (Roby, 1988, p.164).

There are, to be sure, forces at work against the kind of discussion which we have in mind, some of which are well beyond our control. First, perhaps most powerful, is the strong sense of obligation that teachers have to "cover" course content. Discussion can often seem so much less efficient as a teaching method than the lecture if we see our job primarily as making sure that a given body of information has been transmitted to our students. If we have stood in front of them and presented them with the requisite facts and theories, we can feel comfortable that we have done our part. We have told them what they have to know, and it is now up to them. Truth to tell, there are many students quite content with such an approach. There are those who, by temperament, prefer to sit and listen. There are those who delay their reading until exam time and so have little to contribute. There are those who grow quickly impatient with discussions that do not have immediate and direct bearing on how they are to be evaluated. All in all, confronted with the difficulties of conducting effective discussions, a straightforward lecture, where we control more of the variables, can seem an attractive teaching alternative. However, the values attributed to genuine classroom discussion are real, and their importance in developing our students as people who actively pursue our subjects and give serious thought to them should not be quickly set aside. The concern for us as university teachers thus becomes one of ensuring that at least some of the time they spend in our courses is spent taking part in genuine discussion that will promote those values. How, then, can we conduct such discussions in our classrooms?

Creating a Classroom Climate that is Conducive to Discussion

The foundation of effective discussion is a classroom climate in which all participants feel that their views will be welcomed, found to be of interest, and respected. Consequently, it is important that you begin to establish such a climate as quickly as you can. Even before you meet your class you might give some thought to the seating arrangements. If you are teaching in a classroom with movable seats, you should think about having them arranged in some fashion that enables as many students as possible to see each other's faces directly. The standard lecture-hall arrangement with all students sitting facing the front of the room is fine for students listening to professors, but you want to create the impression that in your class students will be encouraged to listen to each other as well as to you. An elongated horseshoe arrangement something like this ⌐⌐ often serves very well.

At your first class meeting, a helpful step toward creating a climate conducive to discussion is to create the impression that you are looking forward to working with these particular students and interested in getting to know them. Your first task will be to learn their names and something about them. A simple way to accomplish this is to distribute 5 x 7 cards and markers and ask them to fold the cards lengthwise, to write their first names on one side of the fold in large letters, and then to prop them up so that you and everyone else in the room can read them. If there is any information that you would find helpful in your teaching (e-mail addresses, home addresses, related courses taken, relevant experiences, and so on) you can ask them to provide that information on the back. Then work through your class list and spend half a minute or so chatting publicly with each student. Ask them any harmless introductory question that comes to mind: where they are from, what school they went to, what their major is. With a group with fewer than twenty students you may wish to have them chat in pairs or trios for a few minutes and then have them introduce each other to the class as a whole. This is time well spent. It not only helps you and the students get to know each other but also in a non-threatening way it immediately involves everyone in the classroom conversation. Very quickly every student has been established as someone who speaks in the group; every voice has been heard. At the end of the class collect the name cards for next time, when you will have volunteers distribute them, thus encouraging the students to get to know each other's names quickly. Keep using the name cards until you are confident that you know most of the names, and do not be embarrassed about having to rely on them for a few weeks. Remember that the name cards are there for everyone in the room, not just you.

Also during your first meeting, if possible, introduce the students to the following sequence, which is very powerful in fostering discussion and one which you may well come to rely on in your teaching. The key is to invite students to address a question in three stages: first as individuals, then as members of a small group, and then last as members of the class. Begin by asking the students to take five minutes to write down their initial thoughts on some relevant question. Then, ask them to form small groups (up to five) to share their thoughts. Then lastly raise the question to the whole class. The advantages of this sequence are many. The first stage gives students time to think about what they have to say on the matter. This is particularly important for reflective students who like to think things over before making their thoughts public and who often find the pace of classroom discussion too fast for them to contribute readily. The second stage greatly increases the opportunity for all students to offer their thoughts in a comfortable setting. As most students tend to locate themselves in classrooms among people they think they will be comfortable with, small groups initially work best if you simply invite students to form them with four or five their neighbours. Then, finally, when we raise the question with the entire class, students have already thought through what they have to say, and they make their contributions with greater confidence, having rehearsed and refined them in the earlier stages.

The question for this first discussion should be one about which you can be fairly confident that all students in the room will have something to say. With a group of beginning university teachers, for example, a useful first discussion topic might well be: "Thinking back over your experiences as a student, what would you suggest to be the qualities of an effective discussion?" As an alternative to a question drawing on past experience, you could provide them with some concrete task to work on which will provide a basis for moving successfully through the individual ▶ small group ▶ whole class sequence. Give them an intriguing problem to solve, preferably one with several possible solutions. Have them consider the grounds which could justify some contentious quotation you have given them. Invite them to choose between two brief statements with opposing points of view. Show them a picture to speculate about. Watch a videotape that will arouse their interest. Give them any task relevant to the concerns of your course that will get them talking to each other. The outcome of the task is less important at this point than the fact that it will provide a shared experience for the students to talk about. If at the end of your first class you see students chatting with each other as they leave, and there are a few lingering on to talk further, some perhaps hoping for a few words with you, you will have made good progress.

Setting Topics for Discussion

When planning for class discussion, you need to consider the kind of questions you will ask to get things under way. Not all questions will work. Look at the following questions:

> In the reading I asked you to do for today, what are the three central arguments which the author puts forward for . . . ?"
> What were the most important events leading up to . . .?"
> Why does introducing X bring about Y?

If these questions simply ask students to reproduce information which they have read or were told in previous lectures, then they will be of limited value in promoting discussion. If the correct answers were explicitly stated or can be readily inferred in texts that the students have read or heard, then they are only being asked to remember, and there will be little to talk about. You may in fact wish to ask questions of this nature to bring information to the fore as a preliminary step to discussion, but in themselves these questions are unlikely to evoke discussion for you. The students' answers will be either right or wrong, and probably brief. On the other hand, if the same questions are actually asking students to *judge* which arguments are central, or to *evaluate* which events were most important, or to *analyze* and then *explain* why X brings about Y, then they are likely to work very well to create discussion. Instead of simply remembering information, the students will then be using that information to think with in order to respond satisfactorily. Their answers will be stronger or weaker, more convincing or less convincing, highly creative or thoroughly conventional, but they will be answers that will support discussion. Keep in mind that it is not necessarily the form of the question that promotes discussion but rather the kinds of mental processing that students have to do to provide answers; *why?* does not in itself prompt thinking if an adequate answer can be produced from memory.

In general, the questions that serve best at beginning discussion are those which are genuinely open to a variety of answers. Among the kinds of questions which generally work well are those which promote thinking in the following ways:

Comparing	How would you compare the discussions that students have in the student union with those they have in classrooms?
Explaining	Why do you think some students say very little in university classes?
Evaluating	What would be the fairest way to evaluate class participation?
Hypothesizing	What might happen if we asked the students to bring their own questions?
Judging	Of the articles we have read, which do you think is the most helpful to a beginning university teacher?
Organizing	How could you organize the classroom so that students might contribute more freely to discussion?

It is also helpful if you get in the habit of asking questions in an invitational manner. If you ask, "What is the most important factor in ....?" or "Why did the author say that . . .?", students may well infer that the desired answer is already formed in your mind and thus see less point in pondering over answers of their own. However, if you tone down the implied certainty of the question and ask, "What *might* be the most important factor in ... ?" or "Why *do you think* the author *might* have said that?", the question seems more open and worth pursuing. A question asked with *might* invites students to explore the matter rather than to state their considered positions. Those, after all, should be seen as outcomes of the discussion rather than its starting-points.

Once discussion is under way, how you respond to student contributions becomes critical. Indeed, your responses are likely to have far greater effect on the quantity and quality of your classroom discussions than the questions or prompts you used to get them started.

Learn to Draw out Contributions
A common fear among beginning teachers is that they will ask a question and no one will volunteer an answer. This turns out hardly ever to be the case, and if you have had a successful first meeting the likelihood of it happening will be even smaller still. However, let us say that it does. You ask the question that you are confident will get the discussion off to a lively start, and no hands go up. What should you do? You will be tempted to ease your embarrassment by offering an answer to your own question; "All right, I'll tell you what I think." Try very hard not to do this, for it will signal to the students that you are ready to do the talking whenever they choose not to. They will have

negotiated a concession from you that you should not yield so readily. Instead, pose your question, look as confident as you can, and wait a few seconds for some volunteers to come forward. If no hands appear, look round the class for expressions or gestures that suggest that those students are indeed thinking about the question and could be nudged into contributing. This is a moment when those name cards will save you: "What are your thoughts, Joanne?" She will give you something. Then: "Interesting. How about yours, Bob?" The discussion will build. Let me point out that following the individual ►group ►class sequence will eliminate any likelihood that you will get no contributions, as you always begin the class discussion with what are really group reports.

Learn to Withdraw and Attend to Managing the Discussion

In the normal course of events you will chair the discussions which take place in your classroom. For much of the time, you will be the one to signal who may take the floor to speak, and once a student has spoken, the floor will return to you. As a polite human being, and an experienced conversationalist, you will almost inevitably feel a need to respond in some way. There is likely to be a great deal that you could say to expand or clarify or refute what has been said. However, in the interest of fostering discussion it will be better if much of the time you refrain from doing so, for nothing suppresses potentially fruitful discussion as quickly or as thoroughly as professors who hold the floor and treat student contributions as springboards for their own comments. Professors who, intentionally or not, dominate the conversation in this way soon convince themselves that their students have remarkably little to say for themselves, a discovery that opens the door for them to dominate even more. If you find yourself starting to talk as soon as students finish, or even before, you will discover that participation will increase if more of the time you hold back and yield the floor more readily. Instead of responding to student contributions with comments of your own, try inviting response directly from other students: "Anyone like to add to what John has just said?"; "Who sees this differently?" You might also try simply nodding, or giving verbal equivalents to nods like "uh huh," "interesting," or "I see" to acknowledge the comment and to signal that the floor is still open for further comment. Often this is all that is needed to encourage the student who has just spoken to go on to elaborate, or to bring forward contributions from other students.

Learn to Hold Back Your Own Thoughts

While many students will make interesting and informed contributions to the discussions in your class, you will also have to deal with answers that are halting and tentative, only partially thought out, perhaps even ill-informed. You will be tempted to take over and put matters right. You may want to compensate for the deficiencies in the answer by providing a fuller and more polished version of your own. Or you may want to expose its inadequacies with a series of rigorous and challenging questions addressed to the student who gave it. Avoid both these temptations. Remember that students watch carefully how you react to their classmates. The first response will convey that the only valued contributions in your class are those that are fully developed, clearly stated, and in line with your thinking. The second may look to them like an inquisition and not something they want to be part of. In either case, you will have sent a message that you plan to control the discussion, and almost surely the participation will be restricted to hardy souls. It is generally more effective in these situations either to encourage the student to tell you more–"Could you help us with a bit more about ...?"–or to invite other students to ask questions–"Is there anything anyone would like Sarah to clarify?" As the discussion progresses the weaknesses and flaws of any one answer are usually overcome, and the contributions you may need to make to the process can be made in ways that will do nothing to suppress it.

Learn to Slow the Pace Down

Typically, when we first start leading classroom discussions, we tend to keep things moving at a brisk pace. We pose a question and then immediately call for answers. We respond to students' answers by immediately asking follow-up questions, or inviting comments from other students, or starting to talk ourselves. We try to keep the conversation rolling along smoothly. However, we would do well to pause and reflect on the fact that it takes time for students to formulate answers to questions of any complexity, and that their thinking does not come forward in smoothly flowing units of speech. Indeed, research into effective classroom discussion tells us that slowing the pace with brief periods of silence, which we have come to call "wait-time," has positive effects on both the quantity and quality of student participation (Rowe, 1974; Tobin, 1987; Dillon, 1990). If we pause strategically for 4-5 seconds during the flow of discussion we can expect the number of students participating to increase and the contributions they make to become longer and more complex. We can expect the students to address more of their comments to other students, to initiate more questions, to offer more alternatives, and to function on higher cognitive levels. So, when you have a thought-provoking question in mind, try waiting for five seconds before you call upon a student to answer. You are likely to find the silence a bit embarrassing, and you may be more comfortable asking the students to take a few seconds to jot down some thoughts on paper, but either way you will be pleasantly surprised at how many more hands you will see and how much more extended and complex the students' responses will be. Another opportunity for wait-time comes after students have spoken. I suggest you try keeping silent for four to five seconds, and see how often they begin talking again and go on to build on their previous comments, or how often another student will carry on the same line of thought, or raise some carefully considered alternative. Initially, pausing for silence in the midst of discussion may be disconcerting, but if you make it part of your teaching repertoire you will be rewarded.

Learn to be Open and Accepting in Manner

As a rule, it does more to promote discussion if you respond to student contributions in as non-judgemental a manner as you can muster. Whatever the thoughts running through your mind as students speak, your public manner should try to convey neutral acceptance and signal that you are willing to listen respectfully to any ideas that are brought forward. Doubtless, you will readily appreciate that criticizing or rejecting student contributions–"No, you're simply wrong about that"; "Surely someone in here has a better understanding of this point?"–can have a suppressing effect on students' willingness to take part in your classes. On the other hand, if it is sincere and not merely a frequent verbal gesture, your praise is likely to have a positive effect on the amount of discussion in your classes. Most students tell us that praise from the instructor is a major factor in their willingness to contribute to class discussion (Nunn, 1996). However, you need to think about just when in the course of discussion you give your praise. As Costa (1990) has astutely observed, praise can work against participation by encouraging students to accept what has been said and think no further. Your praise–"That's a superb insight, Rob!"–may shut down discussion of the question prematurely. There may, of course, be good reason to praise Rob for his insight, but it is probably better if you do so either in the late stages of the discussion or in the hall after class.

Keeping Discussion Productive: Purpose, Focus, and Depth

Many students take a very results-oriented approach to their educational experiences and have very little interest in classes which do not pay clear dividends for their progress as measured by grades on assignments and examinations. From this point of view, many students appear to look on class discussion, at least as they have experienced it, as having limited value. This attitude likely underlies Nunn's finding that 80% of the students she studied wanted discussion held to less than 40% of class time, and 50% wanted less than 20% (Nunn, 1996, p. 257). These results need to be seen in light of the evidence that much of the "discussion" which the students experienced, at university and before, is likely to have been recitation rather than the genuine discussion which we are hoping to achieve. Nevertheless, as university instructors we have an obligation to use instructional time productively. This means that our discussions should have three qualities: purpose, focus, and depth.

First of all, you need to have a clear idea of what exactly it is that you want your discussions to accomplish. It is particularly important that you have thought about how exactly the discussion you are planning will relate to the course content that is being presented in lectures and assigned readings. Students have to experience something in the discussion beyond a simple airing of content that they have already heard or read if they are to see any value in it. Is the discussion to help to clarify material covered in lectures that is known to be particularly difficult for students to master? Is it to pose problems that ask them to apply a principle? Is it to encourage them to think critically about certain claims that are made in articles they have read? Is it to provide opportunity for considering points of view that are different from those presented in their textbooks? Whatever the purpose you set, make sure that you make it evident to the students at the very beginning. Keep in mind, too, that it usually engages even the most grade-oriented students when you put forward a question in the form that it took on some previous year's test or examination.

Once the discussion is under way, you need to keep it focussed on the question at hand. Learn how to bring students whose contributions are wandering off into sidetracks gently but firmly back into the main line of discussion. It can be helpful in this regard if you write the question to be considered on the board, on an overhead transparency, or on chart paper and then keep brief notes of the points that are made. The list gives you something concrete to bring the wandering speaker's attention back to; "How would you like me to record the point you're making?" The student will often reconsider the comment, and if not, either then or later, someone will question its relevance. You can also use the list to pause periodically and take stock. Don't worry if you let a few points slip along the way, as you can turn to the class and ask, "Is there anything I have overlooked? Anything we should add?" You are likely to find a list of points made helpful not only in keeping discussion in focus but also in creating a momentum and a sense that progress is being made.

Keep in mind that active participation is not enough in itself. If your class discussions are to be productive over the long run, you need to ensure that they do not descend to mere "bull" or "chat" sessions in which students happily participate in voicing their opinions freely, but are seldom held to account for supporting evidence or logic. However satisfying students find it to 'speak their minds' for a while, they learn little from discussions which do not call upon them to support their views or which fail to challenge them with thoughtfully articulated positions that differ from their own. You will not learn much from them either, and all concerned will lose interest. You need to ensure that does not happen.

Conclusion

Leading productive discussion is a very complex and difficult form of teaching. You will likely experience an empty feeling at the end of more of your class discussions than you would like. You may find yourself irritated that many students did not take part and appeared rather uninterested. You will be uneasy at all the loose ends that the discussion left lying around. You may even feel a bit guilty about some of the remarks you made or let pass. It can be a messy and frustrating business, this class discussion, and no doubt that fact helps to account for the comparative infrequency of its occurrence. It is so much easier to tell students what you know and think, to retreat to the more controlled world of the lecture. Keep it always in mind that discussion can do more to stimulate students' minds and interests than any other form of teaching we know, and that under the surface much more learning is taking place than we may think. Do not be surprised if, at the end of term, some of those silent students who seemed not much interested drop by to tell you how much they enjoyed your classes.

To Further Teaching:

Barnes, C. P. (1983). Questioning in college classrooms. In C. L. Ellner & C. P. Barnes (eds.), Studies of college teaching (pp. 61-82). Lexington, MA: D. C. Heath.

Bligh, D. (2000). What's the Use of Lecture? San Francisco: Jossey-Bass.

Brookfield, S. D. (1999). Discussion as a Way of Teaching: Tools and techniques for democratic classrooms (First Edition). San Francisco: Jossey-Bass.

Costa, A. L. Teacher behaviors that promote discussion. In W. W. Wilen (ed.), Teaching and learning through discussion: The theory, research and practice of the discussion method (pp. 45-77). Springfield, IL: Charles C. Thomas.

Dillon, J. T. (1990). Conducting discussions by alternatives to questioning. In W. W. Wilen (ed.), Teaching and learning through discussion: The theory, research and practice of the discussion method (pp. 79-96). Springfield, IL: Charles C. Thomas.

Fischer, C. G., & Grant, G. E. (1983). Intellectual levels in college classrooms. In C. L. Ellner & C. P. Barnes (eds.), Studies of college teaching (pp. 47-60). Lexington, MA: D. C. Heath.

Gall, J. P., & Gall, M. D. (1990). Outcomes of the discussion method. In W. W. Wilen (ed.), Teaching and learning through discussion: The theory, research and practice of the discussion method (pp. 25-44). Springfield, IL: Charles C. Thomas.

Karp, D., & Yoels, W. (1976). The college classroom: Some observations on the meaning of student participation. Sociology and Social Research, 60(4), 421-439.

Nunn, C. E. (1996). Discussion in the college classroom. Journal of Higher Education, 67(3), 243-266.

Roby, T. W. (1988). Models of discussion. In J. T. Dillon (ed.), Questioning and discussion: A multidisciplinary study (pp. 163-191). Norwood, NJ: Ablex.

Rowe, M. B. (1974). Wait-time and rewards as instructional variables, their influence on language, logic and fate control. Journal of Research in Science Teaching, 11, 81-94.

Smith, D. G. (1983). Instruction and outcomes in an undergraduate setting. In C. L. Ellner & C. P. Barnes (eds.), Studies of college teaching (pp. 83-116). Lexington, MA: D. C. Heath.

Tobin, K. (1987). The role of wait-time in higher cognitive level learning. Review of Educational Research, 57, 69-95.

Three-D Instruction: Discussion, Debate and Drama
by Larry Glassford

Discussion is a form of teaching that many instructors strive to perfect, and there are as many different styles of teaching as there are personalities. Building trust in a classroom of students, so that they will feel comfortable discussing without fear of recourse, is often best accomplished by 'being yourself'. Glassford's own educational framework, developed through experience and time, invites readers to experiment with his ideas about 'community building'. A fear-free classroom with open access to opinion and discussion is generated from the type of community that Egbo and Shantz encourage instructors to build.

Too often, as university professors, we simply assume our pre-ordained place is at the top of the instructional food-chain. Was not the entire school system designed to serve us? Despite growing evidence that three hours per week of professorial monologue, with perhaps a perfunctory pause for "any questions?" here and there, is just about the least effective method of teaching imaginable, university departments abound with cranky academics convinced that such is the natural way to instruct our undergraduates. In the face of our own failure to ignite learning in the lecture halls, we rhetorical relics blame everyone but ourselves. "The students are deficient in intelligence, or character, or both," we reason. "They will not read, cannot write, and do not think," we conclude. "The schools from which they graduated did not teach them the basic 3 Rs, let alone the sophisticated skills required to master my brilliantly taught courses," we titans of traditionalism we assume. "What can one expect of this generation of students when their naive high school teachers have foolishly emphasized context over content, self-esteem over skills, and process over product?" So goes our argument.

Let us assume that you, a newly hired academic, intend to be different. You still remember what it was like to struggle through snowdrifts to an early morning lecture, only to discover your prof was actually reading his lecture verbatim from the textbook. "I came for this?" you muttered incredulously. The dreadful monotone delivery was simply the crowning touch. As you squinted around the half-empty lecture hall, packed to the rafters on the first day of the course, when the syllabus was distributed, and not ever since, you asked yourself, "why are we doing this?" Now that you are teaching such a course, things will be different. Or will they?

Strange as it may seem, some students actually come to like the dry, old lecture format. For one thing, they know what to expect: show up for tests, organize a rotating class attendance scheme with a friend so you always get the lecture notes, turn in your essays and reports on time, study for the exam with the course syllabus beside you for guidance as to the prof's biases, thank this same professor in person or on the bottom of your exam paper for her patience and insight, and you are in pretty good shape. Just as some prisoners reputedly come to accept their chains, so some undergraduates decide they prefer the familiar, albeit boring rhythm of a traditional lecture course to a more demanding format that encourages genuine discussion. So, unless you, the novice instructor, learn a few things about effective teaching, you too may quickly retreat to the tired old lecture format in the face of apparent student resistance to the idea that they should contribute in new ways to the success of their own classes.

A good place to start is to decide exactly what you want the students to learn from taking your course. If you're not careful, the following three items may be what they actually learn. First, the prof is always right, and on the rare occasion when it is revealed that he is not, refer to the first clause in this sentence. Second, the key to academic success is memorization of endless facts, punctuality in completing assignments, and remembering to use all aspects of the proper essay or report format. Third, plagiarization is wrong for students, especially if you get caught. Doubtless you would prefer a different list of student outcomes, nowadays commonly referred to as "learning expectations." Under the heading of knowledge, you would doubtless generate an impressive list of concepts that the students should understand, and be able to apply. Such in-depth comprehension would go far beyond the rote recall of memorized definitions and facts. In addition, you will want the students to utilize, and further develop, such thinking skills as analysis, interpretation and inference, not to mention communication skills in print and oral form, perhaps using other media as well. If that is what you want the students to know and be able to do, then you must construct teaching strategies as if that is really so. Lecturing from the textbook in a dull monotone is not developing thinking skills, though it may be mildly useful in developing patience and fortitude. Furthermore, if you are really serious about them, then you must tailor your evaluation procedures to fit the learning expectations as well. University students quickly learn to deconstruct the rhetoric of a course syllabus. Racing past the lengthy, and in your mind at least, impressive list of course objectives, their eyes come to rest upon the marking plan. Where the marks are, there also are the priorities of all but your most idealistic students. An awareness of the combined effect of tuition fees and opportunity costs renders most of today's students into dedicated pragmatists. The stakes are too high for it to be otherwise. So, make sure the "words" of your course goals, and the "music" of your teaching strategies and evaluation strategies, match.

It helps to know the multiple facets of your teaching role. Leaving aside the other key roles involved in being a university professor, namely to be engaged in meaningful scholarly activity, and to provide service to the academic and general communities, there are at least four key aspects of your identity as a course instructor. Your students expect these, and benefit from their presence, even though they are ideas that are rarely articulated.

You will not be surprised to read here that it helps to be an expert in your field. **Knowledge expertise** is widely seen as essential to the success of university teaching. As a new entrant to the field, you are probably fresh from the triumph of successfully defending your doctoral dissertation. You are at work on oral presentations and written papers and articles, possibly even a book. Earlier in your Ph.D. program, you demonstrated mastery over a broad spectrum of literature in your field. You *are* an expert. For now. Beware of the judgment of the Canadian humourist and economics professor, Stephen Leacock, however. He likened the Ph. D. degree to a final test, one in which you are examined and determined to be completely full of knowledge. For the rest of your life, then, there will be no room in your brain for any new ideas. Obviously, being a knowledge expert requires staying abreast of new developments in your field. It also requires reviewing information you once knew automatically but no longer use, except for teaching. Rust can corrode the memory, just as it corrodes unprotected metal. There is nothing more pathetic than the has-been professor who used to know, but fails to realize she no longer is in the know.

You are not likely to be surprised by the second facet of your teaching role either. It pays to be an effective **communicator**. We are not all stand-up comedians, or dramatic actors. Students do not expect that we should be, though they appreciate humour and drama as much as any audience would. But we can all come prepared - armed with whatever props and audio-visual resources are appropriate to the lecture, lesson or learning experience we have planned. We can all learn to vary the tone of our voice, employ pauses to good effect, and utilize a mike if our voices don't project to the far reaches of our classroom. We may lack the raconteur's gift for story telling, or the talk show host's spontaneous wit, but change-of-pace humour comes in many forms. Funny stories may be read, comical cartoons can be shown, and even professorial "dullness" or "absent-mindedness" can be celebrated until it becomes a reliable in-joke shared with your class. In my own case, I make sure to inform my students, early and often, that I am a die-hard Toronto Maple Leaf fan. This invariably draws a smile from the class - some out of sympathy, some out of humour at the plight of my perpetually hapless heroes. You may be surprised to learn that time devoted to creating a community of learners in your lecture-hall will improve teaching effectiveness. Many things in a modern mass university conspire against the goal of class community-building. Class sizes, particularly in first and, increasingly, second years are large. Classrooms offer immovable chairs, which is bad enough. Worse, they are usually arranged theatre-style, reinforcing audience passivity. Individualized timetables promote choice, but at the cost of atomization. Each person is left feeling alone in a sea of humanity. Cost accountants and some "techies" even look forward eagerly to the day when students are physically separated, each in their own home, linked only via their computers. Despite these barriers, the fact remains that most humans - our students included - seem to crave community. Again, we are not all gifted charismatics, able to put people at ease in our presence with little effort. Most of us lack the photographic memories necessary to quickly master our huge class lists. But we can try. There are techniques - name cards, seating plans, self-identification policies for oral questions - that can begin to break down the anonymity. Another aspect of being a classroom **community-builder** is facilitating the creation of student-student relationships. We are not talking deep, lasting friendships here. Nevertheless, if I as a student become personally acquainted with a few of the people who habitually sit around me in a large lecture hall, that can both increase the likelihood that I will continue to attend class, and promote in me a deeper level of participation in the learning opportunities being presented by my professor. Knowledge expert...communicator...community builder...isn't that enough? Actually, it is not sufficient - necessary, but not sufficient. As the only person paid to be in that classroom or lecture-hall, you have a special responsibility as the **orchestrator of learning**. Certainly the students have responsibilities, too, but it is your course, and you are in charge. Take another look at your course expectations. If all you want is for the students to know what you know, then perhaps being a knowledgeable, dynamic and caring lecturer would be enough in the short run. But you will not always be there for them. Surely, you want your students to acquire skills as well as content, so that they will be lifelong, self-starting learners. And, not every learner learns best through passive listening and note-taking. In fact, few do.

So what are your options? Happily, they are myriad. Let us assume for the moment that you prefer direct teaching, and quite like traditional lecturing. Yet, you are aware of its limitations. You have a range of choices to perk up those chalk-and-talk lectures: colour-print handouts, overhead transparencies, PowerPoint-style computer enhancements, audiotapes, videotapes, even live television and internet hookups. Guest speakers can provide variety as well as authenticity. Don't just talk the talk. Do a personal, live demonstration of a key point. Better yet, involve one or more volunteers from your student audience in a joint demonstration. Routine factual-recall question-and-answer sequences fit into this category as well. These types of review questions do not engage the students in much higher-level thinking, but they do involve some students in the live action, and they also provide the rest of the passive audience with a new supporting cast of characters, thereby supplementing your own role as feature performer. One step beyond direct instruction is indirect instruction. Many university lecturers imagine themselves in this role, almost as a latter-day Socrates, engaging the handful of students sitting at their feet in stimulating discussion of the enduring complexities of their chosen subjects. It is a bit of a stretch to project this classic image onto a class of 500 anonymous undergraduates, but the fantasy endures. Effective socratic questioning is difficult to do - as much art as it is science. The key is in the quality of the questions, both the initial focussing query, that launches the discussion, and the followup probing questions, which clarify, challenge and stimulate, as required. A classic error made by many a would-be Socrates is to talk too much. Facilitate the discussion, yes, but do not dominate it. The point is to involve the students in the discussion - both those who contribute to the oral exchange of views, and those others who are moved to think more deeply themselves through witnessing the class discussion.

Again, indirect instruction need not be totally oral discussion. You may use props such as maps, photographs, diagrams, clippings, textbook illustrations, audiotapes, videotapes, cartoons, tools and other objects of interest to provoke thought and discussion. Good old problem-solving need not be restricted to the teachers of math, physics or economics. Any subject is a potential source of puzzles, dilemmas and issues that can be turned into problems that need solving. For a change of pace, and to encourage real thinking, briefly describe a problem (for the auditory learners), supplemented with a print document (for the visual learners), then give each student time to think, and then to write out a few thoughts. Now, begin the discussion. More hands will go up, and more answers will actually contribute important thoughts, because more student minds are now engaged in the topic.

Individual study has its place. In fact, researching for reports and essays away from the classroom is a key part of most university courses. For this very reason, it is a shame to throw away the real possibilities for productive interactive discussion during scarce class time. Rather than a series of one-on-one "chess games" involving a master player (yourself) moving about the room playing against each student individually, and with many a player missed, why not get the students to "play chess" with one another simultaneously? Can you feel the collective productivity rising dramatically, with this one simple change in strategy? As the professor, you are now less directly involved, but more of real value is getting done, if you have planned well, and set things up properly. There are many techniques available for such interactive instruction. A very simple one is entitled "think, pair and share." As its name implies, two students are presented with a topic or problem to think about, individually. After a few moments, they pair up, and share their thoughts. This may, if you wish, then lead to a period of socratic discussion(indirect instruction), and then back into a straight lecture (direct instruction).

Debates can be a formalized version of interactive instruction, if properly set up. The word "debate," in common usage, frequently refers simply to an involved or heated discussion. Some professors like to stir up such mock debates by deliberately playing the "devil's advocate," arguing vehemently against the conventional wisdom on a given topic. Frequently, the hope is that the students will thereby be shocked or provoked into thought, and then on to oral participation. While the technique certainly has its place in an instructor's repertoire, it is well to remember that such devil's-advocate debates are inherently teacher-centred, and may occasionally serve no purpose other than to flatter the vanity of an oversized academic ego. Oxford-style debates, on the other hand, involve only a few students actively, while the others in the class remain in their passive role. One option is to schedule such formal debates over several classes, while holding them to strict time limits, so they don't eat up all your instructional time, yet everyone is actively involved at least once. Another option is to mimic the think-pair-and-share strategy described in the previous paragraph. Divide the students into groups of six, meaning two opposing teams of three, and allocate small sections of the room to each debating group. Then, get out of their way, and let the debates begin. The noise level will shoot up, but so too is the active participation rate. Budget some class time at the end for a reporting stage, when representatives from several of the debates summarize the key points that were voiced. A short followup written assignment requiring each student to summarize the key points for both the "Pro" and "Con" viewpoints can do wonders to encourage both participation and attendance, not to mention active listening skills.

A final method of instruction you should be aware of is experiential learning. Hands-on lab experiments have given the sciences and engineering a competitive advantage in this area for many years. Why should they have all the fun? One approach is to get out of the classroom or lecture hall altogether, and organize a field trip or other off-campus experience. This might involve measuring the impact of shoreline erosion in geography, touring a prison in criminology, attending a meeting of city council in politics, or attending a special museum display in fine art. All such activities, if carefully planned, provide obvious learning opportunities. However, the difficulties inherent in making arrangements, securing permissions and covering costs necessarily limit the possibility of this form of experiential leaning for most instructors.

Another option worth exploring is to create your own experiential learning opportunities right in the classroom. Role play has many possibilities. On a small scale students can, with the aid of role cards and scenario handouts, replicate situations and circumstances from the past, present or future. As with the simultaneous debating strategy described earlier, each student can be actively engaged in a small-group role play, while their peers take part in similar dialogues all around them. Oral debriefing and a written assignment can follow such a learning activity, to reinforce key points, and encourage attentiveness. Students who would rather die than perform in front of the whole class are generally both able and willing to take part in simultaneous small-group role plays. Those who simply freeze up in such situations can be enlisted as observers, and given anecdotal or checklist forms to complete. No one's talents need go to waste.

On a larger scale, you may wish to try your hand at an orchestrated simulation activity. For example, a politics course on political parties might lend itself to an ongoing simulation of a mock party's leadership race. Some students become leadership candidates, others role play their key organizers, and still others act as the voting delegates, each one initially uncommited to any candidate. As the course progresses, a few minutes of each class can be saved for the ongoing simulation, with perhaps one whole period near the end of term devoted to the candidate speeches and delegate voting. Indirectly, the simulation will deepen students' understanding of the whole leadership selection process in party politics today. This comprehension will be sharpened by a structured debriefing, in good socratic style, after the simulation has been wound up. Direct evaluation could consist of a followup creative assignment, chosen from among these options: an ongoing reflective journal with a series of entries as the simulation unfolds; a post-simulation memoir, in the form of a first-person article written as if for a current magazine; a post-simulation interview ostensibly produced for a radio or television current-affairs program. This extended learning activity has worked very well for me. Other subjects will permit other dramatic possibilities.

As the instructor, you must not only be able to see the learning potential in this form of experiential instruction, but also be willing to buck the initial opposition from doubting colleagues, some students, and perhaps even your own conscience. How can something that is this much fun possibly be a legitimate form of learning? There is a bit of the calvinist naysayer in most of us. Why not let the results speak for themselves? And after each try, collect feedback from the students, and implement the feasible suggestions for improvement. Before long, these dramatic recreations will make your course a campus legend, even though you're not an accomplished standup entertainer or dramatic actor, and never will be.

Discussion, debate, drama...the three "d"s of effective university teaching. Each of them has its place in your repertoire. While none is easy to pull off in the typical lecture hall, the good news is that you get better at implementing them with repetition. Practice may not make you perfect, but it will see you consistently improve your proficiency over time. Socrates, watch out.

Teaching for Improved Learning
by Ian Crawford

The following two chapters provide a concise summary of The Art of Inquiry (Hudspith et al, 2002) and Active Learning (Cameron, 2002). These are wonderful, in-depth resources to consult for a more thorough examination of the subject matter. "Chickering's 7 Principles" is also alluded to within this section. Crawford, a popular instructor in his own right, describes five "approaches to good teaching practice" that include a positive learning environment (also described by Shantz and Glassford), activating prior knowledge (what do they already know, as outlined in Smith and Oakley's chapters), encouraging active learning, promoting cooperation among students, and giving prompt feedback (as Ableser and Clovis also suggest). Although Crawford draws examples from the humanities, he is actually a scientist by profession, and prefers his students "do", rather than "hear" or "see". This is part of active learning. Why enquiry rather than the case method? Crawford argues, as does Hudspith and Jenkins (2002), that enquiry motivates students to become responsible for their own learning. It allows each individual to apply content material, and make it immediately relevant, to his/her own physical world. Enquiry is to discussion what the case method is to the lecture. Many examples of improving learning and active learning are provided by Crawford in this short space. Concept mapping, and the "one-minute paper", are also described in this chapter.

There is a well-known aphorism that states that he who can does, while he who cannot, teaches. The truth is that those who can "do", cannot automatically teach. Good teachers are able to do and to teach. The intent of this chapter is to offer some suggestions to help those highly proficient in a content area to transfer this subject expertise into improved teaching skills.

Learning and Teaching Defined

There are as many definitions of learning and teaching as there are individuals willing to define them. Simply stated, learning is a cognitive change. Teaching is helping students make a cognitive change. As a consequence of learning, students are able to know facts, to understand and apply concepts, to analyze problems and situations, to make judgements, to solve problems, and to become creative in new areas. Learning and teaching require activity. Learning is a process of changing what one knows by constructing patterns of action to solve problems of meaning. Teaching involves the creation of an environment which fosters this construction on the part of the individual. In this view of learning and teaching, teachers promote the essence of education - to draw out rather than to put in.

Teaching as a Metaphor

The use of a metaphor, and a consideration of its imagery, is helpful in formulating a richer understanding of the role of a teacher. The metaphor of the teacher as a partner conveys persons of different strengths (teacher and student) working together to achieve similar ends. The teacher as an explorer conveys the uncovering and describing to others of hitherto unknown aspects. Two common metaphors for teaching are teaching as gardening and teaching as conducting.

In the metaphor of teaching as gardening, the student is perceived as a plant. Every plant has the ability to bloom, yet not every plant will bloom at the same time or to the same extent. Each plant will need personal attention to reach its full potential. Not every plant is alike; yet, each plant contributes to the beauty or utility of the garden. In the hands of a good teacher, students grow and ideas are sown, germinated, pruned, and displayed.

In the metaphor of teaching as conducting, the teacher is the conductor and the students are the orchestra. Each student plays a different instrument and at differing levels of ability. The role of the teacher is to get each to play as well as possible while working together to produce a performance of lasting quality.

As you consider your role as a teacher which metaphor will be reflective of you? Are you the gardener, the conductor, or someone else of your own creation?

Approaches to Good Teaching Practice

Whichever metaphor you choose has to reflect good teaching practice. Five approaches to good teaching practice are the following:

1. Create a positive learning environment.
2. Activate prior knowledge.
3. Encourage active learning.
4. Promote cooperation among students.
5. Give prompt feedback.

Create a positive learning environment

Good teaching practice focuses upon students. The teacher listens to them, responds to their needs, and pushes them to excel. Learning and teaching should be enjoyable. If a student can find relevance between the subject matter and everyday life or future usefulness then s/he is more likely to enjoy learning.

At the beginning of your course discuss the applications of the course content to aspects students know and care about. You could put students into pairs or small groups of three or four to brainstorm possible examples of real world applications of the course content. In an introductory biology course, for example, students could be asked to list the various careers such as anthropologist, botanist, coroner, dentist, forester, nurse, physician, teacher, veterinarian, which require biology as a foundation. Students are motivated to learn material that connects with their experiences, interests, and personal goals. Most students care about what they will be doing when they graduate. Bring in a practising professional in your subject area to talk about how s/he uses the course material on the job (Brent & Felder, 1999, p.16).

Activate prior knowledge

Students bring a variety of experiences to the classroom. Capitalize on this resource. Select a question or activity that will activate prior knowledge and hook students for the lesson. Gagnon and Collay (2001) recommend the following:

> For example, one of your colleagues uses the movie Dead Poets Society as a motivation for a unit on poetry or on teenage tendencies toward self-destruction. You might consider modifying this activity by just showing a video clip of the teacher encouraging students to tear pages out of their textbooks that describes rating poetry on a rather sterile matrix about style, and then use the clip as a springboard to a discussion about whether poetry needs passion or prescription to capture readers' attention (p.62).

This quotation reveals that an effective teacher provokes a realm of knowledge and a habit of mind from her or his students. Effective teaching creates an environment marked by finding new meaning in familiar circumstances. Above all, it identifies the importance of active learning.

Encourage active learning

Learning is not a spectator sport. Students do not learn as much as they are capable of learning by sitting and listening. They must be encouraged to discuss what they are learning and apply it to their lives and interests. In other words, students should be exposed to hands-on, minds-on experiences.

Students learn by creating, doing, designing, solving and writing. Passivity dampens students' motivation and curiosity. Pose questions. As much as possible, do not tell students something when you can ask them or create an environment in which they can uncover what you want them to know. Encourage students to suggest approaches to a problem or to predict the results of an experiment.

Promote cooperation among students

Active learning often promotes learning between student and student. As Hartman and Glasgow (2002) stated:

> When students work in cooperation with other students, they often get more out of learning than they do when they work on their own or even when they work with the teacher. When students are isolated from each other and compete with each other, they are less involved in learning, their learning is not as deep and they have fewer opportunities to improve their thinking. Students who work cooperatively learn more and produce higher-level subject-area knowledge, and they tend to retain and apply what they have learned when working on difficult tasks

more effectively than do students who work individually (p.120). Effective learning is collaborative and social. Sharing one's ideas and responding to the ideas of others sharpens thinking and deepens understanding.

Give prompt feedback

Students need to know what they know and what they can do well. They also need to know what they do not know and what they cannot do well. An important part of good teaching practice is promoting learning through feedback. What type of feedback works best? Danielson (1996) identified effective feedback as accurate, constructive, specific, substantive, and timely. Silverman (1992) found that achievement increased when feedback was corrective, descriptive, encouraging, prescriptive, and outcome-focused.

Caring about students

Felder, Woods, Stice, and Rugarcia (2000) stated that "the social environment in a class - the nature and quality of interactions between the students and the instructor and among the students - can have a profound effect on the quality of learning that takes place in the class"(p. 35). Students perform better when they believe that an instructor is concerned about them. Some suggestions to help develop a caring attitude include:

1. Learning the students' names.
2. Making yourself available.
3. Avoiding sarcastic or belittling comments.
4. Collecting periodic feedback and responding to it.
5. Giving choices or options whenever possible in tests, assignments, and activities.

Motivating Students

Good teaching practice involves using instruction that motivates students. Five strategies effective in motivating students include:

1. Building upon the students' strengths and interests.
2. Varying teaching methods.
3. Specifying assessment criteria.
4. Providing samples of exemplary work.
5. Soliciting student reactions.

Building upon the students' strengths and interests

Find out the reason for students taking your course and their expectations for the course. Use this information to correlate your assignments, lecture examples, case studies, or supplementary reading with the students' responses. Motivation is enhanced when students realize that the course content is relevant and useful to them. Examples to consider include providing students with a news clipping, magazine article, or TV/video clip that relates to the course content, and using enhancing resources such as simulations, case studies, or video conferencing with an expert or credible source.

Varying teaching methods

Variety reawakens student involvement and interest. Plan to use as many teaching strategies as possible throughout your course. Five main instructional categories with representative examples are:

1. Direct instruction (guest speakers, handouts, lecture, multimedia)
2. Indirect instruction (concept mapping, inquiry, problem solving)
3. Interactive instruction (cooperative learning, debates, forums, panels, open discussions, role playing, tutorial groups)
4. Experiential learning (dramatizations, field trips, games, model buildings, simulations)
5. Individual study (assigned questions, book reviews, papers, reports)

Specifying assessment criteria

Use a rubric to indicate specifically to the students what they have to do to earn a particular grade. A rubric is generally characterized as a set of guidelines for assessment that identify the characteristics and /or dimension being assessed along with specific performance criteria. One example of performance levels for the criterion of organization in a rubric for student presentations is:

1. Level One- poor organization and lack of preparation
2. Level Two- signs of organization but some parts do not seem to fit the topic
3. Level Three- organized, logical and interesting
4. Level Four- very well organized, logical, interesting, and lively

Providing samples of exemplary work

Sharing exemplary work gives students an idea of what to try to emulate. This sharing can be accomplished by providing access to copies of best papers and exams, projects, reports and the like. Be sure to have the approval of the authors of these exemplary materials prior to using them and determine whether they wish their identity to be known.

Soliciting student reactions

Student reaction can be achieved in a variety of ways. Stop the class with two or three minutes remaining and have the students respond on an index card to a question such as, "What needs to be explained again next class?" A variation on this is to use a prepared sheet referred to as a "ticket-at-the-door", in which the student responds to specific stems or questions such as, "I wish you had spent more time on...", or "One thing I did not understand today was...". By looking these over before the next class you could respond to the students' expressed thoughts.

Engage Students in Reflection

Reflection is the act of describing to ourselves what we have already felt, seen, and talked about; how we are making new meaning, adding to our current understanding, or enhancing current knowledge within a learning episode; and what we will do or think about because of that learning episode (Gagnon & Collay, 2001, p. 104).

Journal entry

Reflection can often occur through writing a journal entry. In a journal entry students keep an ongoing record of their reflections lesson by lesson. This journal can be collected periodically or at the end of the course. Students in a graduate course in education could be given the following instructions for preparing a journal:

1. Faithfully recording regular, detailed and honest entries in a diary format.
2. Revealing candid, personal thoughts about the educational issues and topics relevant to the course.
3. Being open to personal growth.

In a reflective personal journal it is expected that you would comment on a number of the aspects covered in class which are important to you. Some things to note down could be your impressions, insights and reflections concerning selected class topics and activities. The journal could also include some entries focusing on non-course-specific matters such as relevant issues in the news, and course-related insights gained from personal reading.

Letter to one's self

A letter to one's self can also elicit reflection. Periodically, students could be asked to write a letter offering reflections on the course and her or his learning in it. Providing for reflection shows the students that you care about how they are learning. Students learn something in every class. They will likely share with you the details on the learning, if asked.

Creating an Effective Teaching Environment

Teaching is the creation of an environment in which the student becomes actively involved in her or his learning. Rosenshine (1997) focused on advances in research on creating an effective teaching environment. Some aspects he considered important included helping students to develop their background knowledge, providing for student processing, and presenting new material in small steps. An instructor following Rosenshine would provide for reading of a variety of materials, and frequent review and discussion. The instructor would provide opportunities for students to organize and summarize information, compare and contrast new material with prior material, and draw connections between known and new material. Material would be presented in small amounts followed by students working in pairs or in small groups of 3-5, quizzing and explaining the new material to each other.

Teaching for Meaningful Understanding

To make sense of new information students need to fit the new information with previously acquired knowledge. This requires a process of personal knowledge construction. Among the features which an instructor can use to contribute to such meaningful understanding are:

1. Organize the lesson into a coherent framework correlating with the previous lesson and leading into the next lesson. This provides bridges within your planning.
2. Ask one or more students to summarize what was covered in the previous lesson. This provides for a brief review and draws links that lead students from the previous lesson to the current one.
3. Use projects, assignments, and/or self-study teaching strategies to help students deal with the content at their own pace.
4. Insert questions throughout the lesson to prompt students to focus on key issues.
5. Throughout the lesson use useful links such as therefore, since, because, and/or, if...then.
6. Be redundant. Summarize periodically and repeat difficult ideas.
7. Consider using non-graded quizzes and problem sets to give students feedback on how they are doing. Post the answers for students to self-check.
8. Provide short breaks. Assign the breaks as needed rather than at predetermined times. Give the break as student attention level wanders or your energy level lags. A break need not be a rest. It could be a change of activity from lecture to small group discussion, question and answer session or developing a concept map of the lesson up to that point.
9. Place a suggestion box in the rear of the room and encourage individual students to give feedback on anything s/he considers would make the class more meaningful.

Use a Variety of Learning Strategies

Good teaching practice involves planning. Planning can be considered as a four step sequence. First you should review what students already know. Next orient the students towards the new learning. Arrange for the students to be active in the lesson, and finally, consolidate the learning. A few suggestions to consider for each of these steps include:

Review what students already know

1. Review previous learning. Ask questions about specific experiences that relate to the new content, such as "Why is chlorine added to the water in a swimming pool?"

2. Use an analogy. In a curriculum course, when highlighting the differences among goals, aims, and objectives, an analogy to travel is helpful. A "goal" is to travel to Winnipeg. An "aim" is to travel to Winnipeg by train. An "objective" is to travel to Winnipeg by train and arrive on Thursday at 3 p.m. The analogy helps students to relate goals, aims, and objectives as statements of intent by varying degree of specificity.

3. Use review questions. Ask questions that act as scaffolding for new learning, such as "What is one way by which a cell is like a factory?" This draws out prior learning.

Orient the students towards the new learning

1. State the intent of the lesson.
2. Show an example of the final product, skill or attitude that the lesson will lead to or promote.
3. Outline the conceptual structure of the lesson. For example, in a survey course in introductory biology the following conceptual framework could provide an overview of the course:

                                                        biosphere

                       ecosystem

            community

         population

      organism

    organ system

   organ

  tissue

  cell

 organelle

macromolecule

molecule

atom

Arrange for the student to be active in the lesson

Teaching is simply the creation of an environment in which the students become active in their learning.

1. Give examples and non-examples of concepts. Science is a spirit of alert scepticism. Science is not a huge body of frightening facts to be mastered by students.
2. Use inquiry approaches.
3. Use group strategies.
4. Keep students involved by asking questions. "What is the difference between...?; What is the purpose of...?; What evidence led you to...?; What is the reason for...?"
5. Lead a discussion.
6. Present a problem.

Consolidate the learning

1. Summarize the lesson.
2. Select one or two students to state what was presented highlighting what each sees as the most important aspect of the lesson.
3. Encourage students to change content into knowledge. Share with students the analogy of "house and home". A house is an assembly of building materials but a home involves creating personal meaning within the physical framework. Content is information. Knowledge is personalizing the content.

Conclusion

There is a difference between teaching static knowledge from a text-book and teaching as creating an environment involving dynamic inquiry and problem-solving practice. Engaging students in the process of their own learning leads to more motivated individuals. This chapter has focused on raising an instructor's capacity for improving learning through teaching.

To further teaching:

Brent, R., & Felder, R. M. (1999). It's a start. College Teaching, 47(1), 14-17.

Cameron, B. J. (2002). Green guide no. 2: Active learning. Halifax: STLHE, Dalhousie University.

Danielson, C. (1996). Enhancing professional practice: A framework for teaching. Alexandria, VA: ASCD.

Elbaum, B., McIntyre, C., & Smith. A. (2002). Essential elements: Prepare, design, and teach your online course. Madison, WI: Atwood Publishing.

Gagnon, G. W., & Collay, M. (2001). Designing for learning. Thousand Oaks, Ca: Corwin.

Gedalof, A. J. (2002). Green Guide No. 1: Teaching large classes. Halifax: STLHE, Dalhousie University.

Hartman, H. J., & Glasgow, N. A. (2002). Tips for the science teacher: Research-based strategies to help students learn. Thousand Oaks, Ca: Corwin.

Hudspith, B., & Jenkins, H. (2002). Green guide no. 3: Teaching the art of inquiry. Halifax: STLHE, Dalhousie University.

Rosenshine, B. (1997). Advances in Research on Instruction. In J. W. Lloyd, E. J. Kameanui, & D. Chard (eds.), Issues in educating students with disabilities (pp. 197-221). Mahwah, NJ: Lawrence Erlbaum.

Silverman, S. (1992). Teacher feedback and achievement in physical education: Interaction with student practice. Teaching and Teacher Education, 8(4), 333-344.

Active Learning
by Ian Crawford

A Shift in Focus

Much of what has constituted university teaching over the years can be summarized as
organizing knowledge in a rational way independent of the learner. As a result, diverse disciplines and taxonomic schemes have been established. The role of the instructor was to present the structure of the disciplines to students. Teaching and learning occurred by "filling the cup". The learner was a vessel to be filled.

A significant shift in thinking about the nature of human learning and the conditions that best promote the varied dimensions of human learning, occurred in the mid twentieth century. This shift involved conclusions that:
1. learning is an active process
2. learning involves language
3. learning is a social activity
4. learning occurs in context
5. learning is not instantaneous - it takes time to learn
6. motivation is a key component in learning.

These conclusions led to the realization that instructors have to focus on the learner in thinking about learning (not solely on the subject or lesson to be taught), and that there is no knowledge independent of the meaning attributed to experience as constructed by the learner. The term "constructivist learning" has been applied to this view of learning. Applefield, Huber and Moallem (2001) wrote that "constructivism proposes that learner conceptions of knowledge are derived from meaning-making search in which learners engage in a process of constructing individual interpretations of the experiences" (p.36). The role of the learner is to build and transform knowledge. But what does it mean to construct knowledge? For the learner to construct meaningful knowledge s/he must become actively involved in making sense of new experiences relating them to what s/he already knows about the topic.

The Rise of Active Learning

The dancer, Isadora Duncan (1926), wrote, "It is one of the great truths that what is impossible to teach the child through words will be learned easily through the language of movement" (p.118). Duncan was offering an early insight into the shift in instructional focus which has been evolving over the last fifty years from "passive" to "active" learning. Indeed, "active learning has a long and distinguished history – from the dialogue of Socrates, to Rabelais's model Renaissance education of Gargantua, to Dewey's reflecting thinking (1930's), to Bruner's discovery method (1960's)" (Rubin & Hebert, 1983, p.26). Good teachers have always engaged students in learning through activities involving discussing, discovering, manipulating, hypothesizing, graphing, problem-solving and the like.

In the traditional approach to higher education, the instructor dispenses content information to students who passively absorb it. According to Felder and Brent (1996), much of what happens in most lectures is "neither teaching nor learning - it is stenography. Instructors recite their course notes and transcribe them onto the board, the students do their best to transcribe as much as they can into their notebooks, and the information flowing from one set of notes to the other does not pass through anyone's brain" (p.44). This mode of instruction is effective for presenting large amounts of information that can be memorized and recalled in the short term. For longer term retention of information, the development of problem-solving and critical thinking skills, the stimulation of interest in the subject area, and increased motivation to study the subject at a deeper level, research has consistently shown (Bonwell & Eison, 1991; McKeachie, 1999; Sutherland & Bonwell, 1996) that instruction involving students more actively is more effective than straight lecturing. In addition, Felder, Woods, Stice and Rugarcia (2000) wrote "active learning methods make classes much more enjoyable for both students and instructors" (p.31). Active learning is becoming more prevalent in all subject areas.

Leonard (2000) listed a series of general recommendations for science faculty members to consider. These included:

1. "Use significantly more active learning" (p.387).
2. "Implement constructivist learning environments in your classroom" (p.387).
3. "Use lab before lecture to teach the same science concepts" (p.388).
4. "Provide your students with a conceptual framework and advance organizers" (p.388).
5. "Accommodate the many ways in which different students learn by using many different approaches" (p.388).

Promoting Active-Student Learning

Active learning refers to anything that students do in a classroom other than passively listening to an instructor lecture. This includes everything from listening to and absorbing the lecturer's key points; to writing activities in which students react to the lecture material; and, to group exercises in which students apply the course material to "real life" situations involving simulations, case studies, and role plays. The possibilities for active involvement are myriad.

In-class exercises

Students learn by doing, not by watching and listening. Even in a large lecture class, students can be engaged in "doing" activities. At different points during the lecture students could be asked to write responses to assigned tasks individually or in groups of two or three. Occasionally the students could be asked to work alone then to form pairs or small groups to improve their individual responses in a "think-pair-share" format. The task need not take more than five minutes. The tasks will, of course, vary but two from biology could be, "Why do elephants have large ears"? or "Why can't amoebae be as large as a basketball"?

Ebert-May, Brewer and Sylvester (1997) described their teaching efforts to involve active learning by all their students. One strategy described involved trying to promote discussion in a large lecture hall.

> First, students interacted frequently with their nearest neighbours and in cooperative groups, then individual students from cooperative groups reported back to the class. At least once each lecture, students were asked to turn to a student seated next to them to complete a task, such as forming an answer to a question or problem from lecture material, developing an example of a concept, or formulating a question about something that they did not understand from the preceding lecture (p.603).

In-class exercises could also occur at the end of a lecture. Students could be asked to write down and hand in a brief statement of the main point of the lecture, a possible exam question on the topic covered, restate an up-coming assignment in their own words, indicate how their point of view on an issue raised in lecture differs or is similar to the point of view of the instructor or author of the textbook, make connections to previously introduced concepts, or relate the issue or content to their own knowledge and experience. The principal benefit to in-class exercises is that they get students acting and reflecting.

Creative writing

Creative writing, whether it be poetry, fiction or drama, involves a personal interaction. It is inherently interpretive and critical in approach. Creative writing is one way to involve students in any subject area in active learning. Vess (1996) has written extensively on the use of creative writing in history.

> Writing assignments which incorporate the framework of creative writing can be adapted to meet the needs of the historian, propel students beyond mere mastery of history. Historical fiction is a genre which can accurately assess the factual knowledge of students, while simultaneously demanding a creative mode of expression which forces students to interact with facts on a personal level (p.46).

In addition, Vess discusses using creative writing in the form of creative autobiography where "students attempt to assume the character, personality and point of view of their chosen subject" (p.46). Vess indicates that students might explore the outbreak of the Black Death in the fourteenth century. Students could be asked to write an autobiography of someone around at the time such as a victim of the plague (gruesome physiological details), a yeoman (able to rise to affluent free peasant status by judicious marriage and by occupying peasant lands made vacant by the plague), an abbot (how to deal with the sudden death of 40 percent of the peasants on the abbey's lands), a working-class woman (occupationally more active due to labour shortage), a religious zealot (scapegoating thus fueling pogroms), a painter (recording what he sees as he travels), or a physician (trying to uncover the cause of the deaths). The resulting sharing of these autobiographies in a story-telling, presentation or role-play format would allow students to explore the Black Death (and the fourteenth century) from a variety of perspectives.

Panel discussions, debates, and role-plays

Panel discussions are useful as a way of involving many members of the class. Groups could be assigned a topic to research and to prepare a presentation. Each panelist is expected to make a short presentation before the floor is opened to questions from the "audience". The students representing the "audience" are also given a role to play. For example, in a presentation in which students are presenting the results of their research into several forms of energy, students in the "audience" could role-play environmentalists, commuters, transportation officials, and so forth.

Debates provide an efficient structure for presentations in which the topic easily divides into opposing views. Students are assigned to teams and given a position to defend. On presentation day they present arguments in support of their position. The opposing side is given an opportunity to rebut the argument. The original presenters then respond to the rebuttal.

Ebert-May, Brewer and Allred (1997) describe a debate on genetic engineering. Background material was shared with all the students. Students prepared position statements arguing in favour of, or in opposition to, genetic engineering from the perspective of a particular interest group. "To ensure a broad range of viewpoints, short, one-page articles (e.g., from such publications as Science, Nature, Science News, and Time) that could be used to support the viewpoints of 12 different interest groups (e.g., lawyers, insurance agents, physicians, research scientists, concerned citizens, and philosophers) were shuffled and distributed in class" (p.604).

In role-plays students are asked to "act out" a part. The role-play can be scripted or open-ended. Role-playing could take the form of a play. In philosophy, students could role-play Socrates or in biology, the Scopes trial.

Critical thinking

Critical thinking is an important student outcome for today's workforce and professional environments. It is also a key element in active learning. As Eison (1999) stated "The secret to transforming students from passive learners into engaged learners? Teaching strategies that motivate students to actually do things connected to their learning - and then think about what they're doing - can make a world of difference" (p.5).

Chambers, Angus, and Carter-Wells (2000) describe a series of activities effective for teaching critical thinking skills, building concepts, and promoting metacognitive awareness. Three of the many activities described use small group discussion stimulated by the instructor's use of topical material.

For example, fortune cookies, horoscopes, and advertisements became the basis of discussion on ambiguity.

Graphic organizers

Good teachers have always found ways to help students learn. Over the years, many structures have been developed to aid the process of meaningful learning. The better known examples are flow charts, time lines, cause and effect charts, Venn diagrams, cycle diagrams and KWL (What I Know; What I Wonder about; What I would like to Learn) charts. Each of these are helpful for students to visualize interrelationships within the topic of concern. Perhaps the best known graphic organizer is concept mapping.

Concept mapping was developed in the early 1970's by Joseph Novak and his colleagues at Cornell University (Novak & Musonda, 1991). Concept maps are two-dimensional representations of a set of concepts. They are idealized representations of content (usually text) structure. In a concept map, the concepts are arranged in hierarchical order with a major concept (the title of the topic under discussion) at the top. The concepts are linked by arrows which are labelled with connecting words or phrases. As the reader travels down the map, the concepts become more specific. The map usually provides examples of the concepts. The understanding of any concept within a map is determined by the connections with other concepts. An example of a concept map follows:

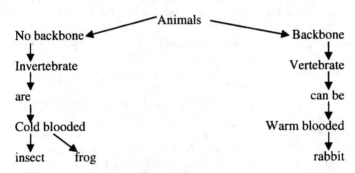

In the previous, very simple example, the value of a concept map in revealing connections is made evident. A concept map can be constructed by an instructor to show the connections. More importantly, a student can be asked to construct a concept map in order to illustrate understanding of a topic by showing the connections within the map. The construction of concept maps helps both teacher and student. Novak and Gowin (1994) reported "students and teachers constructing concept maps often remark that they recognize new relationships and hence new meanings or, at least meanings they did not consciously hold before making the map" (p.17). This discovery of new relationships is particularly important for students who often possess an incomplete understanding of a topic and are unable to integrate all the components to form a meaningful overview.

Concept maps are useful in assessment. A student's concept map can help the instructor to identify any misconceptions. In a test situation, students could be given a list of concepts and asked to map them. In addition, students could be asked to add other concepts of their own choosing. Hartman and Glasgow (2002, p. 206) give an example of a concept map quiz on sedimentary rocks. In the concept map, students fill in the empty spaces with the following concepts: roundness, biochemical, packing, elastic, size, rock fragments, chemical sphericity, chemical precipitates, sorting chemical.

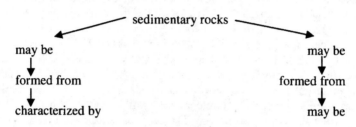

sedimentary rocks

may be   may be

formed from   formed from

characterized by   may be

As shown, concept maps or other graphic organizers can provide an alternative form of assessment.

Inquiry teaching

Inquiry teaching encourages students to take responsibility for their own learning. The instructor's role is that of facilitator. The strategy consists of two branches: guided and unguided inquiry. The instructional process moves from guided to unguided inquiry as students become more adept at identifying and analyzing problems and in structuring solutions.

Inquiry teaching requires prior learning on the part of the student. Bevevino, Dengal and Adams (1999) describe an inquiry approach leading students to determine the causes of World War I. They indicate that the instructor would introduce "concepts such as territorialism, expansionism, employment, wages, economic and natural resource factors, tilting the balance of power, the struggle for economic dominance of power, and mediation strategies" (p.277). In addition, "concepts related to conflict between nations, such as imperialism, nationalism, industrial growth, colonialism, and militarism" (p.277) would have to be introduced. Possessing this background knowledge, students are asked to analyze historical antecedents of World War I:

1389	The Ottoman Empire conquers Serbia.
1850 - 1914	Europe experiences the pinnacle of nationalism.
1862 - 1890	Bismarck dominates European affairs.
1890	Kaiser Wilhelm ascends to power, demanding that Bismarck resign.
1912	Serbia gains independence from Turkish rule, yet many Serbs live in territories (e.g., Bosnia) ruled by Austria-Hungary.
1914	Archduke Ferdinand is assassinated on June 28. (P.277)

The students are then asked to review treaties made prior to the war:

1881	Bismarck signs an alliance with Austria-Hungary and Russia.
1882	The Triple Alliance of Germany, Austria-Hungary, and Italy is formed.
1894	Wilhelm reaffirms the alliance with Austria-Hungary and Italy but excludes Russia.
1894	France and Russia sign an alliance creating a rival block.
1904	France signs the "Entente Cordiale" with Great Britain, leading to close military and diplomatic ties.
1907	Great Britain signs an alliance with Russia.
1905 - 1911	Competition for colonies brings Germany and France to the brink of war.
1912	Balkan states attack the Ottoman Empire (P.278).

Students are asked to analyze conditions and events occurring in Germany, France, and England from 1900 to 1913 related to territorialism, employment, availability of economic and natural resources, personalities, and attempts at mediation. The students' goal is to determine the causes for World War I (p.278).

Inquiry teaching encourages students to develop their own frames of thought. It allows students to personalize and contextualize certain aspects of the subject area. Through the inquiry approach learning the subject area becomes a personally interesting and internalized experience.

Conclusion

Research on cognitive learning suggests that although individual students learn in different ways, all meaningful learning - learning that emphasizes understanding - requires active involvement of the learner. Accordingly, "chalk and talk" teaching is not the ideal strategy for an instructor to use. Good teaching practice requires the use of a variety of teaching strategies that promote active learning on the part of the student.

To further teaching:

Applefield, J. M., Huber, R., & Moalen, M. (2001). Constructivism in theory and practice: Toward a better understanding. The High School Journal, 84(2), 35-53.

Bevevina, M. M., Dengel, J., & Adams, K. (1999). Constructivism theory in the classroom: Internalizing concepts through inquiry learning. The Clearing House, 72(5), 275-278.

Chambers, A., Angus, K. B., & Carter-Wells, J. (2000). Creative and active strategies to promote critical thinking. Claremont Reading Conference Yearbook, 2000, 58-69.

Duncan, I. (1926). The art of dance. New York: Theatre Arts Books.

Ebert-May, D., Brewer, C., & Allred, S. (1997). Innovation in large lectures - teaching for active learning. BioScience, 47, 601-607.

Felder, R. M., & Brent, R. (1996). Navigating the bumpy road to student-centred instruction.
College Teaching, 44, 43-47.

Felder, R. M., Woods, D. R., Stice, J. E., & Rugarcie, A. (2000). The future of engineering education: Teaching methods that work. Chemical Engineering Education, 34(1), 26-39.

Hartman, H. J., & Glasgow, N. A. (2002). Tips for the science teacher: Research-based strategies to help students learn. Thousand Oaks, CA: Corwin.

Leonard, W. H. (2000). How do college students best learn science? Journal of College Science Teaching, 29(6), 385-388.

McKeachie, W. J. (1999). Teaching tips: Strategies, research, and theory for college and university teachers (Tenth Edition). Boston: Houghton Mifflin.

Novak, J. D., & Gowin, D. B. (1984). Learning how to learn. Cambridge: Cambridge University Press.

Novak, J. D., & Musonda, D. (1991). A twelve-year longitudinal study of science concept learning. American Educational Research Journal, 28(1), 117-153.

Rubin, L., & Hebert, C. (1998). Model for active learning: collaborative peer teaching. College Teaching, 46, 26-30.

Sutherland, T. E., & Bonwell, C. C. (1996). Using active learning in college classrooms: A range of options for faculty. San Francisco: Jossey-Bass.

Voss, D. (1996). Creative writing and the historian: An active learning model for teaching the craft of history. The History Teacher, 30, 45-53.

Food, Fun, and Flatulence in Biochemistry Classes: An Example of "Improving Learning"
by Lana Lee

I have been teaching third year biochemistry courses that focus on protein and nucleic acid chemistry and metabolism. The students are biology or biochemistry students with future aspirations as biologists, biochemists, doctors, dentists, pharmacists, veterinarians, and chiropractors. This chapter describes how I, as a professor, use food and current events to enhance the delivery of the course. These general examples from my classes may be applied to related courses. Although students do not always respond with laughter at my jokes, I believe some of the anecdotes, topics, and demonstrations are memorable. – Lana Lee

Live demonstrations are frequently incorporated into chemistry lectures to increase the interest of students; correspondingly, I have developed demonstrations to enhance the presentation of biochemistry. In particular, I have found that food can attract, awaken, and stimulate sleepy students. I cannot recall any student refusing the free food I have offered in any of my courses.

Kidneys, Sausages, and Jello

My Protein and Nucleic Acid Chemistry course deals with isolation and characterization. Dialysis is a basic biochemical method used to remove salts from large macromolecules such as proteins. To demonstrate this technique, I add a volume of blue dextran, a very large molecule bound to a blue dye, to an equivalent volume of dinitrophenol, a small yellow compound. The resulting green solution is inserted into dialysis tubing, secured, and submerged into a flask of water. At the next lecture, the tubing is examined and contains only the blue material. The yellow molecules have diffused out of the membrane and into the water. I stress the correlation between this basic technique to kidney failure. Kidneys normally remove small toxic molecules from our systems. Patients who suffer from kidney failure must undergo extensive dialysis treatment to detoxify their blood. The patient's blood is circulated through membranes and the toxic molecules are removed. I then circulate an artificial kidney, and point out the dialysis membranes in the unit. The combination of theory, experimentation, and linkage to a medical condition, fully reinforces the technique in their minds.

Food can be used to complement the presentations of this technique. I ask my students, "How is Polish sausage related to dialysis?" After a few moments of bewildering silence, I describe the physical nature of dialysis tubing and compare it to sausage casing in frankfurters and Polish sausage. Most students are eager to taste the slices of Polish coil I distribute. They must remove the casing which is comparable to dialysis tubing, before eating it. This action reinforces the concept of dialysis in their minds; they may never look at Polish coil the same way ever again.

Gel electrophoresis is another basic biochemical method used to determine the sizes of proteins and/or DNA. To reinforce the idea of the physical nature of the gel, I distribute Jello jigglers for students to nibble. These tastings are designed to be fun and to establish firmly in the students' minds details of the various techniques.

Cookies, Chips, and Fat Metabolism

Sugar chemistry is often discussed in metabolism courses. One obvious topic would be a discussion of the causes and therapies of diabetes, where glucose uptake is compromised. To extend this topic, I have discussed fructose, a sugar substitute frequently found in fructose cookies available in most health food stores. Thus, a taste test comparing Nabisco's Oreo cookies with chocolate cream-filled fructose sandwich cookies has become standard fare in my course. Two male and two female volunteers are asked to stand at the front of the class, face the blackboard and sample an unidentified cookie. In addition to eating the cookies, they enjoy the reverse position by which they assign grades of A, B, C, or D to each cookie. They are given the second cookie and asked to rate it as well. I won't divulge the results here; one has to perform their own experiment! The students in the audience then usually devour the remaining cookies.

To liven up fat metabolism lectures, I have included a similar taste test on potato chips. Proctor and Gamble has developed Olean as a zero calorie fat substitute used in Pringles potato chips. After presenting the chemistry and rationale behind the low caloric value of Olean laden chips, I do warn the students about the potential side effect of diarrhea. Personally I have eaten twenty such chips and have not yet suffered. Again I administer a comparable taste test of the Olean versus vegetable oil chips, and it has always lead to laughter in the classroom.

Biochemistry Headliners
Murder by mail with anthrax and murder in a Tokyo subway with sarin

Current events and news topics keep the students interested. Unfortunately, at the time of writing, exposure to anthrax has recently been on the front page of newspapers and magazines as the cause of several deaths in the United States. The discussion of the essential proteins of anthrax, their structures, and possible therapies leads to an understanding of how their current course material can be applied to front page news.

Other events in the news provide topics to keep the material fresh. A few years ago, terrorists exposed selected Tokyo subway stations with the neurotoxin Sarin, resulting in the suffocation and death of many innocent victims. I discuss the structure of Sarin, its target, mode of action, and therapy. The connection between the target enzyme and nerve impulses is made.

Biochemistry saves a convicted murderer

Furthermore, amino acid metabolism can be a challenge to teach. In this case, I present the story of Pat Stallings who was accused and convicted of murdering her infant son. This child exhibited uncontrollable vomiting and difficulty in breathing, symptoms often associated with ethylene glycol poisoning. In prison, she performed the best biochemical experiment she could have ever conducted - she became pregnant again. Right after birth, the second child was immediately removed; however, he too developed similar symptoms. Dr. William Sly, a biochemist, came to the rescue and confirmed his suspicions that a defect in amino acid metabolism, methyl malonic acidimia, was the true cause of the infant's death. The convicted murderer, Pat Stallings was subsequently released. The case history, reactions, control, medical issues, and the apparent lack of quality control increases the interest level of the students.

DNA and ostriches

There appears to be a genetic component in some inherited diseases such as Lou Gehrig's disease, Huntington's chorea, breast cancer, and colon cancer. I ask my students the following rhetorical questions: "If one of your parents dies of a genetically inherited disease, for which there may or may not be a cure, would you request to have your own DNA analyzed now to detect the presence of the DNA lesion?" "Would you decide to behave as an ostrich, bury your head in the sand, and not request such a determination?" There is no one correct answer; each individual must consider life expectancy, health insurance, life insurance, and quality of life issues. It is a thought provoking exercise.

After students learn the basic reactions, I try to sustain students' interest by focusing on their regulation, and the clinical aspects whenever possible.

Flatulence - Biochemistry in Action

Although there is no active demonstration involved here, (thank heavens), I also venture into asking probing questions such as, "As third year biology or biochemistry students, have you ever in class discussed the biochemistry of farting?" To date, the answer has always been a resounding "no!" I simply present the basic physiology, bacteriology, biochemistry, and chemistry of flatulence by asking and answering the following questions: "What gases are produced? What volumes are normally discharged daily? What over the counter medications are available? How do they work?" I end the lecture with a reading of the delightful children's illustrated book, *The Gas We Pass, The Story of Farts* (Cho, 1978). The students laugh, and the students learn.

Summary

This chapter has focused on the introduction of food and current news to biochemistry lessons. Although the examples have been quite specific, the general approach is applicable to any course. My fundamental advice is to introduce relevant, modern examples in class in the form of demonstrations and research. Moreover, the instructor's positive attitude towards the material can potentially become infectious. Have fun!

To Further Teaching:

The following list consists of selected references, and serves as a basic starting point for some of the examples mentioned above.

American Chemical Society. What's that Stuff? Chemical and Engineering News. Washington, D.C.

Cho, S. (1978). The gas we pass: The story of farts. Brooklyn: Kane/Miller Book Publishers.

The Howard Hughes Medical Institute. Arousing the Fury of the Immune System. Chevy Chase, Maryland. Retrieved from www.hhmi.org.

The National Human Genome Research Institute. Exploring Our Molecular Selves. Retrieved from www.nhgri.nih.gov

Schwarcz, J. (1999). Radar, Hula Hoops and Playful Pigs. Toronto: ECW Press.

The U.S. Department of Health and Human Services. The structures of life (pamphlet). Bethesda, Maryland. Retrieved from http://www.nigms.nih.gov

Mentoring First Year Students: An Example of a Formal Program
by Geri Salinitri

"The mentorship program has provided me with the opportunity to strengthen my skills as a teacher while providing guidance to a first-year student. Through this program, I developed an open relationship with my student and I was able to give her sound advice and direction which she benefited from greatly. I truly believe that all students could benefit from a mentorship program regardless of their year or academic standing. I wish that there had been such a program in place when I entered university."
Melanie Marshall, PreService Teacher Mentor

Strategies for increasing student retention are among the most important issues facing universities today. Universal recognition of higher education, as a prerequisite to success, ... means that there is an increasing demand for higher education for everyone (Paul, 2001). With more students entering university, a diversity of learning styles becomes apparent revealing various factors which adversely affect the transition of these first year students from high school to university and college. These factors include:

- Inability to meet the academic standards of the university,
- Inability to adapt to the new social and academic environment,
- Changes in personal goals and aspirations,
- Lack of clearly defined goals and motivation,
- Priority of other commitments, such as work or family,
- Financial difficulty,
- Incongruence between the institution's orientation approach and that desired by the individual. (Paul, 2001)

This translates into a growing need for improved academic programs and advising that will improve student retention particularly with *at-risk* students (those whose /Grade 12 admittance average is less than 70%). Universities and colleges not only need to accept these at risk students but also ease the transition by providing them with the tools, knowledge and confidence necessary to successfully fulfill graduation requirements.

These students are a challenge because they generally have poor study habits; study alone; don't seek help and/or know where to find help. They are a reactive group and often find themselves dropping out because they are unable to acquire the necessary tools for success.

This chapter explores the concepts and practices of a formal mentoring program designed for first year *at-risk* university students. Beginning with a brief overview of mentoring, as it relates to this program currently in place at the University of Windsor, followed by the roles, and responsibilities of the participants and ending with the identification of measures that foster good mentoring practices, the focus here is on design, strategies, implementation and ongoing assessment of such a program. This is just one example of a formal mentoring program. Mentoring, at the University of Windsor, has proven to be a successful way of retaining students, and increasing the likelihood of student success.

Mentoring Defined

"The mentorship program is having a profound effect on my personal philosophy as an educator. I have developed skills, along with my student, at a personal level that can translate into a classroom setting and be applied to the whole class easily and effectively. These skill will benefit the students and myself equally and immensely."

Ian Cullion, PreService Teacher Mentor

The term mentor stems from Greek mythology through to Homer's Odyssey. The original mentor/protégé relationship was that of Mentor, a trusted servant of Odysseus, who was left to look after the well being of Odysseus' son Telemachus. This relationship involved the education and guidance of Telemachus.

Today mentoring has become synonymous with role model, coach, guide, sponsor, friend and adviser. Not surprisingly, Carr (2001) identifies mentoring, coaching, teaching, and supervision as having many common components. For instance, each uses the same interpersonal skills, involves learning, affects career development, and the roles are often interchangeable.

Mentoring is both a learning process and a teaching process. The mentor/protégé relationship is one of mutual empowerment. Mentor is synonymous with leadership. Mentoring is about creating an enduring and meaningful relationship with another person. The focus is on the quality of that relationship and factors such as mutual respect, willingness to learn from each other and the use of deeper interpersonal skills. Mentoring is distinguishable from other retention activities because of its emphasis on learning in general and mutual learning in particular. In this relationship both the mentor and the student take responsibility for maximizing the learning activity. For the relationship to work there needs to be a concrete value component for both the mentor and the student.

Rationale for a Formal Education Mentoring Program

Mentoring seems like a natural solution to retaining students at risk; however, most mentoring programs fail because the mentors chosen are either professors in the student's discipline, or other, more successful students in the student's course of study. With the former relationship - Professor as mentor - there is an imbalance of power. The student is always consciously aware that their Professor-Mentor is a colleague in the academic department to which the student is dependent upon for grades. Ultimately, no matter how trusting the relationship, the student would be unlikely to approach this mentor if an academic crisis, or other, were to occur. In the latter relationship - Student as Mentor - there is not enough expertise in the discipline for the relationship to be worthwhile. No matter how senior and how successful, the students chosen to mentor other students at risk are still simply students themselves. They have no experience teaching; they have no formal psychological training; they possess no original expertise in the field. While students as mentors may be successful socially, and while there is no imbalance of power in the relationship. There is still not enough discipline expertise to be worthwhile to the student at risk of academic failure.

One solution to the above problem with mentoring relationships, described below in this formal program, is to select a preservice teacher as the mentor. This 'student teacher' already has a degree, and possesses training in 'how to teach other students'. As a result, the preservice teacher is a student herself, thus, no imbalance of power exists; and s/he possesses both expertise in the program of study (having successfully completed it herself), as well as experience teaching and advising students. This relationship works - the expertise and equity to make a mentoring relationship work are both found in a PreService Teacher Mentor.

This formal program is designed to complement existing retention programs and link mentors from various faculties with at-risk students from undergraduate programs in the Faculties of Science and Arts and Social Sciences. Unlike many existing peer mentoring programs, this program matches trained candidates, from the Faculty of Education, as mentors to the at-risk Grade 12 students entering University. The mentor candidates attend a credit class program with expectations and evaluation criteria that removes the "altruism" issue from the formula. Both mentor and student receive personal gains by participating in the program. Using teacher candidates as mentors also bridges the gap between student/peer relationship and student/faculty relationship. This provides the required experience and wisdom missing from a peer/peer mentorship without inducing the anxiety associated with student/faculty mentorship.

The mentors treat the relationship as a professional responsibility that is intrinsic to the foundation of their teaching philosophy. As such, they are responsible for initiating regular meetings in a professional setting during class hours. They must also trace the students development by follow up on suggested strategies from previous meetings. These meetings are crucial considering the adversities faced by their students which may include social and personal issues, motivation, academic or management problems.

This program is composed of a triadic, interfaculty approach. The roles of each member of the triad will be expanded in the next few sections. The following diagram illustrates the roles of each member of the triad.

Coordinator (oversees the program and monitors the mentors through a credit course criteria)	Academic Advisor (provides the tools and timelines for the mentor/student relationship as well as academic counselling)

Mentor ———————————————— Student

Program Goals

- ❑ To help students develop the knowledge, skills, and attitudes necessary for successful completion of their academic goals
- ❑ To encourage students' development of supportive relationships with other students, faculty, and staff.
- ❑ To advance students' knowledge about campus services
- ❑ To promote students' self confidences
- ❑ To develop students' leadership skills so that they may achieve academic success

Role of the Coordinator

- ❑ To recruit mentor candidates (either experienced students or professors)
- ❑ To interview candidates as potential mentors
- ❑ To design on going strategies to maintain the momentum of the program
- ❑ To provide monthly meetings with the academic advisor and mentor in an open forum for debate and trouble shooting

Role of the Academic Advisor

- ❑ To provide the mentors with the tools necessary in understanding the culture of university environment
- ❑ To make mentors aware of the retention programs, workshops and support services
- ❑ To provide academic counseling for students
- ❑ To interview students for the program and provide a profile for the student

Joint Role of the Coordinator and Academic Advisor

- ❑ To implement, design and assess the program
- ❑ To recruit potential students
- ❑ To match mentor candidates with students
- ❑ To troubleshoot problems in relationships
- ❑ To provide ongoing assessment of the program

Overall Expectations of Mentors

- ❑ Serve as role models and direct student to academic and personal campus advisors
- ❑ Help student understand and adjust to the demands of university life
- ❑ Inform student about academic policies, rules and procedures within the Faculties of Science and Arts and Social Sciences, support services, university services, campus organizations and university activities
- ❑ Help students assess their learning skills and create a plan to improve those skills
- ❑ Direct students to training workshops to improve their problem-solving skills and techniques
- ❑ Participate in organizing events for students
- ❑ Meet with their advisor biweekly to submit logs and discuss progress
- ❑ Maintain professionalism and confidentiality
- ❑ Establish a safe, nurturing environment
- ❑ Motivate student to set realistic education goals – short term and long term
- ❑ Maintain professional ethics throughout the program

Specific Expectations

- ❑ Keep a journal logging each meeting with the student
- ❑ Meet with the student weekly at a convenient time
- ❑ Contact student by email or by phone
- ❑ Promote confidentiality with ethical guidelines
- ❑ Apply practical strategies to assist student in enhancing their learning
- ❑ Create timelines
- ❑ Complete a contact report after each meeting
- ❑ Inform students about tutoring opportunities
- ❑ Assist student to evaluate their learning skills and create a plan of action to improve their skills using the appropriate resources offered by the University

❑ Maintain a journal assessing the program providing feedback for the student and the instructor

❑ Prepare a final report to be presented to faculty administration involved in the program

The Mentor Do's and Don'ts

DO	Don'ts
• Praise student when deserved • Communicate • Be punctual • Be a good role model • Follow the rules of the program • Be honest • Strive for mutual respect • Show initiative • Show compassion and concern • Maintain professionalism • Meet in a professional environment during appropriate times	• Don't judge • Don't be late • Don't disappoint someone that is counting on you • Don't use poor language, written or oral • Don't dress inappropriately • Don't' try to force your beliefs or values onto the student • Don't let the student talk you into something that you know is against the rules

Expectations of the Student

❑ Provide consent to participate and commit to the program

❑ Meet with their mentor weekly

❑ Participate in workshops and/or social events on campus

❑ Participate in the program for 2 semesters

❑ Keep their mentor informed of changes

Monitoring process

❑ Consistent and weekly scheduled meetings with mentor and student

❑ Tracking system of meetings (log sheet)

❑ Written records of each meeting

❑ Monthly meetings with mentors and the administrators (coordinator and academic advisor) of the program

A sample pamphlet sent to the schools to inform them of the transitional program available is illustrated below.

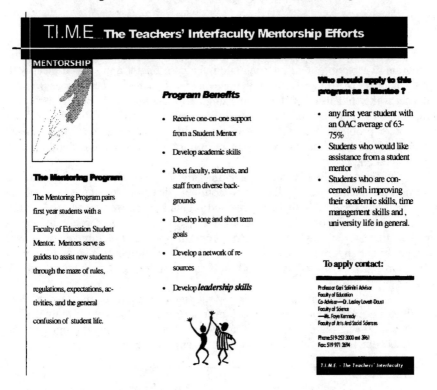

T.I.M.E. The Teachers' Interfaculty Mentorship Efforts

MENTORSHIP

The Mentoring Program

The Mentoring Program pairs first year students with a

Faculty of Education Student Mentor. Mentors serve as guides to assist new students through the maze of rules, regulations, expectations, activities, and the general confusion of student life.

Program Benefits

- Receive one-on-one support from a Student Mentor
- Develop academic skills
- Meet faculty, students, and staff from diverse backgrounds
- Develop long and short term goals
- Develop a network of resources
- Develop *leadership skills*

Who should apply to this program as a Mentee ?

- any first year student with an OAC average of 63-75%
- Students who would like assistance from a student mentor
- Students who are concerned with improving their academic skills, time management skills and, university life in general.

To apply contact:

Professor Geri Salinitri Advisor
Faculty of Education
Co-Advisor—Dr. Lesley Lovett-Doust
Faculty of Science
—Ms. Faye Kennedy
Faculty of Arts And Social Sciences

Phone 519-253-3000 ext 3961
Fax: 519 971 3694

T.I.M.E. - The Teachers' Interfaculty

Matching Mentors with Students

All mentors and students are interviewed. Students are required to complete a demographic questionnaire that will help in matching them with a suitable mentor. Once both parties have been interviewed, the mentors and students are ultimately matched by program choices. Undecided major students are matched with Social Science and Liberal Arts majors.

Subject specific majors are matched with each other. Ethnic background and gender are taken into consideration when pairing if it is a concern is displayed by the student, or the coordinator feels that the match is advantageous in eliminating confusion or misunderstandings due to cultural diversity. The coordinator attempts to match those with common interests.

The student's needs must be the primary consideration in any match. Mentors are selected to respond to these needs. Assessment reveals students through the questionnaire as well as the interview process. The mentor must provide empathy, and be able to assess skills in order to provide manageable steps. Ultimately, it is the job of the mentor to use those strategies to improve student's skills, and that of the coordinator to monitor the progress.

Training and Orientation

Mentors and students who choose to participate need to understand the program expectation. During orientation, the coordinator and advisor meet with the students. An open forum is held to address such expectations as well as concerns the student might have regarding participation, and hopefully welcome them into in the program. Issues of confidentiality, safety, possible termination, and other problems that can arise in the relationship are addressed. Students should be given incentives to participate in the form of positive recognition and reinforcement.

The coordinator and academic advisor should conduct a training session for mentors. It should offer a complete discussion of the criteria of the program, the types of activities, rules and regulations as well as an open forum for discussion and questions. The meeting should consist of role-playing, an explanation of the institution's culture, program goals, and required commitment and termination procedures. This is a time to familiarize the mentor with program participants, advisors, and staff to encourage and facilitate feedback during the program.

Following the initial pairing, the mentor contacts the student and facilitates content and process by asking questions and actively listening. The mentor follows a plan of action set up by the advisor. A sample program plan, as it has been implemented at our institution, appears below.

MENTOR WILL:

- ☐ provide a positive student role model for other students to emulate
- ☐ assist new students in becoming more knowledgeable of academic policies, rules and procedures within the Faculty of Arts and Social Sciences, support services, university services, campus organizations and university activities
- ☐ refer students to proper faculty or staff when necessary

Weekly Schedule for Mentors:

Week 1

- ☐ provide the Passport to Graduation and the Workbook –
- ☐ explain the S.I.S. and ensure the student is attending the courses registered in
- ☐ review final exam schedule for conflicts
- ☐ explain how to make course changes within the first 10 days of classes
- ☐ discuss any questions or concerns the student has

Week 2

- ☐ remind student of last day, , for course changes and late course adds
- ☐ explain STEPS and encourage to take all seminars, NOW
- ☐ walk student over to my office, Room 110 CHT, explain about bulletin board and brochures
- ☐ explain importance of going to all classes, keeping up with readings and reviewing constantly
- ☐ have student for next week's appointment have the yellow workbook completed with goals and time schedule

---

	☐	discuss any questions or concerns the student has
Week 3		
	☐	inform student of the 2 writing centres and their differences, 478 Sunset is the Academic Writing Centre and Room 2126 CHN is the Writing Development Centre
	☐	work on student's yellow workbook - - goals and time schedule
	☐	make sure the student meets with each professor
	☐	discuss any questions or concerns the student has
Week 4		
	☐	discuss and possibly walk the student to the library
	☐	let the student know of free services available on campus - - use the Passport to Graduation (i.e. medical services, psychological services, resume writing; etc.)
	☐	remind student of work study program - - applications and information available in the Awards Office
	☐	go briefly through the University of Windsor Undergraduate Calendar with the student
	☐	discuss any questions or concerns the student has
Week 5		
	☐	prepare students for mid-terms and writing papers
	☐	review section 1 of the Passport to Graduation
	☐	have student meet with their program counselor yet, if not, the student needs to do so this week (for undecided and Liberal and Professional Studies they would see me for program counseling)
	☐	discuss any questions or concerns the student has
Week 6		
	☐	review section 2 of the Passport to Graduation
	☐	go over how the student felt the meeting with the program counselor went
	☐	remind the student of preparation tips for midterms
	☐	remind the student if he/she has any problems, questions or concerns about anything, he/she needs to deal with it ASAP regardless of how small or big it may seem (i.e. stress over mid terms)
	☐	discuss any questions or concerns the student has
Week 7		
	☐	review section 3 of the Passport to Graduation
	☐	remind student when mid-term grade returned if grade lower than expected have student talk to professor about test (review test with professor)
	☐	remind student if not taken any of the STEPS, to do so
	☐	is the student comfortable with using the library and other resources available on campus
	☐	discuss any questions or concerns the student has
Week 8		
	☐	review section 4 of the Passport to Graduation
	☐	remind student last day to withdraw from a
	☐	if they failed a mid-term have them see me immediately before the drop date deadline
		discuss any questions or concerns the student has
Week 9		

		explain the DARS and how to read it (if student needs help, have them see their counselor)
	☐	make sure the student knows how to check on the S.I.S. for registration date and time for Winter registration
	☐	discuss any questions or concerns the student has

Week 10

	☐	registration for Winter term will be starting shortly, if not already,
	☐	see if student needs help with reading the timetable
	☐	make sure student makes an appointment to see program counselor before selecting courses and registering for the Winter term (for undecided and LAPS it would be me)
	☐	discuss any questions or concerns the student has

Week 11

	☐	prepare students for registration for Winter term - remind student to check registration date and time on the S.I.S.
	☐	discuss preparation for finals - taking STEPS if not already done so, talking to professors or T.A. if needs help in classes
	☐	discuss any questions or concerns the student has

Week 12

	☐	remind student only 2 weeks left of classes - has the student picked up the exam schedule from the Registrar's Office (the schedule tells where the exams are)
	☐	remind student to register on time as classes will fill up
	☐	if student has forgotten P.I.N. - will need to go to Registrar's Office
	☐	discuss any questions or concerns the student has

Week 13

	☐	wish students good luck
	☐	last meeting of the semester, set up date and time for week 1 of Winter term,
	☐	classes start
	☐	discuss any questions or concerns the student has

Throughout the program the mentor is accountable to the student and administrators who hold regular formal support meetings. These meetings are mandatory and crucial to the success of the program. Issues, brainstorm suggestions are conducted and the program progress is evaluated. This meeting is facilitated by the advisor following an agenda and open ended discussion. Mentors exchange constructive approaches that can be applied to the developmental stages of the relationship. Thus, mentors are kept on track in their facilitation goals for the student.

As the relationship develops, there should be mutual responsibility between the partners, the student should begin to take on more responsibility for what transpires and the mentor should share perspectives and knowledge. As the first academic year draws to a close, the mentor checks in with the student, maintains an encouraging perspective and establishes goals for the student to become independent, and academically and personally confident in their decision-making skills.

At the end of the year, a presentation and report are required from the mentors to his/her peers regarding the program, its effect on them as prospective teachers, and the future of mentorship in the secondary school setting. The mentors reflectively share what they have learned from their own experiences, and in particular, what meaning that learning has had and the actions that have happened as a result. Once hired, as teachers, these candidates will bring with them the skills necessary to mentor high school students in their transition from high school to University. The potential of the program is far reaching. Not only will these mentors facilitate the at-risk first year students in attaining academic success, and social skills but they will bring these skills first hand into the high school setting hopefully preparing the future post secondary students for continued academic success.

Support and Positive Reinforcement

"This is an excellent program. I am glad that you have it here. I wouldn't have bothered going through the workbooks or going to workshops on my own. The push is very good. I'm doing pretty good. I know where I am going with what I want to do. It may sound confident but if I don't know I can as Heather (mentor). I came in with poor grades and now I am in good standing, surprisingly." -Stephanie, Student

The Mentorship program is concerned with providing an environment that is conducive to student learning and positive experiences. The goal of the mentorship program is to ensure that students are facilitated in their development of personal and academic skills that are necessary to complete the degree requirements, and to attain their career goals. The mentor assesses the student's needs and links the student to established on-campus programs, through the academic advisor.

The mentoring program should be designed to enhance or supplement the programs for retention that are already in place in the university. The program needs to facilitate and encourage the movement of undergraduate students toward full awareness of retention programs and participation in strategic support from the onset of their academic year. In its initial stage the mentorship program should diagnose the individual needs of the student. The mentor and student, under the direction of the academic advisor, should develop a plan of action for participation in selected programs that would help meet those needs. The mentorship should reinforce the strategies developed in the workshop programs provided. Follow up sessions and reflective discussion will lead to progress toward a successful first year at university.

Successful mentoring initiatives also require visible support and involvement from the highest levels of the institution, beginning with the deans of the participating faculties. The goals of the mentorship program should match the goals of the undergraduate program, by providing a learning environment conducive to meet academic, career and personal success. The program should be customized to meet the needs of beginning students. The academic advisor should provide the coordinator and the mentors with the tools to facilitate the process.

Communication among all participants is vital. The coordinator and academic advisor are responsible to the program for providing regular information regarding changes in policy, personnel or strategies. They also need to inform the mentors of the program's positive effects and successes. This should stimulate enthusiasm for what is being done and will maintain the desired momentum. Open communication contributes to a sense of collaboration, involvement, and program outcomes.

Social gatherings including the mentor-student partners, the staff of the program, and the supporting deans of the involved faculties, provide opportunities for recognition and acknowledgement of the participants. This recognition and acknowledgement are crucial to the success of the program. The participants deserve and need positive feedback regarding their achievements and contributions. The mentors' commitment needs to be recognized while student achievement needs to be cited. Public ceremonies inform the university or college community of the program's positive effects and can become an effective recruiting tool as well.

Letters of appreciation and recommendation are provided for candidate portfolios which will assist in their future job interviews. Notes of congratulations are sent to the students to encourage persistence in academic and personal skills development. Demonstrated success enhances recruitment and funding efforts that allow the program to grow and reach more at risk students.

Program Assessment Strategies

Frequent monitoring of the program will keep it running effectively and efficiently. Students and mentors meet on campus near the coordinators office for immediate feedback to increase their confidence levels. Meetings are conducted face-to-face on a weekly basis. The partners will exchange phone numbers and email to handle emergency situations encountered between the weekly face-to-face sessions. Log sheets and journals are essential to analyze progress and detect subtle changes in the mentor-student relationship. Log sheets generally note the dates and frequency of the meeting. Journals note activities, general perceptions of the relationship, problems or concerns, and follow-up activities.

Group meetings for mentors are also necessary to maintain a positive momentum for the program. These meetings allow for sharing problems, ideas and feelings about the program. They can include role playing to improve communication and listening skills as well as brainstorming about possible solutions. A supportive network is maintained within the mentor group. Pedagogy and best practices are introduced by the coordinator and advisor in training the mentors. Mentor programs have recently been introduced in high schools to provide this type of mentorship for all students. In preparing these candidates for mentoring programs, the rewards becomes significant. This is reflected on their sense of responsibility to the student. The momentum is maintained as they change from mentor to teacher and advisor.

It is also important to have the student assess the progress of the relationship. This can be done with a one-on-one interview with the academic advisor and/or coordinator to ensure privacy and forthright communication. The students can fill out a mentor assessment that will only be exclusively analyzed by the coordinator. An example of such an assessment follows:

Mentor Evaluation Form

Please evaluate your Mentor on the following items using the provided scale to indicate how well the Mentor performed over the course of this first semester. This is anonymous and is used for ongoing assessment of the program. Your honesty is important in maintaining a strong effective program.

(1) Strongly Disagree; (2) Disagree; (3) Neutral; (4) Agree; (5) Strongly agree

_____ 1. Comes prepared for mentoring meetings

_____ 2. Prompt for mentoring meetings

_____ 3. Manner is courteous and professional

_____ 4. Communicates effectively

_____ 5. Suggests ideas for discussion

_____ 6. Helps plan strategies for short term goals

_____ 7. Helps plan strategies for long term goals

_____ 8. Guides you toward academic success

_____ 9. Listens effectively

_____ 10. Contacts you at appropriate times for meeting

_____ 11. Your sessions are always face-to-face

_____ 12. Has made himself/ herself available by phone or email regarding any concerns

_____ 13. Shows a genuine concern to help you in becoming a successful student

_____ 14. Has provided you with alternative choices to approach a problem

_____ 15. Helps you self-evaluate your progress

_____ 16. Provides positive support and encouragement

Overall:

Please write any additional comment on the back of this form. Thank you.

Conclusion

"The mentorship program at The University of Windsor proved to be an excellent choice as a first year student to help stay on the right track. As a first year student moving away to University and not knowing what to expect, my mentor provided me with advice and always listened. While in the mentorship program I have learned some valuable skills such as time management which any University student will tell you is essential. This is an excellent program and I would recommend it for any first year students just to make sure you are going in the right direction." -Lora, Student

The mentorship program should be a mutual learning experience for all participants. Success or failure should not solely be rated by academic achievement of the students. By keeping the students in the program for the committed two terms, success is evidenced by the student's completion of the academic program and her/his increased confidence. On-going assessment of all aspects of a mentoring program is necessary for its improvement and continued success. It is the interfaculty collaborative efforts that strengthen the goals of retention and transitional first year student success through mentoring.

To Further Teaching:

Carr, R. (2001). Dancing with Roles: Differences between a coach, a mentor and a therapist. Compass:A Magazine for Peer Assistance, Mentorship and Coaching, 15(1), 5-7.

Conway, D. (2001). The design and implementation of a mentoring scheme for first year computer science students. Retrieved April 4, 2001, from http://www.csse.monash.edu.au/~damina/papers/HTML/Mentoring.html

Paul, R. (2001). State of the University Address, University of Windsor. Retrieved January 26, 2001, from http://athena.uwindsor.ca/units/president/president.nsf

"Pain? or Gain?": Strategies and Best Practices for Using Online Courseware
by Wayne Tousignant

Online Course sites have become a fashionable accessory for faculty across many campuses in the last few years. Unfortunately, there are many that resemble empty storefronts, very little content or activity beyond the guarded gate or password protected entrance. The abundance of "Facade Course Sites" as I call them, could be the direct result of the "Pain" factor greatly outweighing the "Gain" factor. The title of the recent movie "Eyes Wide Shut", not the content - just the title, comes to mind when I think of my first experiences and those shared with me by colleagues, all early adopters of the "Promised Land". New technology or good technology should lessen the load on faculty not increase it. Negative experiences or road blocks can quickly stifle any enthusiasm for moving away from face-to-face delivery to an electronic arena that can provide more challenges than benefits. There are numerous ways that courses can successfully incorporate web support, from basic HTML, to expensive off-the-shelf products, to home grown solutions. An example of the "courseware" product used at the University of Windsor is illustrated below in Figure 1.
Fig. 1

UNIVERSITY
of WINDSOR

ANNOUNCEMENTS

LECTURES

Art Major Projects

RESOURCES

INFORMATION

Required READINGS

Assignment #2

STICK or Art
Discussion

GRADES

E-MAIL Instructor

Virtual Course 13

Previous Next Expand Collapse Search Help

General Methodology - Art
80-303, Section 01- 04

▼Announcement
   What is Expected and When?
   Grades for JI 80-302 students
   Important Notice about Projects
   Attention former students / Lesson plans
▼Course Outline
   Course Outline
▼Required Readings
   Ministry of Education Documents

Each internet courseware, however, shares some basic commonalities; information, email, announcements, lectures, resources, discussion, assignments, and the need to be as simple to use as email. This chapter will not compare products, but will share concerns and best practices that can be applied to the common components that make up most online courseware or course kits and assist in shifting the balance towards "Gain" experiences.

Blueprint -Course Outline

I recommend to faculty interested in having a web presence that no matter what means they plan to use to distribute the information, to do the math first, and then develop a strategy before writing the course outline. In other words, first consider the number of students in the class, 15 or 150. The class of 15 does not present as many problems as the class that I taught last semester. The 174 students in my recent Faculty of Education Art course, posted 1519 submissions to the course kit and sent 112 email messages to the course mailbox. All of which, I, the instructor, read online, monitored, responded to when necessary, and graded. Course outline guidelines for size and a recommended number of submissions for each assignment ensured that the submissions were an appropriate size to read online. This course consisted of a blended delivery approach that combined on-line material and activities with traditional face-to-face contact. The course outline informs students on how communication will be handled, responsibilities, and expectations. Code of conduct issues, unfortunately, are not left behind in the transition from high school to college or university, and faculty have found that students have used course kit discussion areas in inappropriate ways.

Every year I ask the students to indicate by a show of hands who knows how to use a computer, then I ask to indicate again by a show of hands who knows how to rename a file or copy and paste from one window to another. The number of hands in the air is not increasing each year, as we might presume. Sure students have good eye and hand coordination to use a mouse for a game or surf the net, but to use this new technology for instruction is as foreign to them as it is to us. Some courseware systems that allow the instructor to show and hide the main elements of the navigation system can introduce the students gradually to a complex site rather than overwhelming them on day one.

Course Information

It is common for Senate bylaws at most universities to require in the academic calendar that a syllabus be handed out to each student by a set date. As more faculty move to course information on-line the paper handout is still necessary as an introduction and to provide access information for the on-line material. A week-to-week schedule is very beneficial to the students to assist them in the course expectations and due dates. Since I switched to the week-by-week format I now find myself using the posted schedule to quickly remind myself of what I will be doing for that class. "Frequently Asked Questions (FAQs)" is a valuable tool that is also found in the "Course Information" area. If one student has a question then it can be assumed that others will also need additional clarification.

Email

You may wonder why I received so few email messages (112) from so many students (174). When I go over the syllabus with the students, I make sure that they are aware of the high student to professor ratio that we will have for that semester. I emphasize this by telling them that if they get an email message from me it is usually good news or bad news and responses to most email messages will be in the form of a posting in the "Frequently Asked Questions (FAQ)" page of the course kit. For an example of such a "FAQs" page see Figure 2 below:

General Methodology - Art (80-303, Section 01-04)

Frequently Asked Questions   Previous Next Expand Collapse Search Help

Title	Modified	Category
Grades	01/07/2002	Additional Info
What are the 7 items for the portfolio	01/07/2002	
I can't remember how many postings I did. Is there a way to find out?	01/07/2002	
I made a submission to the "stick" discussion. When I went back to view my submission, it was not there!	01/07/2002	
Minimum of 4 postings but is this a minimum of 4 postings in each discussion?	11/16/2001	
Criteria for 2nd Assignment Grade?	09/10/2001	
How do I contact the Instructor?	07/27/2001	
How can I read off-line, so that I am not paying for Internet access?	09/20/99	

Fig. 2

It is very common for my students to send a thank you message for any personal email that I send to them. I will usually respond to emails within one business day, if the above "FAQs" section does not cover the answer. Students do not take it for granted that they have unlimited access to me and appreciate my time spent responding to their individual questions. I have offloaded some of the administrative communication tasks to the students. The following example is what I would recommend to include in your course outline:

1. You may use any e-mail system for this course; however, you are required to send an e-mail message to the course mailbox by the 2nd class. In this message, under "Subject" please type "my info". In addition, be sure to include in your message your full name, your preferred first name, your student number, your email address, and your major.

2. If you change your e-mail system (eg. U of W to HotMail), resubmit the above information.
3. Please note all course-related messages should be sent to the course mailbox; important personal messages should be sent to the instructor's personal mailbox, _____ @ _____.
4. Each student is responsible for checking the "Announcements" and "FAQs" in the "Course Kit" before each class."

As the messages arrive, I will mark and move the email messages flagged "my info" into a folder of the "Course Kit" mailbox labeled "Student Info" without opening them. When I need to contact a student, it is then a simple task of searching for a first or last name and opening the most recent "my info" message from that student and clicking on the reply button. What I have done over the years is make each student responsible for maintaining a current class address book. It is very common for students to change their email address more that once in a semester, change their last name through marriage and provide information that may correct an error on the class list provided by the office.

E-mail provides the students with an option to face-to-face communication from embarrassing, personal or crisis situations. The general consensus of faculty using e-mail as a teaching tool is that the normally quiet in-class students are now communicating. The additional mailbox provided for each course is also viewed as a significant bonus for many professors who have personal mailboxes that are constantly over their size limit. I am unfortunately a member of this group. Several of my colleagues started out by answering every email message as they came in and quickly switched to answering questions during set office hours and discovered that students started to send second messages to disregard the first message because they found the answer in the course kit.

E-mail provides the students with an option to face-to-face communication about embarrassing, personal or crisis situations. The general consensus of faculty using this e-mail as a teaching tool is that the normally quiet in class students are now communicating. The additional mailbox provided for each course is also viewed as a significant bonus for many faculty who have personal mailboxes that are constantly over their set size limit.

Announcements
There is nothing that shows a lack of interest more than a Web site that is overrun with outdated messages. It is also quite common to start out a new kit with a flurry of energy and activity and suddenly pull a disappearing act, leaving the students wondering what happened. Remember the strategy or plan with which we started. The students are very receptive to pattern and change. Pace yourself. You should try to set a specific time each week to post at least one announcement. Fewer office hours and no more lineups at my door are among the many benefits of online discussions. Being online has almost eliminated face-to-face meetings. I now spend the time assisting numerous students in less

time. I still do, however, have a face-to-face meeting at the end of each semester, because I feel that it is important to provide each student with this opportunity at least once.

Lectures

It has become a common and effective practice for faculty to make the lecture notes available for students before each lecture in the 3 per page handout format (Fig. 1). The students would print the handout before class and use the handout to write in emphasized lecture points discussed during the lecture. The Acrobat .pdf file as an attachment is becoming a popular format for the task of making the handouts available for several reasons. This format downloads faster, provides a magnification tool for visually impaired students, a search engine for quick review, is easy to update or replace documents, and provides high quality print capabilities. An attachment for a Microsoft word document that is 881 KB in size is only 267 KB as an attached Adobe Acrobat portable document file.

Resources

The Resource area of many kits can become a dumpsite and needs to be managed as well as the lecture area. Remember that the more links that you provide directly impacts the number of links that need to be monitored and maintained. It is quite common for URLs to change on a regular basis as servers are replaced with newer equipment. It is also important to realize that an abundance of resources makes it difficult for the students to know which links are most relevant to the course. Be realistic in regard to your students' time and flag or limit the number of links.

Discussion

A threaded discussion typically facilitates an ongoing exchange of topical information among students enrolled in a course. This type of communication is asynchronous (not in actual real time) and has been used as a tool for connecting students with content experts, external community, and members of collaborative projects throughout the world. Time zones and different schedules are accommodated well by this type of communication. Faculty members using this tool have reported code of conduct issues by student participants and the issue of who is responsible for monitoring and correcting inappropriate conduct is one that is worth considering. My own approach to such situations is to email the author of the posting to inform them that the content of the posting is in my opinion inappropriate and reflects poorly on the perception of them by others. I include in the message that I am not supportive of censorship and that I recommend that the author reply to my message to authorize me to edit or remove the content in question. Fortunately, I have never had to take action beyond this initial response, but I have assisted colleagues who have found it necessary to report some very serious incidents to a department head or dean. A system that requires each student to have a unique username and password provides a level of accountability that open or guest name systems do not provide.

Multiple discussion areas within the same course site are now becoming very common. This provides an identifiable structure for the students to be casual or informal in discussion areas such as "the Lounge" compared to a "Required Readings" discussion. Each discussion area should include a message from the instructor to indicate the type of participation that is expected within each discussion area. The role or level of participation of the facilitator or instructor in each discussion area should also be clearly identified.

Chat

Internet (IRQ) chat is a synchronous (real-time) communication that is very popular amongst teenagers but has relatively little presence or worth as a consistent component of most on-line courses. This type of communication demands that students be available at a common time to participate. This is difficult to orchestrate compared to an asynchronous threaded discussion. Conflicting time schedules, limits on the number of participants and the difficulty of managing the meeting all contribute to the decision against providing access to this type of tool. It is however becoming a common practice for students to use chat to establish study groups; especially during exam preparation periods.

Assignments

A paperless environment can be wonderful for more reasons than the classic problem of which assignment the dog has eaten recently. A courseware system lives on a server that is backed up on a daily basis and will time stamp each assignment submission. The student has the ability to then look to see that his/her submission is actually there, which can be quite comforting minutes before a deadline. This is another example of offloading the responsibility to the students to use the course site for the confirmation of assignment submissions. If you plan on reading the assignments online, make sure that the students are instructed to keep them to an appropriate length. Viewers or filters are available with some courseware systems. The benefit of this is that a viewer will not only provide access to documents for which you do not have the software, but it also eliminates the risk of acquiring a virus by detaching documents. This, however, may limit your ability to do corrections directly on assignments that you intend to return to the students.

If a student asks to meet with me about his/her final grade, I do so only at a time when I have access to the "Instructor tools" of the courseware. Each document submitted by the student is at my fingertips and retrievable within seconds by using a search engine. Have you ever had the experience of marking hundreds of papers over two or three days and then wondering about consistency of grading? With electronic submissions it is possible to go back quickly and search all the submissions for similar content such as how many submissions made reference to a specific law, quote, reference or other important material covered in the course content.

What do the Students Want?

The students over the years have consistently communicated that online courseware should be user-friendly, fast, and reliable. Students have commented that sites that are overloaded with graphics are slow and are not printer friendly.

A common navigation system, or for all faculty to use the same system, is the preference of the many students surveyed. They also want faculty to realize that participation in a single course kit is no longer a novelty and is becoming a very time consuming to monitor and participate in multiple sites. Within specific areas of study (Faculty of Education) some students might be responsible for monitoring and participating in more than a dozen different course sites.

What Can Go Wrong?

There are courseware systems that allow students to replicate or copy the site content to their own computer. This can be beneficial for students with slow internet access or for whom internet service is unavailable. However it can also create a situation where the students do not have the most recent version of the content because they have not accessed the actual site and updated or replicated their copy.

Conclusion

I have finished the Faculty of Education course that I teach over the past six years with the course evaluation and an anonymous voluntary survey. The survey was designed to acquire feedback from 353 future educators on their experience with using the online courseware for the course. The final question on the survey asks, "Would you use this teaching tool?" Over 90 percent responded "yes".

==

**Making the Large Class "Smaller"—
Some Principles to Consider When Teaching Triple-Digit Classes**
by Larry Morton

I picture Socrates seated and speaking to a few interested disciples; I picture Stalin standing and speaking to the fearful, the conscripted, and the disinterested. Then I wonder if there's something quite sinister about the large group—the large class. The large class is just not a very appealing environment for teachers or for students. Having taught larger classes (100, 200, 300+ students) now for over a dozen years, the first thing that comes to my mind when thinking of the larger class is that it has been quite a learning experience— more so for me than my students, I fear. When I first began teaching the large class I found it a stressful experience, in contrast to the smaller graduate and undergraduate classes that were really enjoyable experiences. The two encounters were radically different and the student ratings showed it. Yet, I kept choosing to teach the larger class. On the one hand, I was interested in understanding and improving the dynamics in the larger class, on the other hand, and perhaps more importantly, I saw it as a wise use of my time. It would be expedient to teach one class of 250 students rather than 10 classes of 25 students each week, would it not?

What I do now in the large class is dramatically different from what I once did. I have found that there are ways of incorporating varied and relatively interesting pedagogical techniques into the larger class. I use technology. I use the Internet. I use cooperative education. I use small groups. I use creative assessment protocols that range from something close to the standard multiple-choice test to various authentic assessments. In effect, I strive to use "small-class" principles in the large class environment. Four of the principles that I have pursued over the past few years will be discussed here. Since many of the more basic strategies (planning, preparation, voice, questioning, notes, and so on) are present in the existing detailed literature (Gedalof, 1998; Green, 2001; Kehoe, 2001; Rogers 2001a, 2001b), I plan to limit my focus to sharing my activities rather than the fundamentals or the theoretical explanations.

Principle #1—Use Media-Based Technology
One could argue that the smallest classroom is one person connected to another either by physical presence or media. The one-on-one format is normal in the private consultations in one's office, or reading a book, or interacting with material on the Internet. It is, however, somewhat mitigated in the large class, however. Nevertheless, it is possible in the large class arrangement to utilize the same dyadic techniques. The dyad can be maintained by using specific media (e.g., the book, the newspaper, the pen, the radio, the film, the TV, the computer, the internet, and so on) to effect these "smallest classrooms." People connect through various media. Students of the 21st Century value media-based connection; at least, I hold the pragmatic view that most contemporary learners

facing the large class experience do favour such media-based, small-class techniques. The specific media favoured, however, are not the pen and book so much as image and Internet. This seems to be the case regardless of the acknowledged merits of critiques of technique (e.g., Ellul, 1964, 1981; Postman, 1992). These "small-class" favoured techniques, if extended to the large classroom, may make for a better learning experience. In fact, technology (particularly, computers and the Internet) seems to be "the" premier pedagogical agenda of the day. Advocates like Papert (1980, 1993), Negroponte (1995) and Turkle (1995) make a fascinating case for technology in education, though perhaps not a thoroughly compelling case (for critical positions see Armstrong & Casement, 1998; Postman, 1992; Stoll, 1999).

This technology finds a natural home in one-on-one settings for sure, but also in the large class. It provides a tool for accessing facts, building databases, systematizing information, communicating with informed people, acquiring resources, and so on. In addition, it provides multi-sensory learning experience, it allows for personal control of learning, and it provides a real independence and empowerment. The learners seem to be in an ideal position to season their knowledge platter as they see fit.

Table 1: Technique in a Technology-Friendly Classroom

Pedagogical Category	Pedagogical Vehicle	Pedagogical Intent	Technological Interfaces	Message
Pre-Class Activities	Music PowerPoint	Entertainment, Information, Discovery	Music, MP3, PowerPoint	"Find the Message"
Sound-Bite Activities	Little Stories Nano-Lessons Projects	Information, Constructivist	Speech, PowerPoint, VCR, MPEG, Drama, Artifacts, etc.	"Build your Message"
WEB[1] Activities	Outline[2] Tour[3] Resources[4]	Information, Technological,	Speech, Photocopies, Video, PowerPoint, WEB-pages, WEB-sites, WEB-Links,	"Medium is Message"
Traditional Activities	Research Review A Story	Information, Literate	PowerPoint, Video, Oral, Audio Tape	"Message in Story"

---

[1] The class Web Site is open (no ID or password is needed to access it). This allows students to use it as a resource even after the class or program is completed. It also may serve as an instructional vehicle beyond the local community.

[2] http://zeus.uwindsor.ca/courses/edfac/morton/new_page_3.htm

[3] http://zeus.uwindsor.ca/courses/edfac/morton/announcements1.htm

[4] http://zeus.uwindsor.ca/courses/edfac/morton/teacher_resources.htm

Several aspects of technology that I now use in a large class (see Table 1) utilize various technological interfaces to link instructor and student in a dyad. In fact, the very first class of the year would include every item mentioned in Table 1.

The techniques are then described in more detail in Table 2. As may be seen in the table the techniques range from simple gimmicks to sophisticated gadgets.

Table 2: My Technological Media-Based Techniques in a Two-Hour Class

Technique	Description
Music (PRE-CLASS)	This is a pre-class activity where music is playing prior to the start of class. It is intended to present a relaxed and welcoming environment. But also, the content of the music is thematically related to the theme of the lecture. (10 minutes)
PPT—PowerPoint (PRE-CLASS)	This is a pre-class activity where a PowerPoint presentation is playing prior to the start of class. It is intended to present interesting, often humorous, information to generate relevant schema and thought. The content is thematically related to the theme of the lecture. (parallels the music for about 10 minutes)
Little Stories (SOUND-BITES)	During the lecture "little stories" are shared (using PowerPoint—text, graphics, cartoons, animation, audio) with the class. The stories relate to personal experiences of self and others (students and teachers previously in the class). (15 minutes)
Sample Projects (SOUND-BITES)	Samples of previous student projects are shared with the class. These are videos (about 5 minutes in length) which are humorous, informative, and illustrative of the technological approach to doing class projects. (15 minutes)
Nano-lessons (SOUND-BITES)	These are brief "lessons" that could potentially equip the student with strategies. An example for student teachers, "Save Your Voice" and use light signals or sound signals to get attention. Or, "Walk Slowly" to deal with discipline problems. The slow pace is intimidating and it will give you time to think about what you are going to do when you reach the source of the problem. (10 minutes)
Gimmicks (SOUND-BITES)	Use of gimmicks to get attention (a bicycle horn, or bell) or to get people talking (a fluff ball thrown into the audience to indicate who responds). (2 minutes)
WEB Outline (WEB)	The syllabus for the course is provided in a printed format, and then displayed on-line so that the hyperlinks to class notes, assignments, and so on, may be demonstrated. (5 minutes)

WEB Tour (WEB)	In addition to the WEB Outline, other WEB pages are viewed. There are pages for notification of cancelled classes, pages for "reminders," "announcements," "updates," "class notes," and so on. (5-10 minutes)
WEB Resources (WEB)	On-line resources related to the lecture topic are shown, briefly. These relate to both informational and practical resources. (3-5 minutes)
The Big Story (TRADITIONAL)	This is an audio story that relates to the lecture theme-a story told by a classic story teller (e.g., W.O. Mitchell in the first class). (25 minutes)
Research (TRADITIONAL)	This involves a PowerPoint presentation of several research studies related to the lecture theme. These are empirical studies over a period of time making an interesting educational point with applications for the teacher. (25 minutes)

The primary media-friendly classroom that I use seats approximately 280 students. It contains a large media projector, a fixed computer, a laptop computer (both with direct connections to the Internet), a VCR, an overhead projector, an opaque projector, an integrated sound system, and all of these work seamlessly from a front-and-center control panel.[5]

A Web resource that I use links students to the online class notes, and related resource links. With respect to the class notes, I post various aspects of the notes on the Web site for a particular lecture. Students can access this material to remind them of information or to fill in gaps in their own lecture notes. I also post notes for downloading in both a PowerPoint format and a MS-Word format for those students who wish to bring an outline to class, or save the information on their own computer as a resource for subsequent review. The on-line notes are sufficiently vague and incomplete that students should come to class to integrate the information—to acquire the critical comments on the material, and the elaboration of the information. Yet the notes are sufficiently clear that a student could go to the on-line notes after a lecture to assist in filling in material missed in the lecture. I do not recommend that the students print out the material as this would be a high paper cost.[6]

Student reaction to the various technologies varies considerably, and in interesting ways. One week following the first class of the year, I asked students to rate a number of specific pedagogical techniques used during the previous class. A cynicism measure was then constructed from the responses of those who did not indicate a favourable view of a particular technique. These cynicism rates for each technique are reported in Figure 1.

---

[5] I also use the same techniques in media-unfriendly classrooms by using portable equipment--a laptop, a VCR hooked up to a video projector, and a ghetto-blaster to amplify sound. Most classrooms also allow for a hookup to the Internet.

[6] It can also be (1) a high ink cost as the notes are usually in colour and many students rely on colour printers, and (2) a high time cost as these student ink-jet printers are slow.

As may be seen in the figure, the least cynicism (approximately 20% of respondents) was expressed with respect to the "Little Stories." Ironically, the most cynicism was expressed with respect to the "Big Story" (approximately 62%). This contrast was the most striking aspect of the data. Techniques that were getting cynical responses from about 40% of the group were the "Nano-lessons," the "WEB Resources," and the "Gimmicks." Techniques that were getting cynical responses from about 30% of the group were the "WEB Outline," the "WEB Tour" and the PowerPoint Presentation of related "Research." The technology was getting a more favourable rating but still the cynicism rate was surprisingly high as far as my personal expectations were concerned.

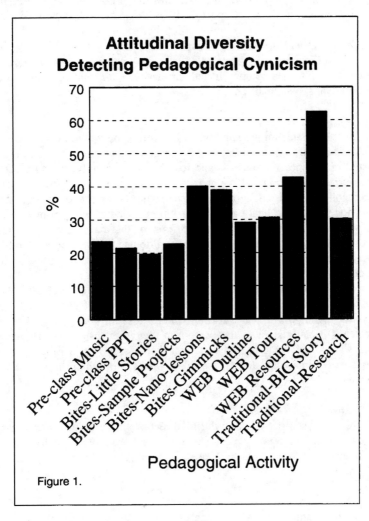

Figure 1.

On the one hand, it may be considered surprising that no one technique appealed to more than 80% of the group, at best. Though these techniques rely heavily on the technology advocated to make learning more palatable to today's "media generation," there was still a substantial cynicism rate. Moreover, this was the first class in the students' program—a time when optimism would be expected to be at its peak. Yet the cynicism rates ranged from 20% to 62%. So it appears that not "all students" are likely to respond favourably to any one thing you do in a large classroom—except maybe letting them go early.

There are a number of factors that could influence such attitudes. Personality, prior educational experiences, learning style, maturity, natural cynicism, and so on, are among the variables that are likely to affect responses to the large class experience. Expect it. Work around it. Work with it.

Principle #2—Use Cooperative Education

I build as much cooperative/collaborative education into the large class as possible. This is accomplished primarily with question and answer, discussion dyads, and small group work.

Question and Answer

I use this technique sparingly. I find it to be a chronic problem in the large class for two reasons. First of all, a large number of students are often not interested in the specific question and lose focus. Secondly, the poor acoustics of the larger classroom also lead to the same loss of focus. Seating arrangements, normal background noise, room design, and so on, make it difficult for students to hear each other from every point in the room. With the added white noise of technology at the front of the classroom, it can also be difficult for the instructor to hear questions. I do use this technique, periodically in a systematic way, but when I do I usually need to repeat the question for the entire class.

An additional problem is that most students are reluctant to ask questions in the large class environment. One gimmick I use when "question and answer" is important is a fluff ball which I toss into the group. The person who catches it can pass it to the person on their right to answer a question or volunteer some information. That person then tosses it to another student for elaboration, commentary, and so on. This works well when the information is "low threat."

Dyads

I use dyads periodically during a lecture and ask students to discuss a point with their neighbours prior to further elaboration in the lecture. This involvement is low threat, and does encourage collaboration, and active participation.

Small Groups

I have students work in small groups (about four to six students per group), ideally in every class. Following a lecture, which may range from 20 minutes to 80 minutes, students work in these small groups on problem solving activities. They draw on the lecture material and the textbook to construct an in-class response to a problem, a case study, or a situation. The response allows them to construct, create, critique, and collaborate in a scholarly fashion.

Peer Teaching

The students are also required to collaborate with their peers in preparing a brief presentation for their classmates[7]. This illustrates for the student the idea that the best way to learn something is to teach it, or be able to teach it. They select a topic to present from a prescribed list which contains some reference material and the date to present. This peer teaching enlivens the class, as students are quite creative in what they present. Of course, students can react negatively to input from their peers so it needs to be carefully balanced with input from the instructor. Time-wise, I aim to allot 20 to 40 minutes per class, in the latter half of the course, to incorporate the student presentations. A variety of presentation formats are possible and encouraged—game show, skits, interviews, mime, puppet show, musical presentations, drama, PowerPoint, lecture, demonstration, video, and so on. The peer teaching opportunities are limited to 10 minutes per group with the recommendation that students aim rather for 5 to 7 minutes. The idea here is the general rule, "Less is More." Since many students are intimidated when addressing a large group they opt to prepare a video presentation and then show the video in class.[8] In the past about 70% opted for this pure video format. Recently it seems that many are becoming more venturesome and are integrating video, PowerPoint, skits, and so on.

Group Testing

One other cooperative education practice that I use in class is periodic group testing. This is explained more fully under the "Assessment" principle. Here I would comment that it is a form of cooperative education that has been viewed favourably by students over the years.

Principle #3—Use Problem-Based Activities

Pre-Class

I use pre-class problems that I post on the Web Site.[9] This year students are not required to visit these "problems" but some choose to do so. I may make it a requirement in the future, but for now I'm just experimenting with the format, and giving students the opportunity to consider the rationale for

---

[7] http://zeus.uwindsor.ca/courses/edfac/morton/topics.htm

[8] Originally I allowed the videos to be shown with no screening. Now I require that they be submitted to me a week in advance so that I may preview them. This serves to remove videos that are too long, may have offensive content, have poor audio quality or camera quality. This practice resulted from a good suggestion made by students who had to sit through some of the poorer presentations. Also, the screening allows me to share some of the striking presentations with other classes so the students end up peer-teaching directed to a much broader range of their peers.

[9] http://zeus.uwindsor.ca/courses/edfac/morton/pre-class_problems.htm

problem-based activity.[10] Each problem is designed to raise questions, or create scenarios, that could be/would be addressed by the material in the subsequent class. The technique can get students thinking about the material in advance. Students can reflect on the situation in a relaxed and prolonged way; they can raise informed questions; and they would activate cognitive schema that would be relevant for the lecture. It is this activation of cognitive schema that I see as most valuable at this time.

In-Class
I use in-class problems following the lecture. These are based on questions, cases, real problems, potential problems, funny problems, and messy problems that could require a temporary solution or plan to deal with the problem. Students work in groups to generate appropriate responses/solutions based on reason, the text, the lecture material, and their personal experiences. These in-class problems could take anywhere from ten minutes to an hour and ten minutes to address. Normally, the response is submitted by the end of class. However, there are times when students get quite involved in the problem and ask for additional time and the opportunity to submit the response later.

Post-Class
I don't schedule post-class problems, but the opportunity does emerge at times. For example, groups of students, or an individual student, may challenge a point in class or ask for clarification. As a result, I may point them in the direction of a possible solution or answer. Another opportunity arises when students ask for a structural change in the course, and I request that they prepare a rationale for their request.

Principle #4—Use a Diversified Assessment Protocol
My assessment strategies have changed considerably from the days when I used the two conventional multiple-choice tests. I like multiple-choice tests. I find value in their objectivity, reliability and ease of computer scoring. However, I use a much more diverse format now without sacrificing the merits of the multiple-choice test.

Multiple-Choice Tests
I schedule four tests for a 16 week course that covers two semesters in our program. I attempt to ensure that each test is low stress, a learning experience, and a formative evaluation technique. Although the final test at the end of the course is summative, I have had students report that it was a learning experience as well[11]. The various test types I use may be seen in Table 3.

---

[10] http://zeus.uwindsor.ca/courses/edfac/morton/new_page_13.htm
[11] http://zeus.uwindsor.ca/courses/edfac/morton/positive.htm

Table 3: Multiple-Choice Test Formats Used in a Larger Class

Name	Type	Material	Format	Process	Use
Formative	Multiple Choice (50-items)	Open-Book: Textbook, notes, dictionary	Groups of 4-6 students	Research, argue, justify, (each student fills out their own scantron sheet and may differ from their group)	Definite (First mid-term) Possible as second semester mid-term, also.
Formative & Summative	Multiple choice (50-items)	Open-Book: Textbook, notes, dictionary	Individual		One Option (December Exam)
Formative	Multiple Choice (1-item)	Open-Book: Textbook, notes, dictionary	Groups of 4-6 students	Each answer is correct but the group must select what they consider the best answer and prepare a rationale for the choice	Possible (as second semester mid-term)
Summative	Multiple Choice (50-items)	Open-Book: Textbook, notes, dictionary	Individual	A summative form of evaluation used at the end of the course typically on selective chapters.	Definite (as Final Exam)
Formative	Multiple Choice (50-items)	Open-Book: Textbook, notes, dictionary	Group or Individual	Students (or groups of students) prepare a series of questions and then I choose a set of 50 to use as the test.	Possible (as second semester mid-term)
Formative	Multiple Choice (10 to 20-items)	Open-Book: Textbook, notes, dictionary	Groups of 4-6 students	Research, argue, justify, (each student fills out their own scantron sheet and may differ from their group)	Can be used as part of a regular class when time is short or a class has been cancelled.

The first test I use is a 50-item multiple-choice test but it is an open-book test and it is done in a small group format. The students are encouraged to treat the textbook as a resource, rather than a compilation of content to be mastered. In the test setting the students have the opportunity to argue for their answers as well as listen to the arguments of others. In the end though, each student fills out his or her own scantron sheet. The tests are computer scored. I find this to be a great learning opportunity for the students. It fact, it is more pedagogy than assessment, yet it does provide a normal distribution of scores. In addition, it is a low stress format and serves to empower students.

The second test (in December's exam slot) is also student empowering. Students have a choice between doing a multiple-choice test or a more authentic assessment (see below). This multiple-choice test is also an open book format but the students who choose to do it must do so individually. Usually students who have an aversion to tests opt for the authentic assessment alternative.

The third test is an opportunity for exploring another creative alternative. For example, I have used a randomly assigned grouping for another multiple-choice test (also open-book) rather than their normal work group. I have used a multiple choice test with only one question on the test and every answer was correct. They then had to write a rationale for the answer they selected as the best answer. Only once did I try this format as it is a problem marking. I have had students work on ideal test questions as an in-class assignment, submit them, and then I used a selection of those questions for the exam.

The final exam is the standard multiple-choice test (again open book) done individually. I have used authentic assessment alternatives as a final exam as well but learned this is not the wisest route. Class attendance drops when students realize that there is no final assessment related to class content. Also, the marking time is considerable and marking is rushed given the grade submission deadlines. Overall, many students do report value in these diverse assessment formats.[12]

Authentic Assessments

One authentic assessment I use requires each student to prepare a series of brochures (one for each chapter studied in the text during the assessment block) where they are required to turn a substantive part of the textbook information into a concise, selective, yet meaningful format for a specific target audience.[13] One aim is to produce a professional quality product that reveals understanding and application. The brochures are then scored by a Teaching Assistant. This year (2001/2002) 61% of the class opted to do the authentic assessment alternative in December. Typically it ranges from 60 to 70 percent.

A rubric, or checklist, is available, but it is not given prior to the assignment. I find that rubrics can function as a disservice to students because they structure their efforts in prescribed or conventional ways and may therefore inhibit creativity. Also, rubrics can push students to try to do too much and end up with a dense artificial product rather than an authentic product. I do post

---

[12] http://zeus.uwindsor.ca/courses/edfac/morton/positive.htm
[13] http://zeus.uwindsor.ca/courses/edfac/morton/brochures.htm

links to the rubrics[14] and marking checklists after the submissions as a form of debriefing.

Another authentic assessment I have used allows students to come up with a creative, yet meaningful, format of their own. Some venturesome students have created Web sites, newspapers, and so on, as alternative formats. This is not an announced opportunity, but I have used it with those with initiative who seek me out with a well-developed rationale for a particular creative alternative.

In-Class Assignments

I have a number of in-class applied assignments for students and these are marked on a scale of 0, 1, or 2. There may be anywhere from seven to 10 during the course and the students are never exactly sure when they will be given. The random in-class assignments do keep the attendance up (although this is not the intent), they give the students feedback on how they are doing, they facilitate cooperative learning, and they align with a constructivist educational philosophy as advocated on the class Web site[15]. These in-class assignments usually account for about 14% of the grade.

Class Presentation

The class presentations become a valuable learning experience for the students—those who prepare them and those who witness them. This project accounts for 10% of the grade. As with the authentic assessment, a rubric, or checklist, is available, but it is not given prior to the presentations. Creativity and authenticity are encouraged rather than prescribed effort or conventional effort. Links to the marking checklists are available after the presentations as a form of debriefing[16].

Self Assessment

I also ask the students to do a self assessment in the second last class. They fill out a survey indicating how they would rate their learning, their contributions, and so on. This accounts for 2-3% of the grade.

Peer Assessment

I ask the students in the second last class to rate the other members of their group. If certain members have not been carrying their share of the burden, have shown up for group activities unprepared, or have been counter productive to the group dynamics their peers have an opportunity to rate their contributions. This accounts for 3-4% of the grade.

Conclusion

Overall, I now find the large class experience a much more enjoyable and rewarding experience. It is still not as enjoyable as the smaller graduate

---

[14] http://zeus.uwindsor.ca/courses/edfac/morton/new_page_101.htm

[15] http://zeus.uwindsor.ca/courses/edfac/morton/constructivism1.htm

[16] http://zeus.uwindsor.ca/courses/edfac/morton/new_page_103.htm

classes, nor is it as rewarding as working one-on-one with a student preparing a thesis or dissertation. However, I look forward to the large classes now. I find value in the experience. The student ratings are still not as good as ratings when teaching a smaller class, but I have learned to live with that. In fact, I have come to expect cynicism, value cynicism, and even do some research on the dynamics of cynicism. At this point, I wonder what I will add next year.

To further teaching:

Armstrong, A. & Casement, C. (1998). The child and the machine. Toronto: Key Porter Books.

Ellul, J. (1964). The technological society. New York: Vintage Books.

Ellul, J. (1981) Perspectives on our age, Jacques Ellul speaks on his life and work. (W. H. Vanderburg, Ed.). Toronto: House of Anansi Press Ltd.

Gedalof, A. J. (1998). Teaching larger classes. Halifax, Canada: Society for Teaching and Learning in Higher Education.

Green, L. (2001). Effective lecturing techniques. In J. Newton, J. Ginsberg, J. Rehner, P. Rogers, S. Sbrizzi, & J. Spencer (eds.). Voices from the classroom: Reflections on teaching and learning in higher education (pp. 184-187). Toronto: Garamond Press.

Kehoe, D. (2001). Improving large-class lecturing. In J. Newton, J. Ginsberg, J. Rehner, P. Rogers, S. Sbrizzi, & J. Spencer (eds.). Voices from the classroom: Reflections on teaching and learning in higher education (pp. 188-195). Toronto: Garamond Press.

Negroponte, N. (1995). Being digital. New York: Vintage Books.

Papert, S. (1980). Mindstorms. New York: Basic Books.

Papert, S. (1993). The children's machine. New York: Basic Books.

Postman, N. (1992). Technopoly. New York: Vintage Books.

Rogers, P. (2001a). Improving student learning in lectures. In J. Newton, J. Ginsberg, J. Rehner, P. Rogers, S. Sbrizzi, & J. Spencer (eds.). Voices from the classroom: Reflections on teaching and learning in higher education (pp. 197-199). Toronto: Garamond Press.

Rogers, P. (2001b). Dead silence... A teacher's nightmare. In J. Newton, J. Ginsberg, J. Rehner, P. Rogers, S. Sbrizzi, & J. Spencer (Eds.). Voices from the classroom: Reflections on teaching and learning in higher education (pp. 200-201). Toronto: Garamond Press.

Stoll, C. (1999). High tech heretic. New York: Doubleday.

Turkle, S. (1995). Life on the screen. New York: Touchstone.

Induction into University Graduate Supervision and Teaching
by Noel Hurley

So you have made the grade and have been hired as a professor to instruct at the undergraduate and graduate level of education. It is your first week on the job, and you have been asked to supervise a thesis by a graduate student who is familiar with your research. As a responsible member of the higher education community, you want to do your share so you agree to take the student as one of those whom you will supervise. You advise the Graduate Studies Co-ordinator in your faculty that you have committed to supervise the student only to be told that you cannot because you do not have graduate faculty status. Welcome to one of the first educational experiences in the university hierarchy of research life.

The attainment of your PhD opens the door to working with graduate students, but, to obtain full status at most universities, you have to have an active research portfolio. To build up a reputation as graduate instructor takes time and requires that a professor earn the respect of graduate students who are registered in that faculty. The first thing that students need to know is that you are there to support them when they need you. This support is probably most effective when it takes the form of mentorship. In many of the sciences, you are assigned graduate students only when you can support them with your own grant money.

Graduate Studies for Junior Professors

This is intended as a guide to success for your career as it relates to graduate studies. At the outset, I have to make a disclaimer that it is based on my own personal experiences as a graduate student at two different universities, and as a professor in graduate programs at three universities, beginning in 1970 to the present. As I say to the students in my pre-service professional studies program in education, "If anything here is useful, take it and incorporate it into your professional practice, if it is not, put it away somewhere so that you can retrieve it later if needed." Your perceptions as to what is worthwhile will have a tendency to change over time, and progress as you pass through the different phases of graduate study instruction and supervision. What is done here is to offer a guide that you can use when dealing with graduate students, taking them from their initial search for a graduate program to the successful completion of a graduate degree.

Guiding Student's Choice of Graduate School

The old phrase "Well begun is half done" does not accurately describe the amount of work necessary to successfully complete a graduate program, but it is critically important to all graduate students to choose a program that is a good match academically and personally. Student preparation for graduate studies ideally should begin when they choose their undergraduate major. The level of achievement attained from a grade perspective will open up entrance possibilities to the top graduate programs in the world or will limit access to less esteemed universities. If their grades have not been fixated at the beginning letter of the alphabet, you should advise your students not to despair because success in any graduate program is less affected by where one studies than by the effort they put into their study. The choice of which university to enter for graduate studies, I feel, is driven by other factors than reputation and status. Some of the first things you should advise students to investigate before they enter a graduate program are:

1. The structure of the graduate program.
2. The length of the program.
3. The tuition cost.
4. The location of the university.
5. The level of financial and professional support that students are likely to receive.
6. The pre-requisite learning necessary to be successful at the target institution.
7. The research culture of the program.
8. The likelihood of the degree leading to a professional career or to a terminal degree in the chosen discipline.

At the personal level, as a graduate instructor, you have to help the student determine whether or not your graduate program has the faculty members who can and will agree to supervise the area of study in which the student wishes to specialize. These are some considerations but not an inclusive list of things of which you have to be cognizant as you advise students as to which degree they should undertake.

Structure of Graduate Faculty or College
Depending on the university in which you work, your graduate program could be operated in a graduate faculty or a college of graduate studies. The nomenclature does not really matter because North American universities have similar models. The Faculty of Graduate Studies supports the development and continuation of graduate programs in that institution. To ensure that the quality of programs offered in graduate studies meet standards of excellence, all new programs are subject to provincial, as well as university, approval. Additionally, in the province of Ontario every graduate program has to submit to a system of rigorous external review on a regular cycle. Based on the opinions of respected scholars from both within the province and from outside the province, the program under review can be approved, modified, or canceled.

Admission to Graduate Programs
Admission to graduate programs might in practice be done at the departmental or program level but the application process is relatively standardized across the whole university to which students are applying. Most

universities require averages during undergraduate degrees to equal or exceed at least B-. Many programs have a number of pre-requisite courses that are essential for entrants. If graduate students do not have these pre-requisites, they are well advised to complete them as they are usually predictive of a successful outcome in those courses for which they are deemed necessary.

Many university students realize that student transition to university life often differs. Weak high school preparation, leaving home for the first time, or less than ideal study habits have limited some students' career aspirations. If your applicants fall into this category, it does not mean they can never get a graduate degree. Sometimes, universities will admit students conditionally to graduate programs even when their averages are not as high as required because the applicant has demonstrated that his/her overall average is not indicative of his/her level of ability at the time of graduate application. In such cases, students are sometimes admitted provisionally and permitted to take up to two graduate courses. If their performance is acceptable, than they can then be admitted to the regular program in graduate studies.

Program Length

There are a number of routes that graduate students can take to attain a Doctor of Philosophy in the various programs of study. The usual route to the terminal degree is to complete a Masters degree after an undergraduate program of studies. In some disciplines, one can obtain direct entry to a Ph.D. program directly from an honours' bachelors program. A more frequent alternative approach is to switch to a Ph.D. program after the first year in a masters program. One can expect most Master's degrees to last two years of full-time study. Ph.D. degrees can take anywhere from three to six years depending on the discipline and the dissertation project undertaken. In rare cases, candidates have been known to complete doctorate degrees in two years. The only certainty when entering a graduate program is that the attainment of a graduate degree will demand time, effort, and perseverance. Your students need to be made fully aware of this upon entry to graduate studies. Some universities offer introductory workshops and short courses to prepare their new graduate students so that their chances to be successful are increased.

Graduate Financial Support and Program Costs

Generally speaking, in the United States, the richer the university one attends, the higher the level of scholarship and financial support that is likely to be available to the graduate student. In Canada, this is not the case because of the universalization of funding approaches. The universities with the highest levels of reputation usually attract the highest achieving students and thus entrance to these programs tends to be more competitive. The size of research grants and the number of grants that professors in graduate faculty hold determine the number and size of research assistantships that are available to graduate students in any program. Most graduate programs guarantee some level of support to any students who enroll in full-time study. Graduate assistantships are available to most graduate students across programs.

Graduate Research Supervision

The most important consideration in the choice of a graduate school is to ensure that the chosen university has the personnel to provide the excellence in graduate supervision necessary to complete quality graduate research. This entails that the university has a professor or professors who are experts in the area in which students wish to pursue graduate research. This expertise has to be supported by an active refereed research portfolio in the area of research interest. The ideal supervisor, in my opinion, is a professor who has a balance in both areas - research and teaching. This might be a practice that as a beginning professor you wish to develop. Supervisors with active research and scholarship are highly valued by students and are usually well positioned to provide excellent mentorship.

Another important attribute of any graduate supervisor is a professor who has time for her/his students. What I mean here by time is not limited to a set appointment schedule, but time for quality scholarly engagements that further the development of the graduate student. The supervisor challenges the position of the student, furthers their thought processes, and encourages thinking in a non-linear fashion.

A graduate student has to be comfortable with the supervisor from an interpersonal relationship perspective. One of my colleagues likens the process of completing a graduate degree with that of the rise and fall frequently attributed to the Christian religion. There are peaks and troughs that one experiences in the process of gaining a graduate degree and these cycles can cause strains in any relationship. It is therefore imperative that the partners in the graduate research have an understanding that will allow them to get through such difficulties. An ideal supervisor-graduate student relationship is one where both parties have respect for one another and from the graduate student's perspective one where the supervisor is encouraging to the candidate.

Getting Off to a Good Start

To be effective in a graduate program, a beginning professor has to be able to establish an acceptable publication record for the discipline in which s/he is employed. A number of common sense acquisitions can facilitate your efforts in this regard. One of the key things to do when entering graduate instruction is to ensure that you have state-of-the-art computer equipment. From the start it is necessary to save information, to document what you have read, develop proper reference citations as to where you have read the material, and to begin an archive of properly indexed data for future retrieval. Most research is data driven. A number of pre-requisite technical skills are essential for success in graduate study and research. Perhaps one of the easiest and most important is the ability to type well. Keyboarding skill, as it has become known in the computer era, is not a luxury but rather a necessity to experience high levels of success. A second technical skill is familiarity and keen knowledge in the use of whichever publication manual is used in the program in which you are participating. Most Arts and Social Sciences graduate programs use the

Publication Manual of the American Psychological Association (APA). In the humanities, frequently the Publication Manual for the Modern Language Association (MLA) is chosen. Key differences exist between the different publication manuals on such things as in text citations, use of commas, and other writing conventions. It is incumbent upon the graduate student instructor to become proficient in whatever manual of style is in use in their program and area of research.

Course of Study

It is vitally important for your students to meet with the program head of your graduate program and map out their intended course of study before taking any courses. Having an initial plan of study does not prevent students from altering their course of studies after they have begun but it will likely save them from having courses superfluous to their needs. This can save the students time and money. In doctoral programs at some institutions, required courses are often tailored to suit individual needs, and it is important as a supervisor that you have input into course selections. One size does not fit all when it comes to useful courses of study for graduate study. The department chair of graduate studies and the supervisor are in the best position to advise graduate students in the courses they should take. Pragmatic choices that further research skills and knowledge in the student's particular area of specialization will optimize resource efficiency.

At the master's level, graduate students are often not certain of the area of a discipline in which they will want to specialize. This is not uncommon at the doctoral level as well. It is important to begin study in courses that will not limit choices later in the student's program. Courses should also equip students with the research skills to allow them to complete their dissertation or thesis when they finish their course requirements. For example, if you anticipate that your graduate student will need to use structural equation modeling then you should endeavor to ensure that s/he takes statistics courses that permit use of these techniques.

Some graduate instructors prefer to have students who are searching for a research area and who go to where their research trail leads them. In many of the sciences, a student's area of research is predetermined by the supervisor's interest, expertise, and funding. However, students will develop their own research questions and studies within the broader context of that faculty member's expertise.

A successful strategy in the completion of courses is to advise students to try to complete as many of their compulsory courses as soon as possible. This will prevent them from being unduly delayed by having to wait for a required course. In my own case, I was delayed in one of my graduate degrees for almost two years because a required course was not offered for two consecutive years because not enough students requested it. Effective pre-planning will prevent such an unfortunate delay and, to that end, you should be as proactive as possible with your students.

Thesis Research

When I asked one of my graduate students what she most looked for in a supervisor, she was relatively quick to respond. Her perception of a good supervisor was one who was congenial and collegial. She further pointed out that this should present itself in being available to the students and that the supervisor has a willingness to share time, experience, and expertise with the student.

Another important point to remember in graduate supervision is that the graduate student has the right to expect any graduate supervisor to have a solid foundation in the area in which they are supervising. The benefit of the supervisor's prior learning can often prevent the graduate student from having to re-invent the wheel for each stage of the journey through the graduate research process. Timely feedback is important to graduate students as they are paying tuition for every semester they are registered in a graduate program. This is particularly important when graduate students are completing thesis research. Frequently, data gathering and ethics approvals are time sensitive with limited windows of opportunity to be successful. Feedback that is related to the graduate student's research should expand the student's scope rather than narrowing it to fit the supervisor's preconceived notion of what should be included. The graduate students should be given enough freedom to use their interest and the existing research literature as a guide for their own research.

Many universities have regulations that outline how the relationships between graduate students and supervisors function and what each should expect from the other. Beginning professors should ensure that their actions fall within the parameters outlined at their institution to avoid any unwarranted problems. Guidelines regarding intellectual property help faculty-graduate student disagreements about ownership of information and authorship on publications.

In summary, perhaps the most important role of the graduate supervisor is to encourage and coach your graduate students to persevere in their journey towards successful completion of their programs. Every student experiences some problems and nearly all require encouragement and perhaps praise to achieve successful completion. Be their friend and be their mentor and you will get back much more than you send out.

HOW WE ASSESS
AFTER WE ASSESS

This section represents a fresh overview of something most of us dread doing - marking. Clovis, Ableser, and Smith approach the job from the more positive perspective of assessment. Assessment involves not just a percentage, or numerical grade, but an overview of qualitative data illustrating the students' and the instructor's development over the period of a course. For e.g., how can we see and measure how much knowledge and which skills have been retained by students as a result of what learning and modelling we have organized for them? How could the teaching have varied or changed to refine the learning and make the course more successful?

Posing assessments as research questions is something Western university professors are used to doing since they are required to publish as a component of their job. Regularly researching and reflecting upon what you are doing (as a student and as a teacher) can make you a more effective, successful instructor.

Re-conceptualizing Assessment at the University Level
by Christopher J. Clovis

Assessment is one of the most difficult, time consuming, and complex parts of teaching. It is initially planned and considered during the course design stage, or when an instructor is creating the course outline. Generally, one does not wish to evaluate someone on something that has not been covered in class, and the form of assessment chosen should be a good measure of the skills the instructor wishes the student to display and apply following her course. How do you do it? And once you do it, how can you be sure that it has been done accurately? Many of the assessment concepts within this chapter are not new to the field. Ableser, in the next chapter for example, provides a list of the multiple types of assessment available to an instructor in higher education. A beginning instructor should choose a form of assessment with which s/he initially feels comfortable. Peer evaluation techniques and concept mapping (as described by Crawford) can be difficult for new faculty, and yet are perceived as fair by students. Gifted students, for example, are accurately identified by peers, but not accurately identified by teachers. If structured, peer evaluation can often be a more accurate indicator of performance than faculty evaluation. Such issues of validity and reliability are continually debated. Clovis suggests one theory here; he encourages readers and new instructors to critically examine forms of assessment in their own field. Is it accurate? Is there an alternative?

Are the terms assessment and evaluation synonymous? If not, how do they differ?

Students and faculty are continually assessing each other. This assessment is based on a variety of criteria including the clarity of the material covered, the presentation or activities pursued, and the meeting of individual and group expectations. From the student's perspective, the assessment of the course is informal and framed by what they perceive the outcome of the course to be. This perception, for some, is founded solely on a primitive course of study and an acceptance of the process within the system. In the end, the value of the course may be based on subjective or nebulous criteria, which can differ for each student. This can pose a problem for faculty.

Student assessment by faculty, on the other hand, should be based on more solid, objective criteria and assessment protocols analysed over time. This information is being used to evaluate the student's final progress. Hence, assessment terms differ in that the former occurs over time and is a collection of individual pieces of work, which can be criterion-referenced; it provides a more complete picture of student growth in understanding. Using this, the student's progress can be effectively and consistently validated.

The primary method used for interpreting the results of student assessment has been to compare the results of a specific individual with a well-defined group of other individuals, e.g. a 'norm group', such as that used in the

Scholarship Aptitude Test (William, 1997). Typically, these norm referenced tests rank individuals numerically based on their individual scores. The inclusion of other assessment tools has reduced the reliance on a single and small number of assessment protocols, e.g. mid and end of term exams, as the primary arbitrator for measuring student learning. Consequentially, norm referencing has given way to cohort-referencing where students are now compared with other students studying at the same time (McGraw, 1996); however, the premise for assessment remains unchanged. The results provided by these protocols are not referenced to standards, and give no indication of what the student knows or can do. Since student scores are determined by the performance of the cohort group, an able student may score low, not necessarily because of individual weakness, but because of the strength or ableness of the cohort s/he is in. Being placed in another group may result in a higher relative score. The consequence of cohort scoring may be the early elimination of individuals who could be extremely successful in that field.

Criterion-referenced assessment arose out of a desire to reduce the impact of cohort or norm referencing on achievement since its focus is on measuring what students can and cannot do. Some advantages of this focus include the sequencing and individualization of instruction, outlining behavioural objectives, reducing unhealthy competition and promoting self-esteem. This style of assessment requires time and thought in developing the criteria for each assigned task so that students know before hand what is expected of them. In the end though, providing the criteria simply provides a measure of acceptable and unacceptable performance. This may, however, produce some unfortunate consequences since greater specification of assessment objectives could result in the narrowing of the curriculum (Smith, 1991). The alternative to criterion-referenced hyper-specification (Popham, cited by William, 1997)) is to resort to more general assessment descriptors. However, students may interpret these descriptors differently resulting in direct comparisons between students which is a common disadvantage associated with norm referencing. Moreover, as criteria are more clearly defined, the greater the likelihood that students will achieve the objectives; and the less meaningful and useful the assessment tool becomes.

To overcome the deficiencies inherent with norm, cohort and criterion-referenced assessment, other protocols have been suggested. These include standard-referenced and construct-referenced assessment (William, 1994), based on the premise that teachers have internalized standards and are able to assess students' work consistently based on those standards. However, in order for these standards to be referenced to performance standards, they have to be articulated. Once expressed, these standards can then be used for making a balanced judgement of individual students' work. Hence, others not involved directly in the instruction process can assess with, consistency and validity, individual students' progress based on the prescribed standard.

In summary, students prior to entering university have been exposed to many types of assessment strategies each focussed on one or more aspects of their development. The standards upon which their work and therefore their academic progress have been judged are well articulated. In typical university courses, the prime assessment protocol used to determine academic progress is usually limited to the exam, which is highly weighted. This may disadvantage many students not necessarily because of ability, in the academic sense, but more an inability to adapt to the more focussed and centred evaluation construct. Thus, like teachers, university faculty need to rethink, re-construct or redefine how they permit students to demonstrate academic achievement, if their goal is to educate.

Alternative Assessment Methods

Students, leaving the primary and secondary level education system, have experienced numerous alternative assessment protocols. These include direct observation, interviews, group projects, concept mapping, journals, performance strategies, open-ended problems, portfolios, demonstrations and role-playing. Many of these tools may not be appropriate in the university setting depending on field of study and particularly in large class settings. However, if there is a reconsideration of the objectives of the course, then some of these approaches may be quite helpful. For instance, if in a first year biology class, one objective may be to develop appropriate laboratory skills. Rather than simply providing a typical investigation, the same lab could be executed as a challenge. Hence, a verification lab could become a discovery or application style activity It would now be possible to assess students ability to analyse, problem solve and think creatively using the training and techniques already acquired.

In lecture rooms where instruction of large groups is being conducted, the easiest method for presenting the knowledge component is through a lecture style approach. This concentrates on the instructor's presentation rather than on the learner. In order to shift the emphasis on to the learner, a different approach must be developed. What follows are a number of techniques which may enhance learning and teaching.

Research has shown the benefits of providing instructional objectives to students. These provide a road map along which they and the instructor will travel through the course. It outlines and highlights the knowledge component that is required but also identifies the skills that will be developed: problem solving, critical thinking, dexterity, be they science, computer, drama or music in nature, behavioural skills such as collaboration, cooperation, time management, etc. Many of these skills are implicit and others explicit, however, in the development of the whole student all of these skills are necessary and should be given some consideration.

In order to encourage the development of these skills, the evaluation protocol should reflect their implied importance. To state, in the instructional objectives, that a certain skill set is important to be successful yet it not be reflected in the evaluation protocol, would indicate to the student the low priority of those skills in achieving success in the course. Hence, stating clear objectives informs the student of his/her responsibilities and makes them aware of the importance of those the objectives in determining a final grade.

Teaching a large group

Classes, where there can be little or no personal contact with the students, are a challenge to teaching and learning and instructors often resort to the process of teaching by definition and explanation. The instructor cannot ascertain the prior knowledge of the group much less individual students; further, he/she has to assume that the students have completed the assigned readings and, more importantly, have understood what they have read. The first indication of the level of understanding may not be obtained until the first test or exam. One way to encourage students to complete the assigned reading prior to class is to use the "One Minute Paper". To use this effectively, the instructor will have to develop a question based on the reading. Depending on the focus of the instructor, the question could be simply based on the knowledge component, an application, indicating a deeper understanding of what was presented, or even transference of knowledge. The question is posed at the beginning of class and allocating a limited amount of time for students to answer the question will encourage students to come to class prepared. Their responses may or may not be graded, however, initial collection and grading of the 'paper' would again encourage students to be prepared since marks are being allocated. Also, since they will not know when the paper will be graded they would always, or at least most of the time, be prepared.

There are a number of advantages to using the "one minute paper' assessment tool: students, for the most part, would come to class prepared and this would permit the instructor to address the implications, historical, social and/or advanced aspects of the work thus enabling the student to construct their own learning. By putting the whole concept into context deeper learning is facilitated. The instructor can now move from defining and explaining to extending and applying the information. An adaptation of the 'one minute paper" would be to permit students to answer the question after a brief discussion with a partner, or complete the question individually, then sharing their understanding with someone else, and then permitting them to write their responses in light of their discussion. Another advantage is that the instructor is now able to leave the stage and circulate among the students. A consequence of this approach is that the instructor must be willing to give the student control of the class for a while and has to develop techniques to re-establish control when necessary. This can be achieved by keeping a strict control on the time allocated for discussion and responding. The net result, however, would be that students will become more involved in the learning process.

Group Work

Although it is not feasible to conduct group work in a large lecture theatre, seminars may be a suitable venue for assigning work that requires the formation of groups. It is recognized that assigning grades to individuals based on a group activity is problematic, particularly in a large class with many groups, where the more persuasive and vocal group members' dominate.

However, if one values collaborative work, then projects have to be well designed to permit the development and practice of the behavioural skills identified in the instructional objectives. The difficulty with this mode of assessment is how to determine individual grades since it is a group effort. Sullivan (2001) suggests the use of structured but open-ended self-assessments by students reflecting on their progress within the group. These reflections are then graded. The rewarding of group work through self-assessment validates individual effort, self-reflection and growth and encourages students to engage more fully in the often difficult and frustrating process of group work.

The use of effective peer (Appendix A) and self-evaluation protocols is critical in determining individual contributions and skill. Such protocols, necessarily, must be designed so that students can honestly reflect on their own development and those of their peers without personalities becoming problematic. This can be achieved by defining clearly the traits that should be considered when reflecting on self and peers with respect to the project. Further, the weight given to particular traits should not be given to the student prior to the evaluation and the peer mark should be assigned openly. That is, each member of the group should see what others have said or what mark has been given and should be given the opportunity to agree or disagree with that mark. Disagreement requires the instructor to become the arbitrator and may decide whether to use the peer assessment in the determination of the overall individual mark.

The use of group work as part of the assessment method requires much more time and effort on the part of the instructor since considerable thought has to be applied in the design of the assessment tool as group, peer and self assessment is now taken into account. These assessment tools, in order to be useful in providing information about the strengths and weaknesses of students, need to be honest. Thus, these protocols must be designed in a non- threatening way so that weaknesses can be identified and worked on and strengths shared.

Concept Maps

The volume of information and knowledge accumulation is increasing exponentially but the available instructional time remains constant, thus it becomes necessary to develop strategies that will permit students to link concepts in ways that leads to individual understanding. One such strategy is the use of concept maps, which permits students to organize abstract knowledge into a form that enhances their understanding. These maps, which provide a pictorial representation of the prescribed knowledge, is designed and constructed by the student and can enhance understanding, recall and application of the material.

The map is broken-down into four parts: the main concept, descriptors, connectors and arrows. The main concept comprises the most general, inclusive and abstract thought. The descriptors, usually nouns, are the key components that are linked to the main concept. The connectors, usually verbs, adverbs and prepositions, connect the descriptors to each other and to the main concept. The arrows designate the direction of the relationship between descriptors. In the end, the arrangement of descriptors, connectors and arrows result in a complete thought or sentence.

Some advantages of this assessment strategy include assessing pre-knowledge of the topic; post knowledge of the topic; consolidate the knowledge base; summarize notes; review content; and as a diagnostic tool to determine students' understanding or misconceptions. Further, it is non-threatening as it can be administered as a game or simply as an instructional tool. It can be used in conjunction with the "One Minute Paper" strategy.

These maps can be used to assess students' understanding but they are difficult to analyse since individual maps differ, hence a clear checklist and rating scale would be necessary. A rating scale could be easily developed giving marks for levels, connected relationships, branching and integration. This strategy is aimed at the patterning of students by enabling them to arrange the material covered pictorially permitting the level of understanding to be determined and misconceptions identified and corrected. Further, since individuals learn in unique ways, this ensures that they clearly articulate what they have learned. One added advantage to the instructor is that the requirement for an exam evaluating content recall may be negated and time can be apportioned more on the higher level thinking skills since the assessment of the map will confirm the absorption of the content.

In conclusion, instructors at the university level should give greater consideration to student educational experience. Coming into the tertiary educational system from a system that is changing and encompassing alternate assessment strategies that recognize and enhance the whole student development to one that is still traditional, students have to reconfigure to a system that focuses on content knowledge. Those who are unable to adapt fail and many do not retain their previous levels of excellence. By adapting the assessment strategies to reflect their previous experience, particularly in first year, may ensure greater success.

To Further Teaching:

McGraw, B. (1996). Their future: Options for reform of the higher school certificate. Department of Education and Training Coordination, Sydney.

Smith, M. L. (1991). Meaning of test preparation. American Educational Research Journal, 28(3), 521-42

Sullivan, S. (2001): Making Group Work Count. Assessment in and of Collaborative Learning.

Developed and edited by the Washington Center's Evaluation Committee. Retrieved Feb. 11, 2002, from
www.evergreen.edu/user/washcntr/resources/acl/b2.html

William, D. (1994). Assessing authentic tasks: Alternatives to mark-schemes. Nordic Studies in Mathematics Education, 2(1), 48-68

William, D. (1997). Construct-referenced assessment of authentic tasks: Alternatives to norms and criteria. 7th Conference of the European Association for Research in Learning and Instruction, Athens, Greece.

Life Beyond Multiple Choice Tests: Alternative and Authentic Assessment
by Judith Ableser

This chapter provides new faculty with an excellent list of the different forms of assessment options. Since there is such a plethora, Ableser encourages readers to try one form of assessment, such as portfolios (where the work a student does is put into a folder and evaluated as a whole, much like a research portfolio); apply it to their own disciplines; and create a customized assessment for their subject and class of students based on that form.

What is assessment?
   "You mean it is not just that multiple choice test?"
- Assessment is actually the gathering of data.
- Evaluation is the interpretation, judgment or decision making that we place on the information we have gathered.

Why assess?
   "You mean there is more to assessment then assigning grades at the end of the semester?"
- Assessment does allow us to evaluate our students and give them a "grade".
- Assessment provides students with feedback.
- Assessment allows us to monitor student progress.
- Assessment allows us to monitor the effectiveness of our instruction.
- Assessment helps us to plan our instruction.

   I have taught child development courses for many years. Generally, my students are education or nursing majors. One year, I noticed that the questions and comments that were coming from the students were very different than previous years. After further investigation, I discovered that more than half of my students were court-ordered to enrol in the class in order to gain visitation rights with their children following child-abuse cases. Although, it did not change my goals and objectives for the course, it most certainly changed the examples I used and the assignments I gave. From that point on, I began each course with the students completing a "personal inventory" that provided me with information about their prior knowledge and experience as it related to the course content. From that information, I was better able to design my instruction to meet my students' needs.

When should we assess?
   "Well, during final exam week of course."
   Good effective instruction involves:
- Ongoing, continuous assessment.
- Pre-assessment to determine prior knowledge, experience and interest.

- Ongoing informal checking for understanding by observing students and asking questions.
- Ongoing monitoring of progress (formative evaluation).
- Final assessment (cumulative evaluation).

What should we assess?
"I expect my students to know everything covered in the text and lecture notes."
- Actually this is a **KEY** question. Before we can decide what we are going to assess, we must decide what it is that is important for the students to learn.
- What we select to assess should be directly related to the outcomes of what we plan to teach and have students learn.

Flow Chart of Designing Curriculum

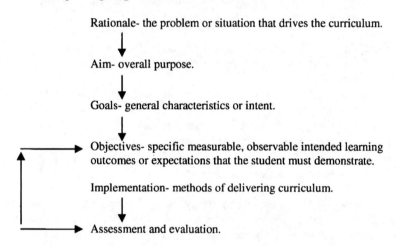

Rationale- the problem or situation that drives the curriculum.

Aim- overall purpose.

Goals- general characteristics or intent.

Objectives- specific measurable, observable intended learning outcomes or expectations that the student must demonstrate.

Implementation- methods of delivering curriculum.

Assessment and evaluation.

Bloom's Taxonomy of Educational Objectives (1956)

Low level thinking
1. Knowledge- facts, definitions, terminology, theories, principles.
   Example- The student will be able to identify, label and describe the function of human heart.

Higher level thinking
2. Comprehension- understanding and interpretation.
   Example- The student will be able describe the conflicts felt between the main characters in the drama.
3. Application-uses the information and applies it in a specific situation.
   Example- the student will apply the assessment strategies to make an acute diagnosis of the situation.

4. Analysis- Breaking down the components.
   Example- the student will be able to compare and contrast the critical elements by creating a Venn diagram.
5. Synthesis- Combining the components to create a new creative form.
   Example- the student will construct a new design by integrating all components in a unique way.
6. Evaluation- The highest level of thinking involves prior levels in order to make informed judgments.
   Example- the student will use evidence from the trial to determine if the party should be found guilty or not.

Stop for a moment and ask yourself this question: What percentage of your course focuses on low level thinking and what percentage on high level thinking? If you are like the majority of us, the vast percent of our time is spent teaching and assessing low level thought. Research indicates (Carnegie Foundation, 1988), however, that in order for us to prepare individuals to meet the intellectual demands of the 21st Century we must be creating critical thinkers who use higher level thinking skills.

I have had discussions with colleagues who insist on testing students' knowledge of the textbook by giving them multiple-choice tests. When I ask them why they are doing this, they argue that it is the only way that they will read the text book, in fact, they claim, it is the only way they will buy the text book. I shrug my shoulders and say, 'I didn't realize that our aim was to make a profit for the publishing company.' I know from years of personal experience, and many sleepless nights that you can cram for exams by studying the text, score extremely high on the test, and forget every single fact within a matter of weeks. I believe that the text book should be a resource and guide for students to be able to use and apply the facts and theories into practical, relevant situations that involve higher level and critical thinking skills.

- Now, we can state that we assess the course objectives that include higher level thinking skills.

What is Authentic Assessment?
"So, you mean the way I was always tested wasn't real/authentic?"
- Authentic Assessment directly measures student's performance through "real life tasks" or situations that resemble "real life situations" (Wiggins, 1989).
- Examples include demonstrations, exhibits, recitals, videotaping performances, fieldwork, debates, experiments on real problems, virtual reality computer simulation activities.
- Authentic assessment is often used synonymously with *performance assessment* and alternative assessments. (In truth, there are differences but for our purposes we will use them interchangeably).

- The key is for alternative assessments to be as "authentic" or "real life" as possible by focusing on the application of knowledge in purposeful, meaningful, relevant ways.
- Generally, students complete an authentic assignment over an extended period of time in which they determine the amount of time that will be needed to successfully demonstrate their skills, performance or knowledge rather than an assigned two hour "testing time".

What's wrong with the good old-fashioned traditional tests?
"If it was good enough for me, why not my students?"
- Generally focuses on low level thinking.
- Does not provide means to assess student's thinking process or progress.
- Does not assess the student's ability to apply knowledge to real world problems and situations.
- Does not involve the student in the evaluation or decision-making process.

Main Types of Authentic Assessment
1. Paper and Pencil
- In some ways can be very similar to traditional assignments or essays that require students to apply their knowledge to some practical situation.
- Completed over a period of time. Case Studies/Application- A problem or situation is presented to the student, in which they must integrate and apply the theory and concepts studied by describing and analyzing the situation, identifying the problem, generating recommendations or alternative solutions or plans. The case study can be a 'written simulation scenario' or may involve a real life situation. For example, a psychology student may be asked to develop a "behavioural intervention plan" for a child based on a detailed description of a student or by observing an actual child and then develop a behavioural plan from the assessment and observational data.

EXAMPLE #1

ASSIGNMENT: Observing Young Children's Social and Emotional Development
OBJECTIVES:
1. To develop check-list/observational tool to assess social and emotional development of children
2. To use observational/interview skills to assess the social and emotional development of children
3. To compare and contrast different children's social and emotional development as compared to developmental norms
4. To gain an understanding of the factors affecting children's social and emotional development.
METHOD:
1. Develop a check-list/inventory/interviewing questions to assess the social and emotional development of young children. Using information from class, including: Erikson's stages, components of temperament, types of play, self-concept, parenting

styles etc. and previously developed assessments (i.e. high scope, Portage, developmental inventories etc.) compile an observational/interview checklist to be used for this assignment.

Length- open

Percent-10%

2. Select a child between 2-8 to observe for your case study. Focusing on the child's social and emotional development complete a case study. Spend 2-4 hours observing the child and interviewing parent/teacher/ child etc. in order to answer and respond to your assessment tool. Tape your interviews and keep anecdotal notes.

3. Paper-
   a) Introduction overview of the child-age, background etc.
      -description of when, where, how collected information (1 page)
   b) Summarize information gathered on the child and compare it with developmental norms
   c) Give interpretations or explanations for your findings (2 pages)
   d) Conclusions-reflect on assignment and on development of assessment tool (1 page) Note: the paper itself is worth 25% of your grade
   e) Remember to include a copy of your assessment tool (checklist, questions asked etc.) as well as your raw data (10% of grade)

(Judith Ableser-CMV assignment)

i.   Journals- Students respond in reflective journals by applying the knowledge covered in the course by describing concrete examples and personal experiences that illustrate the concepts and ways in which to solve or understand them. For example, a nursing student could use anecdotal recording of his/her placement and relate how certain experiences connect theory with practice.

ii.   Graphic Representation of Concepts- Students create flow charts, graphic organizers, hierarchical charts illustrating the concepts used in class in order to design a visual framework that demonstrates the problem solving process for a given situation.

iii.   Annotated Bibliographies- Students complete a bibliography of resources that includes a brief summary or description of the reference.

Performance Assessment

- Directly measures student's skill or understanding through direct observation of demonstration in a real life situation or simulation of situation.

- Criteria for mastery or level of competence are documented through the use of checklists or rating scales used by "observer" (instructor, advisor, and peer) to evaluate.

- Music recital, performing arts presentation, multimedia presentation, experiment, role play, mock trial, debates, public speaking presentations, student teaching, internship.

EXAMPLE #2

A. Major Memorandum

Students will use the skills developed during the Fall term to research a new legal problem. The results of the research will be communicated in memorandum form using appropriate citation for case, statute and secondary sources. Plain Language writing is required. The legal problem researched will form the basis of the factum which will be prepared in February 2003 and the oral argument which will be presented to the *Supreme Moot Court of Windsor* in March, 2003.

B. Factum

1. Working Factum

During the preparation of the Major Memorandum, students selected a partner with whom they wished to work during the oral advocacy portion of the course. The week after the Major Memorandum is submitted for marking, students will be presented with a written decision called the "Moot Judgment". This is the decision of the trial judge (or the appellate bench) who has decided the case which has been researched for the Major Memorandum.

Student pairs are now divided into teams of **appellants and respondents**. If their client was unsuccessful at trial, appellants will find reasons to appeal the decision of the lower court to the **Supreme Moot Court of Windsor**. If their client was successful at trial, respondents will argue that the appeal should be dismissed and the decision of the lower court upheld.

In support of their argument to be made at Moot Court, student partners will write a jointly prepared Factum, which is a brief synthesis of the law and facts. Appellant partners will use their factum as a basis for their oral argument that the decision of the lower court was incorrect. Respondent partners will use their Factum as a basis for their oral argument that the decision of the lower court was correct. One factum will be submitted per each appellant team. One factum will be submitted per each respondent team. The correct method of citation is required.

2. Amended Factum

Good factum writing is a difficult task. Because beginning law students often have difficulty anticipating how a factum will be used by the judges who hear the argument, students will have an opportunity to submit an amended copy of their factum following their Moot Court presentation. Students must indicate what changes they made to the second draft and why amendments were made (and were not made) to the working copy.

Both members of the Factum team will receive the same grade on the Factum. Please note the penalty for handing in assignments after the date and time due. The working draft of the Factum constitutes 15% of the final mark. The amended draft of the Factum constitutes 5% the final mark for this course

C. Letter of Opinion

Working individually or with your Moot partner, students will be required to prepare a Letter of Opinion reporting the progress of their client's case based on the Major Memorandum fact pattern. A Peer Evaluation format will be used.

D. Moot Court Presentation

Students will prepare and present oral argument before the Supreme Moot Court of Windsor, which will be specially convened to hear appeals. Moot presentations will begin in March and continue until all student pairs have presented their oral argument. A marking scheme of "Pass with Distinction", "Pass" or "Fail" will be used to evaluate the presentation. Each student must pass the moot presentation in order to successfully complete the requirements of the Legal Writing and Research course. Students who receive a "Fail" must successfully upgrade to a

"Pass".

(From Moira McCarney, Faculty of Law, University of Windsor)

Portfolios
- A sampling of student's work over time demonstrating the growth and development of skills and competencies.
- Student selects which samples and artifacts to include that best demonstrates their learning process and performance.
- Should include self-reflection or self-evaluation component by student.
- Instructor may provide guidelines or criteria to use.
- May be handed in to instructor or "reviewer" for evaluation or may be presented by student through an interview or conference with reviewer.

i. Student Teaching Portfolio: In addition to observing the student teacher interacting in the classroom (performance assessment) the student may be asked to submit a portfolio demonstrating their competencies. Based on the learning outcomes or objectives of the course, the student provides evidence of how each objective was successfully met. For example, the student may take pictures of them working in classrooms to illustrate interaction skills, or may include sample lesson plans or other examples.

EXAMPLE #3

Performance indicators (weight)	B+	A-	A	A+
Artifacts (2)	Includes a few required artifacts	Includes some required artifacts	Includes most required artifacts	Includes all required artifacts, as well as additional relevant material
Organization (2)	A collection of artifacts with no clear organization; lacking a table of contents, introduction/ purpose, conclusion, and/or growth plan.	A collection of artifacts which is organized; including a table of contents, an introduction, purpose, conclusion, and/or growth plan; artifacts are unrelated in theme or purpose.	A collection of artifacts which is effectively organized; including a table of contents, an introduction, a purpose, conclusion, and/or growth plan; artifacts are somewhat related in theme or purpose.	A collection of artifacts which is thoughtfully organized; including a table of contents, an introduction/pur pose, a conclusion, and a growth plan; artifacts are clearly related in theme and purpose.
Analysis of teaching and learning (3)	Simple descriptions of artifacts, with little understanding of their relationship to theory, student learning, teaching practice, personal learning, and/or teaching experiences.	Clear and somewhat supported descriptions of artifacts, with some understanding of their relationship to theory, student learning, teaching practice, personal learning, and/or teaching experiences.	Clear and well supported descriptions and explanations of artifacts, with adequate understanding of their relationship to theory, student learning, teaching practice, personal learning, and/or teaching experiences.	Insightful and articulate descriptions and explanations of artifacts, with in-depth understanding of their relationship to theory, student learning, teaching practice, personal learning, and teaching experiences.
Writing mechanics (1)	Little evidence of proofreading and revision of spelling, punctuation, and sentence structure, making it difficult to discern meaning.	Some evidence of proofreading and revision of spelling; punctuation and sentence structure that detracts the reader from the meaning.	Careful proofreading and revision of spelling, punctuation, and sentence structure, which enables the reader to focus on the meaning.	Critical proofreading and revision of spelling, punctuation, and sentence structure which enhances the meaning of the text.
Overall communica tion about personal and profession al growth (2)	An unfocussed learner who analyses some experiences and makes connections between some learning experiences.	A focused learner who briefly analyses all experiences and makes connections between some learning experiences.	A conscientious learner who critically analyses, evaluates, and synthesizes most learning experiences.	A reflective learner who critically analyses, evaluates, and synthesizes all learning experiences.

(Portfolio assignment from Dr. Pat Rogers, York University.)

EXAMPLE #4

Biology and Science Methodology
Portfolio Evaluation

Name:_____

THE PORTFOLIO DOCUMENT:
SECTION ONE: Resume, Professional Goals and Philosophy
THE CANDIDATE INCLUDES: (Circle one)
1. Resume Yes No
2. Professional Goals Yes No

FOR THE REMAINING ITEMS SCORE THE CANDIDATES PERFORMANCES AS:
(5=excellent; 4=above average; 3=average;2=below average;1=no performance)

SECTION TWO: Leadership for Good Classrooms and Schools
THE CANDIDATE:
4. Evidence of Classroom Management   5 4 3 2 1
5. Evidence of Pedagogy   5 4 3 2 1
6. Evidence of Leadership   5 4 3 2 1

SECTION THREE: Candidate's Role in Strategic Leadership
THE CANDIDATE:
7. Demonstrates his/her prof. Growth   5 4 3 2 1
8. Demonstrates teaching strategies employed   5 4 3 2 1
9. Addresses relevant competencies   5 4 3 2 1

SECTION FOUR: Candidate's Role in Instructional Leadership
THE CANDIDATE:
10. Discusses his/her prof. Growth through best practices   5 4 3 2 1
11. Supports his/her narrative with documentation   5 4 3 2 1
12. Addresses relevant competencies   5 4 3 2 1

SECTION FIVE: Candidate's Role in Organizational Leadership
THE CANDIDATE:
13. Demonstrate organizational skills in lesson planning   5 4 3 2 1
14. Uses resources effectively   5 4 3 2 1
15. Addresses relevant competencies   5 4 3 2 1

SECTION SIX: Candidate's Role in Political and Community Leadership
THE CANDIDATE:
16. Discussed his/her prof. growth through volunteer experience   5 4 3 2 1
17. Supports his/her narrative with documentation   5 4 3 2 1
18. Addresses relevant competencies   5 4 3 2 1

COMMENTS:

ii.   Writing Process Portfolios: Rather than turning in the "finished product" the student submits samples of their writing in progress. For example, the student would submit their initial brain storming or planning ideas, a rough draft, a revised piece of work that illustrates content changes, an edited version that includes grammatical and structural corrections and the finished product. The student may include a self-reflection of the process that analyzes and evaluates each step.

iii. Work Samples: A collection of work (art, design, architectural plans, construction) collected over time that includes explanation, reflection and evaluation by student.

Computer Simulation- Virtual Reality

- Through the use of computers and multimedia technology it is possible to recreate or simulate a "real life problem" or situation for the student to solve that requires precise skill and precession. In many cases, it is unrealistic, unethical and dangerous for a student to truly perform a skill in the "real world" but could simulate it through a computer or virtual reality situation.
- Common examples include pilots learning to fly or land a plane through flight simulation or medical students performing surgical procedures through a virtual reality simulation exercise.

Additional Alternative Assessments

Student Personal Response- At the beginning of each course that I teach, I give the students a form entitled "Student Personal Response" which asks questions relating to their prior knowledge and experience and general questions about the course. I collect and read their responses in order to better meet their needs and interests but I do not mark the papers. At the end of the semester I give them a similar questionnaire to complete. I then return their original response and have them compare their answers in order for them to become aware of how their have grown and developed throughout the course.

EXAMPLE #5

STUDENT OVERVIEW
NAME: STUDENT NUMBER: ADDRESS: PHONE: EMAIL: EDUCATIONAL BACKGROUND: WORK EXPERIENCE: VOLUNTEER EXPERIENCE: WHY ARE YOU TAKING THIS COURSE?   SPECIAL INTERESTS:

EXAMPLE #6

PERSONAL RESPONSE- NURSING

NAME: DATE:

1) WHY DO YOU WANT TO BE A NURSE?

2) IF YOU COULDN'T BE A NURSE, WHAT WOULD YOU DO?

3) WHO OR WHAT INFLUENCED YOU IN YOUR DECISION TO BECOME A NURSE?

4) LIST CHARACTERISTICS OF A QUALITY NURSE. Rank them.

5) LIST YOUR STRENGTHS THAT WILL MAKE YOU A GOOD NURSE. Rank them.

6) WHAT SKILLS DO YOU FEEL YOU NEED TO DEVELOP?

7) HOW DO YOU PLAN TO DEVELOP THESE SKILLS?

8) DESCRIBE THE ROLE OF A NURSE.

9) WHAT CHANGES DO YOU BELIEVE ARE NEEDED IN THE HEALTH CARE PROFESSIONS TO IMPROVE THE QUALITY OF CARE?

Pre-test/Post-test Inventory

In addition to the Personal Response that I use at the beginning of each semester, I give my students a "Pretest". This consists of a list of all the terms and concepts that I plan to cover in the course and are in the textbook. Usually, it only takes a few moments to complete because most of the terms are left blank. Once again, I do not mark the test, but review it to determine what prior knowledge my students do have. I return the papers to them and tell them that I expect them to fill in each term with a definition or example once we cover that concept in the curse or read it in the text. This is one way that encourages them to complete all the readings. At the end of the semester, I check to see how complete the Inventory is. I do not evaluate each concept or term but give them marks for participation if the inventory is completed.

EXAMPLE #7

WHAT DO YOU KNOW?- LINGUISTICS

Name:
DEFINE AND GIVE AN EXAMPLE OF EACH.
1. LANGUAGE ARTS
2. INTEGRATED CURRICULUM
3. CONSTRUCTIVIST THEORY

4.	SOCIOLINGUISTIC
5.	ZONE OF PROXIMAL DEVELOPMENT
6.	SCAFFOLDING
7.	BLOOM'S TAXONOMY
8.	EMERGENT LITERACY
9.	WHOLE LANGUAGE

Reflective Practice

Through the use of journals or as written response and the end of an assignment, I ask my students to reflect on the experience (essay, lesson, project, demonstration) by discussing what they have learned and how they can apply this into their own personal and professional situations.

What are the Main Advantages to Authentic/Alternative Assessments?

- Assesses relevant, practical "real life" problems.
- Applies higher level thinking skills.
- Involves student reflection and active participation.
- It is more interesting and engaging.
- It is more meaningful.
- Allows students and professors to see growth and progress.
- Focuses on strengths and competencies.
- Motivates students.

What are the Disadvantages?

- Takes longer for the student to do.
- Takes longer for the professor to mark.
- Much more complex marking.
- Requires developing rubrics / criterion for evaluation in order to reduce subjective evaluation.
- Cannot rely on textbook test bank for test.

Ways to minimize the Disadvantages

- Encourage group work to reduce marking load.
- Encourage peer evaluation of some work.
- Include some self-evaluation.
- Do not write on the actual assignments (if they involve actual written work). Create a scoring rubric in where you use checkmarks and provide some space for general comments. (See below).
- Develop strong rubrics with clear defined criteria and involve other professionals or graduate students to assist with marking.

Portfolios are commonly used in teacher education as part of an exit interview. Each student demonstrates their competencies through a variety of methods by presenting their portfolio to a professional team. Often the faculty will bring in master teachers and principals to review students' work and provide them with detailed rubrics or checklists to use for evaluation purposes.

- Team up with other professors to develop an integrated cumulative project for a number of courses.
- Plan your time well. Drink lots of caffeine.

Some years, I have more than 250 students in any given semester which makes marking authentic assessments a challenge as each student is to complete three assignments. I am committed to using authentic/alternative assessments because I believe I must practice what I preach. I make sure that I arrange to papers to be turned in just before breaks or when I can clear my schedule of any other commitments.

However, when I first look at the boxes of work it seems like a daunting, never-ending task. I swear that I am crazy and will never do this again. But, I slowly proceed and reward myself as a complete a pile of work. Once I have finished all the marking I can share the sense of accomplishment that my students feel when they turn in their assignments.

How to Evaluate Authentic/Alternative Assessments

- Task is to develop a method to evaluate what student has done.
- Although not using objective, standardized scoring it is essential to develop standards or levels of competency that is consistent, equitable and clearly reflects the objectives of the course and the assessment.
  1) Anecdotal recording
     - notes and comments while observing students.
     - generally must then be turned into more objective.
     - form of measurement if going to be used as part of an evaluation.
  2) Mastery Learning
     - successful or not successful.
     - completed or not.
     - Generally, in most mastery learning situations, the student may turn in a piece of work to be evaluated and can make revisions or changes until the work has been successfully mastered.
     - The goal here is that by the end of the semester the student will have mastered the skill or concept.
     - Therefore, in mastery learning situations it is possible for everyone to get an "A" even if initially the work was not successfully mastered.
  3) Checklists
     - a compiled list of descriptions of behaviours/ attributes that are observed in the student's work or performance.
     - generally, the reviewer simply notes if the behaviour/attribute is present or not but does not put any judgment or value to the quality of what has been observed.
     - behaviours that are specific or clearly occur versus do not occur are good examples to be included in a check list.

4) Rating Scales
- expand upon check lists by attributing value or judgment to the behaviours observed or assessed
- quantitative scores or qualitative measures may be used for the ratings
- - for example:

5-excellent	or	consistently observed
4-well done		usually observed
3-average		occasionally observed
2-below average		rarely observed
1-poor		never observed

EXAMPLE #8: Science and Biology Methodology

Science & Biology Methodology
Unit of Study Criteria Evaluation

Name:_____

1. Unit overview
   i. Strands, activity titles   1   2   3   4
   ii. Prior knowledge   1   2   3   4
   iii. Summary of unit planning notes   1   2   3   4
   iv. Resources   1   2   3   4
   v. Assessment and evaluation   1   2   3   4

2. Activity Information
   i. Description   1   2   3   4
   ii. Planning notes   1   2   3   4
   iii. Strand   1   2   3   4
   iv. Expectations   1   2   3   4
   v. Prior knowledge   1   2   3   4
   vi. Teaching strategies   1   2   3   4
   vii. Accommodations   1   2   3   4
   viii. Resources   1   2   3   4
   ix. Appendices   1   2   3   4

3. Methodology
   i. Teaching/learning strategies   1   2   3   4
   ii. Problem solving/Thinking   1   2   3   4
   iii. Activity based   1   2   3   4
   iv. Grade level appropriate   1   2   3   4

4. Content
   i. Quality   1   2   3   4
   ii. Language usage   1   2   3   4
   iii. Writing style   1   2   3   4
   iv. Examples   1   2   3   4
   v. Safe practices   1   2   3   4
   vi. Connections   1   2   3   4

5. Assessment and Evaluation
   i.   Tools   1   2   3   4
   ii. Criteria   1   2   3   4
   iii. Activity appropriate   1   2   3   4

6. Overall impression of Unit   1   2   3   4

(Geri Salinitri, University of Windsor, 2002)

Rubrics
- scoring guides that make it explicit the criterion to evaluate
- detailed descriptions of levels of criterion that are used to determine ratings
- provides objective, reliable and consistent way of evaluating items that may otherwise be judged in a subjective manner.

I always give my students a copy of the rubric when I handout and review the assignment. This allows for them to know exactly what it is that I am expecting of them and, as they are doing their work, can check to see that they have each criterion met.

Evaluation Criterion- levels of competency
- Exemplary
- Proficient
- Minimally Competent
- Little evidence of Competence

EXAMPLE #9: Mathematics Rubric

Note: A student whose achievement is below 50% at the end of a course will obtain a credit for the course.
(Ministry of Education-Ontario Curriculum 2000)

Achievement Chart- Grades 11 and 12, Mathematics Rubric

Categories	50-59% level 1 below standard	60-69% level 2 minimal standard	70-79% level 3 standard	80-100% level 4 above standard
Knowl./Understand. -understanding concepts -performing algorithms	**The student:** -demonstrates limited understanding of concepts -performs only simple algorithms accurately by hand and by using technology	-demonstrates some understanding of concepts -performs algorithms with inconsistent accuracy by hand, mentally, and using technology	-demonstrates considerable understanding of concepts -performs algorithms accurately by hand, mentally , and by using technology	-demonstrates thorough understanding of concepts -selects the most efficient algorithm and performs it accurately by hand, mentally, and by using technology
Thinking/Inquiry/ Problem Solving -reasoning -applying the steps of an inquiry/problem solving process (e.g. formulating questions; selecting strategies, resources, technology, and tools; representing in mathematical form; interpreting information and forming conclusions; reflecting on reasonableness of results)	**The student:** -follows simple mathematical arguments -applies the steps of an inquiry/problem-solving process with limited effectiveness	-follows arguments of moderate complexity and makes simple arguments -applies the steps of an inquiry/problem-solving process with moderate effectiveness	-follows arguments of considerable complexity, judges the validity of arguments, and makes arguments of some complexity -applies the steps of an inquiry/problem-solving process with considerable effectiveness	-follows complex arguments, judges the validity of arguments, and makes complex arguments -applies the steps of an inquiry/proble m-solving process with a high degree of effectiveness and poses extending questions
Communication -communicating reasoning orally, in writing, and graphically -using mathematical language, symbols, visuals, and conventions	**The student:** -communicates with limited clarity and limited justification of reasoning -infrequently uses mathematical language, symbols, visuals, and conventions correctly	-communicates with some clarity and some justification of reasoning -uses mathematical language, symbols, visuals, and conventions correctly some of the time	-communicates with considerable clarity and considerable justification for reasoning -uses mathematical language, symbols, visuals, and conventions correctly most of the time	- communicates concisely with a high degree of clarity and full justification of reasoning -routinely uses mathematical language, symbols, visuals, and conventions correctly and effectively

Categories	50-59% level 1 below standard	60-69% level 2 minimal standard	70-79% level 3 standard	80-100% level 4 above standard
Application -applying concepts and procedures relating to familiar and unfamiliar settings	**The student** -applies concepts and procedures to solve simple problems relating to familiar settings	-applies concepts and procedures to solve problems of some complexity relating to familiar settings	-applies concepts and procedures to solve complex problems relating to familiar settings; recognizes major mathematical concepts and procedures relating to applications in unfamiliar settings	-applies concepts and procedures to solve complex problems relating to familiar and unfamiliar settings

Diverse Learners
- Students have different learning styles (Dunn and Dunn, 1978), a variety of multiple intelligences (Gardner, 1991), and personal preferences.
- Students may have any number of special needs; it is important to offer a variety of assessment techniques.
- Never rely on only one measurement. Every course should include several different assessments at different points throughout the course.
- Give students choices in some of the assessments (both in the type of assessment and the way in which they will complete it.)

In many of my classes, I give my students a group assignment because I feel it is important for them to learn to work co-operatively and they can generate more ideas by building upon each other's thoughts. However, I realize that for some students, it is almost impossible to successfully complete a group project due to personality traits, time constraints, or other intervening factors. I, therefore, give them the option of completing the same activity on their own stating that the extra time spent in completing more work is often less taxing then coordinating and arranging to work together. Some professors offer the students the option of doing a cumulative project or writing a more traditional exam.

The Last Word
- Now that you have read this entire section, proceed slowly.
- Do not feel that you have to throw-out old reliable ways of testing.
- Quality traditional tests can continue to be part of your overall assessment package.
- Evolve slowly using alternative/authentic assessments.
- Find the ones that work for you, for your students and for the objectives of the course.

- Meaningful teaching and assessment will help students become productive, competent individuals.
- Enjoy the journey.

Authentic Assessment vs. Traditional Assessment

AUTHENTIC ASSESSMENT
- Portfolios, demonstrations, field work, performances, simulations, case studies, essays, assignments, lab report
- Student takes an active role in process focuses on process and product
- Qualitative
- Interpretive
- Process and integrated learning
- High level thinking/content
- Use of rubric/criterion levels for evaluation to create standards
- Part of teaching and learning process
- Self-referenced- shows competency and mastery of individual's learning and performance
- Generally occurs over extended time

TRADITIONAL ASSESSMENT
- Multiple choice tests, true-false short answer, fill in the blanks
- External-teacher driven focuses on grade or score
- Quantitative
- Objective
- Standardized
- Low level thinking/content
- End product/outcome
- Isolated facts
- Norm/criterion referenced-compares students to others
- Generally occurs at a specific time

To Further Teaching:

Bloom, B., Englehart, M., Furst, E., Hill, W., & Krathwohl,D. (1956). Taxonomy of educational objectives: Handbook I: Cognitive domain. New York: David McKay.

Carnegie Foundation (1988). The conditions of teaching: A state by state analysis. New Jersey: Princeton.

DunnR., & Dunn, K. (1978) Teaching students through their individual learning styles. Reston,VA: Reston.

Gardner, H. (1991). The unschooled mind: How children think and schools should teach. NewYork: Basic Books.

Herman, J. Aschbacher, P., & Inters, L. (1992). A practical guide to alternative assessment. Alexandria,VA: Association for Supervision and Curriculum Development.

Jacobson , D., Eggen, P., & Kauchak, D. (1999). Methods for teaching: Promoting student learning. New Jersey: Prentice-Hall.

Mitchell, R. (1992). Portfolios. In R. Mitchell (ed.). Testing for learning: New approaches to evaluation can improve American schools (pp.103-131). New York: Free Press.

Ornstein, A., & Hunkins, F. (1998). Curriculum: Foundations, principles and issues. Boston: Allyn and Bacon.

Posner, G., & Rudnitsky, A. (1997). Course design: A guide to curriculum development for teachers. NewYork: Longman Press.

Wiggens, G. (1989). A true test: Toward more authentic and equitable assessment. Phi Delta Kappan, May 1989, 703-713.

Publishing Your Teaching
by Kara Smith

There are many wonderful teachers in colleges and universities across North America. Teaching is a rewarding life experience when done well. One thing both teacher and researcher find difficult is balancing roles between publishing research and developing courses. One way to ensure that good teaching is rewarded is to publish the teaching. Whether this is in the form of original research, a collection of teaching ideas, or a text book, publishing the "scholarship of teaching" allows institutions to provide credit for their esteemed teachers (Kreber, 2001). Publishing also allows instructors and colleagues to feel a greater sense of accomplishment.

One of the foremost concerns of new faculty is publishing. Yet most professors in Canada work for "teaching institutions", where a great percentage of their job consists of preparing and delivering courses to undergraduate students. One might ask, "How can I possibly find the time to do research when so much of my time is spent trying to create thoroughly interesting courses for students?" This is a common problem for academics. Happily, a great deal of the energy and work you put into creating intriguing courses and inquiry-driven students is of interest to peers and colleagues; that is, peers and colleagues in the field of teaching and learning in higher education".

There is an entire canon of research, both general, and discipline-specific, on teaching related issues in colleges and universities. This chapter will cover those peer-reviewed journals used for tenure and promotion, and book proposals; however, there are also many fine newsletters and on-line journals which are highly respected in the fields, and have very high standards for publication. The following part of this chapter will take you, the instructor-researcher, through the process of educational research, journal submission, and book proposals.

Six Basic Steps to Publishing Your Teaching
A problem expressed as a question
Inquiry into teaching begins much like any other research. The researcher starts with a burning question to which he/she needs to find an answer. For example, if you are finding that there is not much discussion in your 8:30 a.m. statistics class, then you might begin with a simply query, such as "How can I generate more discussion in my statistics class?"

This simplistic start may well lead you into further analysis of the problem. For instance, you may question if your undergraduate students are tired. How late do they usually go to bed? Is the topic dry? If so, what methods might I employ to make it more relevant and intriguing for them? What issues, within statistics, would be useful to them in their own lives [to create more discussion]? Each of the aforementioned questions is a research problem in itself. Some are larger than others, but all are very valid questions. The key to a good query is that it must assist your teaching, and it must be an issue that is unique to the field of teaching. That is, your particular research question and answer must approach a teaching and/or learning problem from a new perspective, or offer a new contribution to the field. Refine your question, then, determine whether your problem, and hypothesis (or possible answer), are unique by reviewing the literature on teaching.

Review the educational literature

The researcher reviews the literature in the field to determine whether there has been suitable data previously collected and disseminated on the problem. Go to your institution's electronic journal database first. In the case of teaching, the database search most frequently used for this purpose is called "ERIC"; however, every subject-specific discipline has its own search engine, and those teaching journals related to that discipline would, almost certainly, appear within your regular search routine. Following a simple key-word search, review those abstracts and articles most closely related to your problem. Even if you do not initially find any suitable information, this initial review will allow you to become familiar with the teaching and learning journals within your area of inquiry. This will allow you to search through the shelves in your own library for the most recent copies of these journals. Many educational researchers find that browsing through the stacks of current journals is more useful than an electronic search, which is not as current as the issues on the shelves, and which may not include everything relevant to the topic. Another advantage of this exercise is that you will quickly become familiar with the journals to which you may be interested in submitting articles on your teaching. For a list of peer-refereed, educational journals specific to teaching see Appendix J.

There are issues in our teaching which are specific to our disciplines, and arise solely as a result of the nature of the subject, such as curriculum; however, Weimer (1993), editor of *The Teaching Professor,* argues that much of the educational discourse within the various teaching-related journals can easily be transplanted or related to other disciplines. That is, many problems in the general field of teaching and learning are universal. Each instructor in higher education shares some of the same pedagogical problems. Weimer argues that it is important for faculty in higher educational settings to pool such research and information. When this is done, the canon of teaching and learning is increased, and information regarding more generic issues can be disseminated widely across the subject areas. A peer-refereed, on-line journal, *Positive Pedagogy*, deals with teaching issues that cross all boundaries, and the following journals are not subject-specific, but cover teaching and learning topics that are of interest to faculty in higher education in general. As compiled by Knapper and Wright (2002), they are:

1. *Active Learning in Higher Education*
2. *Canadian Journal of Higher Education*
3. *Higher Education*

4. *Higher Education Research and Development*
5. *Innovations in Education and Training International*
6. *Innovative Higher Education*
7. *Journal of Higher Education*
8. *Journal on Excellence in College Teaching*
9. *Quality in Higher Education*
10. *Review of Higher Education*
11. *Studies in Higher Education*
12. *Teaching in Higher Education*
13. *International Journal for Academic Development*
14. *Journal of Faculty Development*
15. *Staff and Educational Development International*

The above lists are extensive, but not exhaustive. For a complete listing of educational journals both within the subject disciplines, and in the general area of teaching and learning, search through Ulrich's *(Ulrich's International Periodicals Directory)*. Any academic journal, newsletter, or magazine is categorized in Ulrich's. To find the subject journal which you may wish to search or to submit, check the "Subject Listings" section of the directory. Check "Education" to find those journals most closely related to your discipline and the subjects you teach. The directory will also tell you which search engines (e.g., ERIC) under which the journal is listed, and if the journal is peer-reviewed or not (a publishing criterion for most tenure-track faculty). "Ulrich's" is available on-line at www.ulrichsweb.com and on CD-ROM at most college and university libraries.

Another rich source of research information can come from other colleagues. If you know of an author in the field of education, or in the teaching discipline which you are hoping to research, seek his/her advice. E-mailing an author who you know works in that area can be a simple method of finding the best known publishing in the field. For example, in my own area of language research, if I needed a quick reading reference list of 'heritage language research' in Canada, I would simply e-mail Professor Jim Cummin at the Ontario Institute for Studies in Education (OISE) and request a list of what he feels are the "most important readings, or authors, on the subject". Someone who has already done a great deal of research and writing in a particular area can often select direct references which a computer and library cannot. Colleagues are an invaluable resource in research.

Following a cursory reading, and literature review, of the research addressing your initial question, you may well find that your approach to the problem, or indeed your problem itself, is unique to the field of higher education. What is unique about it? Having answered this question, you now have a topic worth writing about and publishing.

Create an ethical research design
Where the instructor is the "participant-observer" of a research design for a particular class or course, educational researchers call this "Action Re-

search". Simply, this means that you will be researching yourself, and/or your students, to find an answer to an educational question. This answer should, in effect, create a change in either your teaching, your course, or your students' learning. This is "Action"; a very real part of teaching. Creswell's textbook on educational Research Design (2002), covers this topic well. In a step-by-step, practical method, he outlines various examples of quantitative (statistical, instrumental) action research, and qualitative (observational, interview, narrative) action research. Specific to teaching, Braskamp, Brandenburg, and Ory (1984) also provide an effective guide to researching your teaching. Select one of these manuals as an outline for educational research design.

Educational research design is much like any other type of research design. You have a question to which you need an answer. To answer the question, you are informed by the current literature addressing issues around that question. Choose a method that will generate the best answer to the problem. For example, if you wish to find out if your 8:30 a.m. statistics students are tired, and, if so, for what reason, you might simply pass out a simple, anonymous questionnaire that asks one, two-part question:

1. Are you tired during the 8:30a.m. section of Statistics? (Yes/ No)
2. If you answered "yes" to 1, why are you tired?

Obviously, this is a rather superficial query; however, for the question asked, it would likely be the best fit for a research design. The form of research design you choose should properly address the question you ask, just as the form of assessment you choose (in the last two chapters) should best address the content you taught.

Whenever human subjects are involved in research, e.g., students and instructors, the research must account for their privacy and human rights. Most institutions have ethics boards which will review a faculty member's research proposal, and offer suggestions for ensuring that any participation is voluntary, that responses will be kept confidential, and that the research will not, in any way, cause any undo harm, discrimination, or suffering. While such a process can sometimes appear cumbersome, it is definitely a benefit for the researcher. Following ethical guidelines can ensure greater participation in your research because students or other instructors do not fear the outcome; it can attach greater respect to your research since it is a type of peer review; and it can alleviate the researcher of liability. Be sure to check your institution's web site for such guidelines, or with the department of faculty or research services on your campus.

Creating a research design which matches the research question (so that you can find and publish your answer), and ensuring that this research will be accepted by colleagues, is one of the central steps in publishing your teaching. Once the literature review and ethical research design is complete, and you have implemented your design, or collected your data, you will need to analyze the findings.

Analyze your findings

Whether you are a quantitative or qualitative researcher, you will already be familiar with one type of data analysis. If your research question required a quantitative design, but you are a qualitative researcher, then you will want to enlist the help of a "quantitative" colleague to properly examine the results of your data. This has been my experience. As a qualitative researcher, I am most comfortable working with text and themes; however, I do recognize the need and value of quantitative data, especially when dealing with large sample sizes. In these cases, I will always enlist the help of one of my more experienced faculty members who works with numbers. He/she is often able to provide me with a course of direction that can collate the results, and a second opinion is invaluable, both when analyzing data and when writing-up results.

When evaluating data, a researcher should always cross-check the findings with the literature review. The time spent reading the literature pertinent to a particular question should not be wasted. At all times of the process, the researcher should always be asking, "how does this affirm, refute, or alter current opinion?" Being capable of answering this question will aid you later in finding a publisher for your work. It will demonstrate precisely to the editor, or publisher, that you are familiar with the research in this area, and that this is how your piece differs and makes a unique contribution to the field.

Writing a paper, or book on your findings

When you are writing up the results of your research query, you should do so fully conscious of the possible publishers for your work. They are your audience. Acknowledge this. Having read through some of the journals, magazines, and newsletters most closely related to your topic, you will probably have surmised which journal may be most interested in your teaching work and which journal is a good fit for your style of writing. Science articles pertaining to Biology, Physics, or Chemistry, for example, have a much different approach to writing than papers within the Social Sciences (e.g., History, English, and Anthropology). Rather than changing writing style, most faculty feel most comfortable writing for a publisher or editor within their discipline. Also, a journal article is a much shorter process than short curriculum units (lesson series), a manual, a text, or a book. Writing a journal article is also a very different process. A journal article, for example, is submitted in whole; a book is submitted as a proposed idea (the full text or book to appear years afterwards). You will often have an idea which one you are writing, article or book, during the research design stage. Some research endeavours are extensive, and require something of book length simply to fully disseminate the material to colleagues; other research is best summarized in an article. Since most professors at "teaching institutions" have little time for research and writing during the academic year, an article is more manageable. What follows are some tips on publishing both an article in a journal and publishing a book.

Each of the journals listed in Appendix B has its own writing and referencing format. Education is categorized as a Social Science. As such, most writing in the field of Education is generally written according to "APA (American Psychological Association) Style". This manual, for example, is written according to the "2001 APA Style Guide"; however, even within "APA writing", there are referencing and formatting distinctions. Check the "Submission Guidelines" in the journal in which you hope to publish prior to writing. Following the writing and referencing requirements of the journal will save you a great deal of time later. At press, there were computer programs available for Microsoft WORD which would automatically change the formatting and referencing in papers to a desired style. You may wish to purchase such software, if you plan on submitting to a large number of different journals.

Journal editors are particularly militant about the length and format in which articles are received for publication. Do not ignore these submission guidelines. It would be a shame if a wonderful idea or contribution were rejected simply due to the fact that the paper was not received in the style requested. Respect details. Incorporating this into your writing will save a great deal of disappointment and/or revisions later.

After you are finished the article you wish to submit, have at least one colleague in the area read it over. Questions this initial, informal reader has about your work will often alert you to areas that need clarifying, expanding, or further referencing. This simple step can also save a great deal of time later.

Morton, who writes in this manual about "Large Classes", suggests that authors submit first to one publisher, or journal, who they suspect will never accept their paper. That is, choose an "aristocratic" journal of superior name and quality. Submit here first. If it is accepted, great! If not, you were expecting rejection anyway so it is not disappointing, and you will have received, in the meanwhile, exemplary reviews which will both inform your revisions, and steel the work against future reviewers.

Since the academic journals listed here require peer review, and since all of the journals listed have a list of their editorial boards and reviewers, it is wise for prospective authors to review the literature written by those reviewers. Where relevant, reference those reviewers. Reviewers, much like students searching for their mark, will check to see if their own work has been acknowledged and referenced within those relevant papers they are reviewing. This is evidence, to the reviewer, but also to the academy, of the breadth of dissemination of knowledge.

Finally, submit the article to a publisher, and, in the meantime, have a plan of where you might try next in case the first submission is rejected (which is not at all uncommon).

I will mention very little here about book publishing, since this area is so vast, and is covered very adequately by a number of manuals and texts on "getting your book published". Knapper and Wright (2002), for example, have much information on this area which is of value to any prospective author in teaching and learning.

If you have an idea for a book, or a manuscript you have been writing for teaching, it is always wise to begin with an inquiry to a publisher. A simple e-mail indicating the topic of the book, and its audience (who would read it), to an educational publisher will indicate to you immediately whether this is something the publisher is interested in or not. This will save you a great deal of time writing a proposal for a particular publisher who is not interested. Editors' names and e-mail addresses can be found on their company web sites. Search here first for contact information and information about the process for submitting book proposals. Knapper and Wright (2002) have compiled a list of the following seven book publishers who frequently accept material in the area of teaching and learning:

1. Anker Publishing: www.ankerpub.com/index.html
2. Jossey-Bass: www.josseybass.com
3. Kogan Page: www.kogan-page.co.uk
4. Magna Publications: www.magnapubs.com
5. New Forums Press: www.newforums.com
6. Open University Press: www.srhe.ac.uk/publicns.htm#SRHEandOpen
7. Sage Publications: www.sagepub.com

There is also a series of "Green Guides", monographs, published by STLHE (Society for Teaching and Learning in Higher Education), and edited by Wright, Université du Québec. This series of short books covers ideas such as, "Teaching the Art of Inquiry, Active Learning, and Teaching Large Classes." Proposals to the "Green Guides" series, or to any one of the above publishers, require the following materials (check individual web sites for detailed format and information):

1. Cover letter (including a brief summary of what the book is about and why people will want to buy and read it)
2. Detailed table of contents (with chapters and subheadings)
3. Projected length (number of pages = 2/3 X (number of double-spaced, 10-point font pages)
4. Biographies of authors or contributors (particularly what they have written before, or their experience in the area)

There are no two pieces of information more important to a book publisher than the audience and the competition. Remember that publishing is a business. Think like a manager of marketing and sales. Who will pay money for this? To whom will we advertise? What other books like this are out on the market and already have a reputation? How is this one any different? Is it less expensive? Is it more thorough? Does it represent an audience that no one has addressed yet? Why does anyone even need to read this information? Can we sell it?

As an academic, being able to market your teaching to the average person, or being able to describe what you do in one or two short sentences, will allow you to publish books. Before you submit a book proposal to a prospective editor, be sure you can describe it and sell it to the person next door.

Submit to a publisher

You are finished. You have researched your teaching topic, analyzed your findings, written a reviewed, and formidable argument that will aid other teachers, and submitted it to a journal or editor. Now you wait. Often editors will contact you to indicate the stage of review of your article or book. For instance, they may e-mail to indicate that it has been received, that it has gone out for review, or that they have received all three reviews. Often, the review process in Education takes between 6-12 months. Following the review process you may receive one of the following four responses back from the publisher:

1. Accepted
2. Accepted with Revisions
3. Revise and Re-submit for Review
4. Rejected

It should be noted that it is uncommon to have an article or book accepted as is, without any suggested revisions. According to the *Canadian Journal of Education*, roughly 80% of all article are returned with the request to "revise and re-submit". Many authors in Education indicate having to re-submit articles to 2 or 3 publishers before they are accepted, and even then there are usually revisions. The process can often feel demoralizing. Try to persevere and your efforts will eventually be rewarded. It is vital to take your reviewers' suggestions into consideration. Some reviews will be much more constructive than others. Try to focus on the practical advice. This can only improve the quality of your work as it is seen by colleagues, and evaluated for tenure and promotion.

As your article, or book, is going through the review process, you may wish to cite it either in a curriculum vitae, for employee reviews, or for another paper you are writing. What do you tell people if you don't know if it has been accepted yet? The following are the guidelines for referencing work as given by CAUT (Canadian Association of University Teachers) and SSHRC (Social Sciences and Humanities Research Council):

1. Completed - Work has been written, but has not been presented or submitted anywhere yet.
2. Submitted - Work has been submitted to one publisher.
3. Accepted - Work has been accepted for publication (either with or without revisions).
4. In Press - Work is at the printers; the release date for public purchase is unknown.

In Tobin's chapter on "Preparing a Course Outline", she mentions Access[©] and Public Lending Rights (PLR). If you have published a book, it is often on file in institutional or public libraries. Since most institutions purchase a licence to photocopy academic materials for educational purposes, as an author, you may register with Access[©] and PLR to have your book(s) searched. Once a year, Access© and PLR will randomly do a search of library records to see which books may have been checked out or put into reserve. You will receive a small commission every time this happens. Welcome to publishing!

Since most of us prepare courses, deliver, teach, and assess for the majority of our year, as academics, it is nice to be recognized for the hard work we do well. By publishing the unique parts of your teaching, you are able to efficiently combine the one part of your job, teaching, into which you put a great deal of energy and time, with the other part of your job, research, that you must complete to become a permanently recognized part of the academy. "Publishing your teaching" allows you to feel that your teaching matters to administration, not just to students. Should you have any questions for one or more of the authors within this manual, please contact us, via e-mail, at the University of Windsor at www.uwindsor.ca. We are always excited to assist new colleagues in the field of educational research.

To further teaching:

Braskamp, L.A., D.C. Brandenburg, and J.C. Ory. (1984). Evaluating teaching effectiveness: A practical guide. Thousand Oaks, CA: Sage Publications.

Creswell, J.C. (2002). Research design: Qualitative, quantitative, and mixed methods approaches. Thousand Oaks, CA: Sage Publications.

Knapper, C., & Wright, A. (2002). Getting published in educational development. Workshop Delivered at 2002 Society for Teaching and Learning in Higher Education (STLHE) Conference, McMaster University, Hamilton, Ontario.

Ulrich's International Periodicals Directory. New York: Bowker Press. Retrieved from www.ulrichsweb.com

Weimer, M. (1993). The disciplinary journals on pedagogy. Change, November/December, 44-51.

APPENDIX A

Value Added Group Participation

Guidelines for Students using the Value Added Group Participation Form
(VAGP)

- All members of the group will receive the assessed project mark. This
  form will permit each member of the group to acknowledge the
  contributions of his/her peers. This numerical acknowledgement will
  be used as a multiplier to the base mark. Hence, your mark cannot
  decrease as a consequence of being honest. Be sure that you judge
  deeds and not personalities. You are not assessing how much you like
  a certain person, but rather, how much he/she contributed to the group
  in helping complete the assigned task. If everyone in the group worked
  equally in an area of participation, then they should all receive the same
  mark for that one item.
- Be honest and avoid hurting people's feelings but do not insult their
  intelligence either. Most people know when their effort could have
  been better. If more than one individual demonstrated the characteristic
  then they should share the acknowledgement equally. You will also
  complete and hand in a self reflection exercise (SEE) prior to the group
  VAGP completion and peer evaluation (PE) of your product. The
  project mark (PE), SEE and VAGP will contribute to your final mark.

Value	Criteria	Value	Criteria
5	Sole contributor in this area	2	Some valuable contribution in this area
4	Major contributor in this area	1	Little valuable contribution in this area
3	Equal contributor in this area	0	No valuable contribution in this area

Criteria

Title	Criteria

Leadership Quotient	Initiated meetings, delegated tasks, maintained timelines, provided encouragement and assistance, kept on task and focused, made final decisions concerning project, is exemplary.
Creativity Quotient	Proposed key ideas, presented novel formats, introduced new information sources and other approaches, brought useful and unique skills to the project, suggested alternative approaches.
Knowledge Quotient	Provided reliable information, resources, background, and outlines on the topic. Understood the issues and provided insight in the preparation, construction and presentation of the material
Effort Quotient	Total involvement in project, worked on assigned tasks and maintained timeline, kept on task, assisted others when necessary, collaborative
Attitude Quotient	Enthusiastic, willing to cooperate, concerned about safety, dependable and trustworthy, willing to learn.

Criteria	Group Members Names					
Leadership Quotient						
Creativity Quotient						
Knowledge Quotient						
Effort Quotient						
Attitude Quotient						

Total						
VAGP Mark						

If you agree with your peers marks sign here	If you disagree with your peers marks sign here and indicate below your concerns

Comments concerning disagreement

APPENDIX B

SUBJECT JOURNALS SPECIFIC TO TEACHING

Agriculture:
NAGTA(National Association of College Teachers of Agriculture) Journal

Architecture:
Journal of Architectural Education

Business:
Journal of Accounting Education
Issues in Accounting Education
Business Education Forum
Journal of Marketing Education
Journal of Management Education

Computer Science:
Computers & Education
Journal of Computer Assisted Learning

Drama:
Drama/Theatre Teacher

English:
College English
Teaching English in the Two-Year College
Research in the Teaching of English
College composition and Communication
English Education
English Leaders Quarterly
The Journalism Educator

Engineering:
Chemical Engineering Education
American Society for Engineering Education

Geographical Science:
Journal of Geography

Journal of Geography in Higher Education
Journal of Geological Education
Journal of Environmental Education

History/Political Science:
Journal of Urban History
OAH Magazine of History
Political Science and Politics

Law:
Journal of Law and Education

Mathematics:
Journal for Research in Mathematics Education
Journal for Research in Mathematics Education Online
School Science and Mathematics
Math Horizons
Math Literacy News
International Journal of Mathematics Education in

Music:
Journal of Research in Music Education

Nursing/ Social Work:
Journal of Nursing Education
Nurse Educator
Journal of Health Occupations Education
Journal of Health Administration Education
Journal of Teaching in Social Work

Philosophy:
Teaching Philosophy

Psychology:

Teaching of Psychology

Physical   Education/Human
Kinetics:

Journal of Teaching in Physical
Education

Religion:
Religious Education

Science:
Science and Technology
The Crucible (Science Teachers
Association of Ontario)
Scientific American
Discover
Journal of Biological Education
American Biology Teacher
Journal of Chemical Education
Journal of College Science
Teaching

Social Science:
Anthropology   and   Education
Quarterly
Teaching Sociology

Women's Studies:
Gender and Education

International Issues:
Compare
Journal of Canadian and
International Education
Comparative Education Review

Bibliography

Adams, M. (1997). Pedagogical frameworks for social justice education. In M. Adams, L. Bell and P. Griffin (eds.). Teaching for diversity and social justice. New York: Routledge.

Applefield, J. M., Huber, R., & Moalen, M. (2001). Constructivism in theory and practice: Toward a better understanding. The High School Journal, 84(2), 35-53.

American Chemical Society. What's that Stuff? Chemical and engineering news. Washington, D.C.

Armstrong, A. & Casement, C. (1998). The child and the machine. Toronto: Key Porter Books.

Barnes, C. P. (1983). Questioning in college classrooms. In C. L. Ellner & C. P. Barnes (eds.), Studies of college teaching (pp. 61-82). Lexington, MA: D. C. Heath.

Bellamy, L., & Guppy, N. (1991). Opportunities and obstacles for women in Canadian higher education. In J. Gaskell, & A. McLaren (eds.). Women and education (second edition). Calgary: Detselig Enterprise.

Bevevina, M. M., Dengel, J., & Adams, K. (1999). Constructivism theory in the classroom: Internalizing concepts through inquiry learning. The Clearing House, 72(5), 275-278.

Bligh, D. (2000). What's the use of lecture? San Francisco: Jossey-Bass.

Bloom, B., Englehart, M., Furst, E., Hill, W., & Krathwohl, D. (1956). Taxonomy of educational objectives: Handbook I: Cognitive domain. New York: David McKay.

Braskamp, L.A., Brandenburg, D. C., and Ory. J. C. (1984). Evaluating teaching effectiveness: A practical guide. Thousand Oaks, CA: Sage Publications.

Brent, R., & Felder, R. M. (1999). It's a start. College Teaching, 47(1), 14-17.

Brookfield, S.D. (1999). Discussion as a way of teaching: Tools and techniques for democratic classrooms (First Edition). San Francisco: Jossey-Bass.

Brookfield, Stephen. (1986). Understanding and facilitating adult learning. San Francisco: Jossey-Bass.

Cameron, B. J. (2002). Green guide no. 2: Active learning. Halifax: STLHE, Dalhousie University.

Carnegie Foundation (1988). The conditions of teaching: A state by state analysis. New Jersey: Princeton.

Carr, R. (2001). Dancing with roles: Differences between a coach, a mentor and a therapist. Compass: A Magazine for Peer Assistance, Mentorship and Coaching, 15(1), 5-7.

Chambers, A., Angus, K.B., & Carter-Wells, J. (2000). Creative and active strategies to promote critical thinking. Claremont Reading Conference Yearbook, 2000, 58-69.

Chickering, A. W. (1974). Commuting versus resident students: overcoming the educational inequities of living off campus. In L. Upcroft, J. Gardner, & Associates. (eds). The freshman year experience. San Francisco: Jossey-Bass.

Cho, S. (1978). The gas we pass: The story of farts. Brooklyn: Kane/Miller Book Publishers.

Conway, D. (2001). The design and implementation of a mentoring scheme for first year computer science students. Retrieved on April 4, 2001, from www.csse.monash.edu.au/~damina/papers/HTML/Mentoring.html.

Corson, D. (1993). Language, minority education and gender: Linking social justice and power. Clevedon, Multilingual Matters/Toronto: OISE Press.

Costa, A. L. (   ). Teacher behaviors that promote discussion. In W. W. Wilen (ed.). Teaching and learning through discussion: The theory, research and practice of the discussion method (pp. 45-77). Springfield, IL: Charles C. Thomas.

Creswell, J. C. (2002). Research design: Qualitative, quantitative, and mixed methods approaches. Thousand Oaks, CA: Sage Publications.

Cummins, J. (2000). *Language, power and pedagogy*. Clevedon: Multilingual Matters.

Danielson, C. (1996). Enhancing professional practice: A framework for teaching. Alexandria, VA: ASCD.

Daresh, J. C., & Playko, M. A. (1995). Supervision as a proactive process concepts and cases (second edition). Prospect Heights: Waveland Press Inc.

Denzine, G., & Pulos, S. (2000). College students' perceptions of faculty approachability. Educational Research Quarterly, 24(1), 56- 66.

Dillon, J. T. (1990). Conducting discussions by alternatives to questioning. In W. W. Wilen (ed.). Teaching and learning through discussion: The theory, research and practice of the discussion method (pp. 79-96). Springfield, IL: Charles C Thomas.

Duncan, I. (1926). The art of dance. New York: Theatre Arts Books.

Dunn, R., & Dunn, K. (1978). Teaching students through their individual learning styles. Reston,VA: Reston.

Ebert-May, D., Brewer, C., & Allred, S. (1997). Innovation in large lectures - teaching for active learning. BioScience, 47, 601-607.

Egbo, B. (1999) Options, relevance and voice: Transforming minority students' educational disempowerment through critical teaching. Paper presented at the annual conference of the Canadian Society for the Study of Education at the Université de Sherbrooke, Quebec, June 7-9, 1999.

Elbaum, B., C. McIntyre, and A. Smith. (2002). Essential elements: Prepare, design, and teach your online course. Madison, WI: Atwood Publishing.

Ellul, J. (1964). The technological society. New York: Vintage Books.

Ellul, J. (1981) Perspectives on our age, Jacques Ellul speaks on his life and work. (W. H. Vanderburg, ed.). Toronto: House of Anansi Press Ltd.

Erickson, B. L., & Strommer, D. W. (1991). Teaching college freshmen. San Francisco: Jossey-Bass.

Felder, R. M., & Brent, R. (1996). Navigating the bumpy road to student-centred instruction. College Teaching, 44, 43-47.

Felder, R. M., Woods, D. R., Stice, J. E., & Rugarcie, A. (2000). The future of engineering education: Teaching methods that work. Chemical Engineering Education, 34(1), 26-39.

Fischer, C. G., & Grant, G. E. (1983). Intellectual levels in college classrooms. In C. L. Ellner & C. P. Barnes (eds.). Studies of college teaching (pp. 47-60). Lexington, MA: D. C. Heath.

Gagnon, G. W., & Collay, M. (2001). Designing for learning. Thousand Oaks, Ca: Corwin.

Gall, J. P., & Gall, M. D. (1990). Outcomes of the discussion method. In W. W. Wilen (ed.). Teaching and learning through discussion: The theory, research and practice of the discussion method (pp. 25-44). Springfield, IL: Charles C. Thomas.

Gardner, H. (1991). The unschooled mind: How children think and schools should teach. NewYork: Basic Books.

Gazda, G. M., Asbury, F. R., Balzer, F. J., Childers, William, C., & Walters, R. P. (1991). Human relations development: A manual for educators (fourth edition). Boston: Allyn and Bacon.

Gedalof, A.J. (1998). Green Guide No. 1: Teaching large classes. Halifax: STLHE, Dalhousie University.

Gibson, L. (1998) Teaching as an encounter with self: Unravelling the mix of personal beliefs, education Ideologies and pedagogical practices. Anthropology and Education Quarterly, 29(3), 360-371.

Gilbert, S. (1995). Quality education: Does class size matter? Research File, 1(1), 1-7.

Glickman, C. D., Gordon, S. P., & Ross-Gordon, J. M. (2001). Supervision and instructions: Leadership a developmental approach (fifth edition). Boston: Allyn & Bacon.

Good, T. L. & Brophy, J. E. (1997). Looking in classrooms (seventh edition). New York: Longman.

Green, L. (2001). Effective lecturing techniques. In J. Newton, J. Ginsberg, J. Rehner, P. Rogers, S. Sbrizzi, & J. Spencer (eds.). Voices from the classroom: Reflections on teaching and learning in higher education (pp. 184-187). Toronto: Garamond Press.

Hartman, H. J., & Glasgow, N. A. (2002). Tips for the science teacher: Research-based strategies to help students learn. Thousand Oaks, Ca: Corwin.

Herman, J., Aschbacher, P., & Inters, L. (1992). A practical guide to alternative assessment. Lexandria, VA: Association for Supervision and Curriculum Development.

Howard Hughes Medical Institute. Arousing the fury of the immune system. Chevy Chase, Maryland. Retrieved from www.hhmi.org

Hurtado, S. M., Clayton-Pedersen, J. A, & Allen, W. (1999). Enacting diverse learning environments: Improving the climate for racial/ethnic diversity in higher education. ASHE-ERIC Higher Education Reports 26(8), 1-116.

Hudspith, B. & Jenkins, H. (2002). Green guide no. 3: Teaching the art of inquiry. Halifax: STLHE, Dalhousie University.

Jacobson , D., Eggen, P., & Kauchak, D. (1999a). Methods for teaching: Promoting student learning. New Jersey: Prentice-Hall.

Jacobsen, D., Eggen, P., & Kauchak, D. (1999b). Methods for teaching: Promoting student learning (fifth edition). New Jersey: Merrill.

Jerowski, S. (1994). Assessment and evaluation. Paper presented at the University of Victoria, Victoria, British Columbia, July, 1994.

Karp, D., & Yoels, W. (1976). The college classroom: Some observations on the meaning of student participation. Sociology and Social Research, 60(4), 421-439.

Kehoe, D. (2001). Improving large-class lecturing. In J. Newton, J. Ginsberg, J. Rehner, P. Rogers, S. Sbrizzi, & J. Spencer (eds.). Voices from the classroom: Reflections on teaching and learning in higher education (pp. 188-195). Toronto: Garamond Press.

Knapper, C., & Wright, A. (2002). Getting published in educational development. Workshop Delivered at 2002 Society for Teaching and Learning in Higher Education (STLHE) Conference, McMaster University, Hamilton, Ontario.

Kolstoe, O. P. (1975). College professoring. Carbondale: Southern Illinois University Press.

Kramarae, C., & Treichler, P. (1990). Power relationships in the classroom. In S. Gabriel and I. Smithson (eds.). Gender in the classroom: Power and pedagogy. Urbana: University of Illinois Press.

Kreber, C. & Cranton, P. (2000). Exploring the scholarships of teaching. The Journal of Higher Education, 71(4), 477-495.

Kreber, C. (ed.) (2001). Scholarship revisited: perspectives on the scholarship of teaching. New Directions for Teaching and Learning, 86. San Francisco: Jossey-Bass.

Lea, M., Spears, R., & de Groot, D. (2001). Knowing me, knowing you: Anonymity effects on social identity processes within groups. Personality & Social Psychology Bulletin, 27, 526-537.

Leonard, W.H. (2000). How do college students best learn science? Journal of College Science Teaching, 29(6), 385-388.

Litner, B., Rossiter, A., & Taylor, M. (1992). The equitable inclusion of women in higher education: some consequences for teaching. Canadian Journal of Education, 17(3), 302.

McGlynn, A.P. (2002). Successful beginnings for college teaching: Engaging your students from the first day. Madison, WI: Atwood Publishing.

McKeachie, W. J. (1994). Teaching tips (ninth edition). Lexington: D. C. Heath and Company.

McKeachie, W. J. (1999). Teaching tips: Strategies, research, and theory for college and university teachers (tenth edition). Boston: Houghton Mifflin.

McKeachie, W. J. (2002). McKeachie's teaching tips (11th edition). Boston: Houghton Mifflin.

Mitchell, R. (1992). Portfolios. In R. Mitchell (ed.) Testing for learning: New approaches to evaluation can improve American schools (pp. 103-131). New York: Free Press.

Moore, K. D. (1995). Classroom teaching skills (third edition). New York: McGraw-Hill Inc.

Myers, E. (1981). Unpublished attrition research studies, St. Cloud State University, St. Cloud, Minn. In L. Noel, R. Levitz, D. Saluri, & Associates (eds.). Increasing student retention (pp. 21). San Francisco: Jossey-Bass.

National Human Genome Research Institute. Exploring our molecular selves. Retrieved from www.nhgri.nih.gov

Negroponte, N. (1995). Being digital. New York: Vintage Books.

Noel, L., Levitz, R., Saluri, D., & Associates. (1986). Increasing student retention. San Francisco: Jossey-Bass.

Novak, J. D., & Gowin, D. B. (1984). Learning how to learn. Cambridge: Cambridge University Press.

Novak, J. D., & Musonda, D. (1991). A twelve-year longitudinal study of science concept learning. American Educational Research Journal, 28(1), 117-153.

Nunn, C. E. (1996). Discussion in the college classroom. Journal of Higher Education, 67(3), 243-266.

Ornstein, A., & Hunkins, F. (1998). Curriculum: Foundations, principles and issues. Boston: Allyn and Bacon.

Paul, R. (2001). State of the university address. University of Windsor. Retrieved on January 26, 2001 from http://athena.uwindsor.ca/units/president/president.nsf

Pocklington, T. & Tupper, A. (2002). No Place to Learn: Why universities aren't working. Vancouver: UBC Press. 55-78.

Posner, G., & Rudnitsky, A. (1997). Course design: A guide to curriculum development for teachers. NewYork: Longman Press.

Papert, S. (1980). Mindstorms. New York: Basic Books.

Papert, S. (1993). The children's machine. New York: Basic Books.

Postman, N. (1992). Technopoly. New York: Vintage Books.

Roby, T. W. (1988). Models of discussion. In J. T. Dillon (ed.). Questioning and discussion: A multidisciplinary study (pp. 163-191). Norwood, NJ: Ablex.

Rogers, P. (2001a). Improving student learning in lectures. In J. Newton, J. Ginsberg, J. Rehner, P. Rogers, S. Sbrizzi, & J. Spencer (eds.). Voices from the classroom: Reflections on teaching and learning in higher education (pp. 197-199). Toronto: Garamond Press.

Rogers, P. (2001b). Dead silence... A teacher's nightmare. In J. Newton, J. Ginsberg, J. Rehner, P. Rogers, S. Sbrizzi, & J. Spencer (eds.). Voices from the classroom: Reflections on teaching and learning in higher education (pp. 200-201). Toronto: Garamond Press.

Rosenshine, B. (1997). Advances in research on instruction. In J. W. Lloyd, E. J. Kameanui, & D. Chard (eds.). Issues in educating students with disabilities (pp. 197-221). Mahwah, NJ: Lawrence Erlbaum.

Rowe, M. B. (1974). Wait-time and rewards as instructional variables, their influence on language, logic and fate control. Journal of Research in Science Teaching, 11, 81-94.

Rubin, L., & Hebert, C. (1998). Model for active learning: collaborative peer teaching. College Teaching, 46, 26-30.

Sacks, P. (1996). Generation X goes to college: An eye-opening account of teaching in postmodern America. Chicago: Open Court Publishing.

Sadker, M. & Sadker, D. (1990). Confronting sexism in the college classroom. In S. Gabriel and I. Smithson (eds.). Gender in the classroom: Power and pedagogy. Urbana: University of Illinois Press.

Schmier, L. (2002). Random thoughts. (A weekly listserv newsletter on teaching). North Dakota University. Retrieved from acadv@listserv.nodak.edu

Schönwetter, D. J. (2002). Becoming a successful student. Communique, 2(2), 23-25.

Schönwetter, D. J. (2002). Equipping teachers with strategies to engage inquiry in first year students. Unpublished paper delivered at 2002 Society for Teaching and Learning in Higher Education (STLHE) Conference, McMaster University, Hamilton, Ontario.

Schwarcz, J. (1999). Radar, hula hoops and playful pigs. Toronto: ECW Press.

Shor, I. (1992). Empowering education: Critical teaching for social change. Chicago: University of Chicago Press.

Silverman, S. (1992). Teacher feedback and achievement in physical education: Interaction with student practice. Teaching and Teacher Education, 8(4), 333-344.

Smith, D. G. (1983). Instruction and outcomes in an undergraduate setting. In C. L. Ellner & C. P. Barnes (eds.), Studies of college teaching (pp. 83-116). Lexington, MA: D. C. Heath.

Smith, D. H., & Malec, M. A. (1995). Learning students' names in sociology classes: Interactive tactics, who uses them, and when. Teaching Sociology, 2, 280-286.

Stoll, C. (1999). High tech heretic. New York: Doubleday.

Sutherland, T. E., & Bonwell, C. C. (1996). Using active learning in college classrooms: A range of options for faculty. San Francisco: Jossey-Bass.

Tatum, D. (1992). Talking about race, learning about racism: The application of racial identity development theory in the Classroom. Harvard Educational Review, 62(1), 1-24.

Teaching and Learning Center, University of Nebraska-Lincoln (n.d.). Learning students' names. Retrieved on January 16, 2002, from www.unl.edu/teaching/Names.html

Timpson, W. M. & Burgoyne, S. (2002). Teaching and performing: Ideas for energizing your classes. Madison, WI: Atwood Publishing.

Tinto, V. (1997). Classrooms as communities: Exploring the educational character of student persistence. Journal of Higher Education 68(6), 599-623.

Tobin, K. (1987). The role of wait-time in higher cognitive level learning. Review of Educational Research, 57, 69-95.

Turkle, S. (1995). Life on the screen. New York: Touchstone.

Ulrich's International Periodicals Directory. New York: Bowker Press. Retrieved on November 12, 2002 from www.ulrichsweb.com

Upcroft, L., Gardner, J., & Associates. (1989). The freshman year experience. San Francisco: Jossey-Bass.

U.S. Department of Health and Human Services. The structures of life (pamphlet). Bethesda, Maryland. Retrieved from http://www.nigms.nih.gov

Voss, D. (1996). Creative writing and the historian: An active learning model for teaching the craft of history. The History Teacher, 30, 45-53.

Weaver, R. (1983). The small group in large classes. The Educational Forum (Fall), 65-73.

Weimer, M. (1993). Change. The Disciplinary Journals on Pedagogy, November/December, 44-51.

Wiggens, G. (1989). A true test: Toward more authentic and equitable assessment. Phi Delta Kappan, May 1989, 703-713.

Wiggins, G., & McTighe, J. (1998). Understanding by design. Alexandria, Association for Supervision and Curriculum Development, The Canadian Copyright Licensing Agency. Retrieved on November 3, 2002 from www.accesscopyright.ca

Williams, (1990). Is the post-secondary classroom a chilly one for women?: A review of the literature. Canadian Journal of Higher Education, 20(3), 30-42.

Young, S. & Shaw, D. (1999). Profiles of effective college and university teachers. Journal of Higher Education,70(6), 670-686.

Contributors

ABLESER, Judith, Ph.D., has been teaching at the university and college level for more than 15 years. She currently teaches special education at the University of Michigan-Flint, U.S.A.

CLOVIS, C.J., Ph.D., is a high school science teacher and adjunct professor at the Faculty of Education, University of Windsor, Canada. His current research interests include the development and utilization of self and peer assessment protocols for high school science programs; the integration of technology into science instruction and its impact on learning, and writing science curricula for students with learning impediments.

CRAWFORD, Ian, Ph.D., teaches at the Faculty of Education, University of Windsor, Canada. Dr. Crawford has taught more than 20,000 students in his distinguished career, and has won Canada's top award for teaching excellence.

EGBO, Benedicta, Ph.D., teaches at the Faculty of Education, University of Windsor, Canada. Her research interests include: transformative pedagogies, literacy, inclusive educational practices, gender and education and, education and social justice. She is the founding editor of the *Journal of Teaching and Learning*.

GLASSFORD, Larry A., Ph.D., teaches history and social studies' curriculum and methods, as well as the politics of education, at the Faculty of Education, University of Windsor, Canada. He has presented papers, published articles, books and reviews in the areas of Canadian political history, citizenship education, cross-disciplinary teaching, and drama in the social sciences.

HURLEY, Noel, Ph.D., teaches at the Faculty of Education, Memorial University of Newfoundland, Canada. He instructs undergraduate and graduate students in the area of educational administration. He completed his studies at Memorial University of Newfoundland and at the University of Ottawa. Dr. Hurley is a native of Newfoundland and has worked in the school system there for more than 20 years. Dr. Hurley is also the Canadian head of the Consortium for Cross Cultural Research in Education at the University of Michigan. He has been an executive member of the Special Interest Group for International Studies of the American Educational Research Association (AERA) since 2003-2006.

LAING, Donald A., Ph.D., is a professor emeritus of the Faculty of Education, University of Windsor, Canada. Dr. Laing has co-edited three volumes of Canadian poetry for schools, and authored books on the art critics Roger Fry and Clive Bell. He has published and delivered many articles and papers on the teaching of English/Language Arts, and his work has appeared in *Canadian Journal of Education, Revue des sciences de l'éducation, Oideas, indirections* and other journals. In recent years Dr. Laing has offered a course on the teaching of Shakespeare as part of the Stratford Festival of Canada's Academy program.

LEE, Lana, A.B., Ph.D., teaches Chemistry and Biochemistry at the Faculty of Science, University of Windsor, Canada. Her research has been funded by NSERC and the Heart and Stroke Foundation and focuses on the determination of protein structure and function in detoxification and blood coagulation systems by nuclear magnetic resonance spectroscopy. She also promotes science by presenting chemistry magic shows to local elementary and high schools.

MORTON, Larry, Ph.D., teaches psychology at the Faculty of Education, University of Windsor, Canada. He has served as the Coordinator of Graduate Studies, and has more than forty publications in diverse areas, yet always finds time to face the challenges of teaching large classes.

OAKLEY, Beth., B.A., B.Ed, is a Transition Support Specialist at the University of Windsor, Canada, and has worked in the Division of Student Development and Support since 1990. She co-ordinates the University 101 course, the summer orientation program for parents, and fall orientation for first year students. In addition, she is an advisor to students with disabilities.

SALINITRI, Geri, Ph.D., teaches at the Faculty of Education, University of Windsor, Canada. Dr. Salinitri's research interests include mentoring programs, induction programs, Science literacy, and Cognition and Learning. She is a 20-year veteran of secondary science and guidance. She is the recipient of both the Chemical Institute of Canada Award for Teaching Excellence, the Prime Minister's Award for Teaching Excellence in Science, Mathematics, and Technology, and the University of Windsor mentoring award.

SHANTZ, Doreen, Ph.D., teaches educational policy and leadership at the Faculty of Education, University of Windsor, Canada. She is currently doing research on parent councils in Canada and New Zealand. She was a former teacher, vice-principal, principal and assistant superintendent with the Waterloo County Board of Education, and is one of the most cooperative and positive teachers one could ever meet.

SMITH, Kara, Ph.D., teaches English language and literacy at the Faculty of Education, University of Windsor, Canada. Her research interests include comparative literacy studies, heritage languages, and children's literature. She has received two accommodations for secondary teaching excellence.

STARR, Elizabeth M., Ph.D., teaches special education at the Faculty of Education, University of Windsor, Canada. Her research interests are primarily in the area of autism spectrum disorders and include parental perceptions of education, positive behavioural support, and other evidence-based educational strategies.

TOBIN, Ruthanne, Ph.D., teaches at the University of Victoria, Canada. Her research includes investigations into differentiation of classroom literacy instruction for learners of diverse abilities, family literacy and classroom communication. She is also an advisor to the National Family Literacy Foundation. Tobin has taught for 10 years in British Columbia public schools.

TOUSIGNANT, Wayne, M.F.A., teaches at the Faculty of Education, University of Windsor, Canada. Since 1980, he has been a media artist and instructional designer in the Centre for Flexible Learning at the University of Windsor.